Real–World Investigations for Social Studies

Inquiries for Middle and High School Students Based on the Ten NCSS Standards

John D. Hoge
University of Georgia

Sherry L. Field
University of Texas at Austin

Stuart J. Foster
University of London

Pat Nickell
Past President, NCSS

PEARSON

Merrill
Prentice Hall

Upper Saddle River, New Jersey
Columbus, Ohio

Library of Congress Cataloging-in-Publication Data
Real world investigations for social studies: inquiries for middle and high school
sudents based on the ten NCSS standards/edited by John D. Hoge . . . [et al.].—
1st ed.

    p. cm.
  ISBN 0-13-095003-3
    1. Social sciences—Study and teaching (Middle school)—United States. 2. Social
sciences—Study and teaching (Secondary)—United States. 3. Social problems—
Study and teaching (Middle school)—United States. 4. Social problems—Study
and teaching (Secondary)—United States. 5. Social problems—United States—Case
studies. 6. Problem solving—United States—Case studies. I. Hoge, John D.
  H62.5.U5 R415 2004
  300'.71'273—dc21

                                      2003011253

Vice President and Executive Publisher: Jeffery W. Johnston
Senior Editor: Linda Ashe Montgomery
Editorial Assistant: Laura Weaver
Production Editor: Mary Harlan
Production Coordinator: Penny Walker, *The GTS Companies*/York, PA Campus
Design Coordinator: Diane C. Lorenzo
Photo Coordinator: Valerie Schultz
Text Design and Illustrations: *The GTS Companies*/York, PA Campus
Cover Design: Dan Eckel
Cover Image: Corbis
Production Manager: Pamela D. Bennett
Director of Marketing: Ann Castel Davis
Marketing Manager: Darcy Betts Prybella
Marketing Coordinator: Tyra Poole

This book was set in Palatino by *The GTS Companies*/York, PA Campus. It was printed and bound by
Courier Kendallville, Inc. The cover was printed by Phoenix Color Corp.

Photo Credits: Corbis, p. 239; Scott Cunningham/Merrill, p. 73; Laima Druskis/PH College, p. 54;
Buddy Endress/Silver Burdett Ginn, p. 121; Courtesy Lynchburg Police Department, p. 225;
KS Studios/Merrill, p. 170; Anthony Magnacca/Merrill, p. 6; PH College, p. 35; Mark Richards/
PhotoEdit, p. 149; Rhoda Sidney/PH College, p. 189; Anne Vega/Merrill, p. 87

Pearson Education Ltd.   Pearson Education Australia Pty. Limited
Pearson Education Singapore Pte. Ltd. Pearson Education North Asia Ltd.
Pearson Education Canada, Ltd.   Pearson Educación de Mexico, S.A. de C.V.
Pearson Education–Japan   Pearson Education Malaysia Pte. Ltd.

10 9 8 7 6 5 4 3 2 1
ISBN: 0-13-095003-3

Preface

Real-World Investigations for Social Studies grew out of a U.S. Department of Education grant that engaged the four author-editors in an exploration of the use of contextual teaching and learning (CTL) to teach social studies. Working with colleagues, doctoral students, teachers, and people in the community, we constructed 10 case studies that were designed to engage middle and high school students in issues-oriented inquiries that met the National Council for the Social Studies (NCSS) curriculum standards (NCSS, 1994).

Writing *Real-World Investigations for Social Studies* was both enjoyable and challenging. Essentially, the editors and authors of this text wanted to achieve a constructive combination of ready-to-implement middle and high school lessons and complementary guidelines for using major social studies instructional methods in support of these classroom lessons. The goal was to offer highly engaging case-based, issues-oriented instructional materials along with supporting methods to demonstrate how the principles of CTL could be used to achieve the 10 NCSS curriculum standards for social studies.

Above all, we wanted to offer ready-to-implement instructional materials that were true to the principles of CTL. In order to help bring CTL into the social studies classroom, each investigation, first and foremost, aims to provide a practical sequence of lessons for teachers to use in middle or high school classrooms. Second, the lessons are designed to take into consideration the teaching and learning styles that many educators and researchers regard as most suited to middle and high school classrooms. Third, the lessons were developed with the intention of making the issues engaging, colorful, provocative, and relevant to the lives and interests of young people. Finally, the cases were designed to develop in middle school children key attributes necessary for undertaking their civic roles and responsibilities. As a result, every investigation requires students, individually and cooperatively, to wrestle with problematic issues, to research and analyze new data, to construct new meanings and understandings, to evaluate different and competing points of view, to reach (albeit tentatively) thoughtful conclusions, and, finally, to explain and defend positions taken. Arguably, no better preparation exists "to help young people develop the ability to make informed and reasoned decisions for the public good as citizens of a culturally diverse, democratic society in an interdependent world" (NCSS, 1994).

However, we also realized that the provision of these exemplary instructional materials offered a powerful platform—and an important opportunity—for teaching essential methods of social studies instruction. Thus, we added an introduction to the methods of CTL and an additional social studies teaching methods focus to teach each chapter's investigation. These materials are designed to offer teachers-in-training a contextually meaningful exposure to important social studies teaching methods. Practicing teachers, curriculum coordinators, and department chairs or curriculum leaders may also find that these methods materials refresh and reinforce their own classroom teaching practices.

Organization of the Text

The 10 chapters of *Real-World Investigations for Social Studies* are structured to match the NCSS curriculum standards. Each chapter begins with an introduction, followed by a discussion of how the case helps students to meet the relevant NCSS curriculum standard. Next, each chapter includes a teaching methods focus that is tailored to its content and NCSS standard. This methods focus is often supported by explicit guidelines for instruction and key links to the lesson content.

Ready-to-implement instructional materials follow, with each chapter offering an overview of its instruction, explicit lesson plans, all necessary handouts, and supporting materials. Teaching procedures have been carefully reviewed and trial taught in middle and high school classrooms.

Overview of the Chapters

CHAPTER 1

The first chapter, "Is America United or Divided by Language?" by Stuart J. Foster, David Clark, and B. Prentiss Woods, challenges students to ask tough questions related to the status of the English language in the United States and to reflect on issues that arise as a result of their Internet research activities. Designed to address NCSS Standard I, Culture, the topic also lends itself readily to a methods focus on teaching controversial issues in a pluralistic society.

CHAPTER 2

A local business scenario is the focus of the second chapter, "Crisis at Blue Ridge Leather: The

Intersection of One Life with Historical Social Structures," by Ronald L. VanSickle. Featuring NCSS Standard II, Time, Continuity, and Change, the investigation provides students an opportunity to learn how historical and existing social structures impact a small business, Blue Ridge Leather. Decision-making and problem-solving teaching methods are featured in this chapter and illustrated throughout the case.

CHAPTER 3

NCSS Standard III, People, Places, and Environments, is at the heart of "The Lake Lanier Land Use Controversy" by Geri Collins. This investigation examines a public issue that is familiar to many communities: land use and environmental change caused by development. A geographic perspective is used to explore this case and is strengthened by the chapter's methods focus on teaching geographic thinking skills.

CHAPTER 4

Individual Development and Identity, NCSS Curriculum Standard IV, is the theme addressed by Sherry L. Field and Pat Nickell in their chapter, "Getting a Job and Keeping It: Expectations in the Workplace." Inspired by the school-to-work movement, the chapter considers issues faced by employees and employers in understanding job requirements, work ethic expectations, and evaluations of work performance. The authors feature teaching methods for using interviewing, as well as character and values education, in the secondary classroom.

CHAPTER 5

Pamela S. Roach's chapter, "Defusing Hate: with Malice Toward None, with Charity for All," advances NCSS Standard V, Individuals, Groups, and Institutions, with the deliberation of a controversial topic: intolerance. The concepts of intolerance, hate, and organized violence illustrate the complexities of hate issues to students and help them to develop a plan to mitigate hatred that might arise in their own surroundings. Because this case study uses a substantial collection of historical photographs, primary source documents, and oral histories, its teaching methods focus is on how to help students analyze historical documents.

CHAPTER 6

Power, Authority, and Governance, NCSS Standard VI, is explored in "Mandatory School Uniforms: A Real-World Exploration of Power, Authority, and Governance," by John D. Hoge and Stuart J. Foster. In

this chapter, the Polk County, Florida, school uniform controversy is presented for deliberation. Students are challenged to research selected issues using resources provided in the case study, in their media center, and on the Internet. Because parties on both sides of the controversy make competing claims, helping students differentiate between fact and opinion was selected as the methods focus for this chapter.

CHAPTER 7

Jon Bauer presents a motivating topic, "Pirates! From the High Seas to High Tech: The Great Debate Over Music Piracy," to address NCSS Standard VII, Production, Distribution, and Consumption. Bauer focuses on a topic of keen interest to all students—music, and its on-line distribution. Challenging students to examine the economic, political, social, and ethical dimensions of music piracy, the chapter adopts a teaching methods focus on current events.

CHAPTER 8

"To Be or Not to Be: The Zoo Is the Question," by Carolyn Lyon, presents concepts that are central to NCSS Standard VIII, Science, Technology, and Society. Students consider biological, ethical, and physical concerns raised by the presence of zoos, and they learn about the work being done by many zoos across the nation to promote the survival of endangered species in order to examine the question "Are zoos morally defensible?" Because of its demanding analysis of the science and morality of zoos, this chapter focuses on methods for teaching higher-order thinking.

CHAPTER 9

NCSS Standard IX, Global Connections, is the theme of the investigation developed by Joseph R. Feinberg and Carolyn Lyon, "Confronting the Cycle of Poverty." Focusing on poverty and its global dimensions, the investigation uses the voices of adults and children living in poverty to inform and awaken students' interest concerning the problem of poverty. Students engaged in this investigation will be challenged to confront their own biases and discover avenues of action to alleviate the suffering of those caught in the cycle of poverty. Feinberg and Lyon selected tips, techniques, and considerations for teaching about children in poverty as the methods focus for this chapter.

CHAPTER 10

Finally, "Connecting Students to Their Communities Through Service," by Joseph R. Feinberg, addresses NCSS Standard X, Civic Ideals and Practices. This investigation connects students in an inspiring way to the service-learning being done by schoolchildren across the country. By examining instances of service-learning, students gain an opportunity to learn the historical contexts of community service, recognize students like themselves who are participating in meaningful community service, and appreciate the long-term possibilities to effect change that are inherent in ongoing community service-learning projects. Methods for using service-learning in middle and high school classrooms serve as the instructional focus of this chapter.

In conclusion, we believe that students and teachers alike will find something meaningful and interesting in each of the chapters. Whether studied as a whole, taught in clusters, or taken one at a time, these investigations will promote the positive attributes of CTL in relevant and accessible ways. By including explicit and context-sensitive attention to major instructional methods of social studies, we hope to support the skillful and thoughtful use of these investigations.

We enjoyed working with each author and author team, and we hope that these case studies will become an important part of middle school social studies teaching and learning.

Acknowledgments

We wish to thank the many people who were involved in this project. These include our editor, Linda Montgomery, and her editorial assistant, Laura Weaver, who carefully shepherded this project through its development; our reviewers: Linda Addo, North Carolina Agricultural and Technical University; V. Robert Agostino, Duquesne University; Janet Elaine Alleman, Michigan State University; Barbara C. Cruz, University of South Florida; Kent Freeland, Morehead State University; Thomas B. Goodkind, University of Connecticut; Carolyn Ledford, East Carolina University; John H. Litcher, Wake Forest University; Sharon Pittser, Newman University; and Jan Waggoner, Southern Illinois University at Carbondale; the classroom teachers who offered feedback; and the many community members who helped provide the real-world contexts for the chapters.

Reference

National Council for the Social Studies. (1994). *Expectations of excellence: Curriculum standards for social studies.* Washington, DC: Author.

Discover the Companion Website Accompanying This Book

THE PRENTICE HALL COMPANION WEBSITE: A VIRTUAL LEARNING ENVIRONMENT

Technology is a constantly growing and changing aspect of our field that is creating a need for content and resources. To address this emerging need, Prentice Hall has developed an online learning environment for students and professors alike–Companion Websites–to support our textbooks.

In creating a Companion Website, our goal is to build on and enhance what the textbook already offers. For this reason, the content for each user-friendly website is organized by topic and provides the professor and student with a variety of meaningful resources. Common features of a Companion Website include:

For the Professor—

Every Companion Website integrates **Syllabus Manager**™, an online syllabus creation and management utility.

- **Syllabus Manager**™ provides you, the instructor, with an easy, step-by-step process to create and revise syllabi, with direct links into Companion Website and other online content without having to learn HTML.
- Students may logon to your syllabus during any study session. All they need to know is the web address for the Companion Website and the password you've assigned to your syllabus.
- After you have created a syllabus using **Syllabus Manager**™, students may enter the syllabus for their course section from any point in the Companion Website.
- Clicking on a date, the student is shown the list of activities for the assignment. The activities for each assignment are linked directly to actual content, saving time for students.
- Adding assignments consists of clicking on the desired due date, then filling in the details of the assignment—name of the assignment, instructions, and whether it is a one-time or repeating assignment.
- In addition, links to other activities can be created easily. If the activity is online, a URL can be entered in the space provided, and it will be linked automatically in the final syllabus.
- Your completed syllabus is hosted on our servers, allowing convenient updates from any computer on the Internet. Changes you make to your syllabus are immediately available to your students at their next logon.

For the Student—

- **Introduction**—General information about each topic covered on the website
- **Organizations**—Links to various pertinent organizations within each topic on the website
- **General Resources**—Links to useful and meaningful websites that allow you to access current Internet information and resources to support what you are learning about instruction
- **Additional Resources**—An additional bank of links for selected topics that are more specifically broken down

- **Lesson Plans**—Links to various sites that help you incorporate theories and practices into the classroom. Some examples include virtual field trips and webquests
- **Assessments**—Links to various means of assessing your students' progress in the classroom
- **Internet Safety**—Information found in each topic to help you keep your students safe on the Internet while in the classroom
- **Learning Network**—A link to Pearson Education's Learning Network, which provides additional information in all fields of teaching
- **Electronic Bluebook**—Send homework or essays directly to your instructor's email with this paperless form
- **Message Board**—Serves as a virtual bulletin board to post—or respond to—questions or comments to/from a national audience
- **Chat**—Real-time chat with anyone who is using the text anywhere in the country—ideal for discussion and study groups, class projects, etc.

To take advantage of these and other resources, please visit the *Real-World Investigations for Social Studies: Inquiries for Middle and High School Students Based on the Ten NCSS Standards* Companion Website at

www.prenhall.com/hoge

Educator Learning Center: An Invaluable Online Resource

Merrill Education and the Association for Supervision and Curriculum Development (ASCD) invite you to take advantage of a new online resource, one that provides access to the top research and proven strategies associated with ASCD and Merrill—the Educator Learning Center. At **www. Educator Learning Center.com** you will find resources that will enhance your students' understanding of course topics and of current educational issues, in addition to being invaluable for further research.

HOW THE EDUCATOR LEARNING CENTER WILL HELP YOUR STUDENTS BECOME BETTER TEACHERS

With the combined resources of Merrill Education and ASCD, you and your students will find a wealth of tools and materials to better prepare them for the classroom.

Research

- More than 600 articles from the ASCD journal *Educational Leadership* discuss everyday issues faced by practicing teachers.
- A direct link on the site to Research Navigator™ gives students access to many of the leading education journals, as well as extensive content detailing the research process.
- Excerpts from Merrill Education texts give your students insights on important topics of instructional methods, diverse populations, assessment, classroom management, technology, and refining classroom practice.

Classroom Practice

- Hundreds of lesson plans and teaching strategies are categorized by content area and age range.
- Case studies and classroom video footage provide virtual field experience for student reflection.
- Computer simulations and other electronic tools keep your students abreast of today's classrooms and current technologies.

LOOK INTO THE VALUE OF EDUCATOR LEARNING CENTER YOURSELF

Preview the value of this educational environment by visiting **www.EducatorLearningCenter.com** and clicking on "Demo." For a free 4-month subscription to the Educator Learning Center in conjunction with this text, simply contact your Merrill/Prentice Hall sales representative.

About the Contributors

Jon Bauer grew up in Wisconsin, Georgia, and Florida and received a B.A. in history, philosophy, and English from the University of Georgia in 1988. He has taught English as a second language and social studies in Hamamatsu, Japan, since 1989, taking 1 year off to backpack with his wife, Hiromi, around the world and another 1½ years off to complete an M.Ed. in social science education at the University of Georgia. He loves Peruvian folk music, Japanese food, and Irish beer. His favorite writer is Kurt Vonnegut. His favorite philosopher is Spinoza. His favorite quote is Mark Twain's "Never let school interfere with your education."

David Clark is a graduate student at the University of Georgia working toward his M.S.Ed. in instructional technology. He received his bachelor's degree from the University of Georgia in 1998 in social science education. Through his work in the Social Science Education Department at UGA, Clark developed a keen interest in educational development and innovative methods of instruction. His attraction to multicultural instruction stems from his diverse educational experiences in grade school in El Paso, Texas, and in high school in the Atlanta, Georgia, area.

Geri Collins has been teaching social studies for the past 11 years, starting with fifth grade and moving to seventh and eighth grades. She received her bachelor's and master's degrees at Mercer University–Atlanta and is currently working toward her Ed.D. in social studies education at the University of Georgia. Her interest in American history and government led to the creation of the unit comprising chapter 3. Her ultimate goal is to help teachers create classroom experiences that can be translated into practical applications.

Sherry L. Field is a Professor of Curriculum and Instruction at The University of Texas at Austin, where she is Program Area Head for Social Studies Education. She has recently served as Chair of the College and University Faculty Assembly of the National Council for the Social Studies, Chair of the Research in Social Studies SIG of the American Educational Research Association, and President of the Society for the Study of Curriculum History. Her research in social studies curriculum and learning has been published in journals such as *Theory and Research in Social Education, Social Education, Middle Level Learner, The Educational Forum,* and *Journal of Supervision and Curriculum.* Currently, she is editor of *Social Studies and the Young Learner.*

Joseph R. Feinberg is an Assistant Professor of secondary curriculum in the Department of Specialty Studies at the University of North Carolina at Wilmington. He completed his Ph.D. in social science education at the University of Georgia. He was formerly a social science teacher for 4 years at Campbell High School in Smyrna, Georgia. A strong supporter of community involvement, Dr. Feinberg sponsored the Cultural Awareness Club and a community service club. He is a recipient of the 2000 Dr. Martin Luther King, Jr., Humanitarian Award.

Stuart J. Foster is a senior lecturer at the Institute of Education, the University of London. He received his doctorate from the University of Texas at Austin. He has published widely on educational history and the teaching and learning of history and the social studies. His contributions in this book reflect his interest in the teaching of controversial issues, the politics of schooling, and the representation of ethnic groups in American education.

John D. Hoge is an associate professor of education at the University of Georgia, where he has taught for the past 14 years while engaging in curriculum development projects, research, and publication activities designed to promote effective elementary and middle school social studies education. Regarding the school uniforms case in chapter 6, he states, "It was a natural for me. It touched so many power, authority, and governance issues and related directly to the lives of the children and parents who experienced it."

Carolyn Lyon is a doctoral student in the Department of Social Science Education at the University of Georgia. Prior to entering graduate school, Ms. Lyon taught history at the secondary level for 5 years. She is listed in the *Who's Who of American High School Teachers* for the year 2000 and is a recipient of the 2002 STAR Teacher Award for Gainesville High School in Gainesville, Georgia.

Pat Nickell is a former elementary teacher, school district administrator, and college professor. She served as president of the National Council for the

Social Studies, 1996–1997, and has an extensive list of published articles, books, book chapters, and curriculum projects to her credit. She coauthored the NCSS Social Studies standards, *Expectations of Excellence*. She is currently a social studies consultant in the state of Florida.

Pamela S. Roach completed her Ph.D. in social science education at the University of Georgia in April 2003. She has a master's degree in political science from the University of Arkansas–Fayetteville. Her dissertation focused on social studies preservice teachers' attitudes toward civic education. She first became interested in hate issues and government influence while she was researching the Little Rock Central crisis of 1957 and plans to conduct research on several aspects of civic education.

Ronald L. VanSickle earned the B.A.Ed. degree in U.S. history at Ball State University. After teaching high school social studies in Indiana, he earned the Ed.D. degree in social studies education at Indiana University–Bloomington. He is now a professor of social science education at the

University of Georgia, where he teaches curriculum, methods, and economic education courses, supervises student teachers, and advises graduate students. He received the George Washington Honor Medal from the Freedoms Foundation at Valley Forge for economic education work. His recent publications appeared in *Social Education, Theory and Research in Social Education*, the *Journal of Research and Development in Education*, and the *Korea Journal of Social Studies Education Research*.

B. Prentiss Woods is a doctoral candidate in social science education at the University of Georgia, where his research interests include the teaching of controversial issues and curricular implications of racial identity. The genesis of his research interests was his 4 years of teaching high school social studies in Rock Hill, South Carolina. Mr. Woods received his bachelor's degree in history and political science from Winthrop University, as well as his master's degrees in social studies teaching and administration and supervision. He also has his master's degree in history from Vanderbilt University.

Contents

NOTE: Every effort has been made to provide accurate and current Internet information in this book. However, the Internet and information posted on it are constantly changing, it is inevitable that some of the Internet addresses listed in this textbook will change.

An Introduction to Contextual Teaching and Learning Methods

by
Stuart J. Foster and Sherry L. Field

This book stems from a growing body of research about contextual teaching and learning (CTL), especially how the principles of contextual teaching and learning connect with social studies curriculum and instruction. *Real-World Investigations for Middle and High School Social Studies* is a series of instructional materials that are eminently practical because they

- can be used easily and immediately by teachers in social studies classrooms;
- can be adapted with specific community and local needs and resources in mind;
- advance the concepts of CTL; and
- are designed around the 10 themes of the National Council for the Social Studies standards (NCSS, 1994).

Naturally, as social studies educators committed to demonstrating the importance of social studies in the school curriculum, we value the notion of instruction that includes CTL, cooperative learning, case-based instruction, and authentic assessment practices in every middle and high school classroom.

CONTEXTUAL TEACHING AND LEARNING

Fundamentally, CTL draws its theoretical base from a variety of approaches including constructivist learning theory, principles of situated cognition, and constructs of expertise, multiple intelligences, and authentic and self-regulated learning (Borko & Putnam, 1998; Brown, Collins, & Duguid, 1989; Ericsson & Smith, 1991; Gardner, 1997; Lave & Wegner, 1991; Vygotsky, 1978). CTL aims to expose students to real-world applications and experiences in the social studies curriculum. It is predicated on the belief that students learn more if they can apply or connect their learning to meaningful contexts in the world outside the classroom (e.g., in the community or in the workplace). In many respects, therefore, CTL does not deviate from practices already employed by many effective teachers. Indeed, its goals are remarkably similar to those aspects of issues-based education (Engle & Ochoa, 1988; Evans & Saxe, 1996; Hunt & Metcalf, 1955; Massialas & Cox, 1966; Oliver & Shaver, 1966) and the NCSS advocacy of teaching and learning that are meaningful, integrative, value-based, challenging, and active (NCSS, 1994). However, recent initiatives in CTL have attempted to build on, expand, and share best practices in more systematic and comprehensive ways across all subjects. Accordingly, based on concepts derived from research and practice, CTL typically incorporates the following 12 key characteristics of teaching and learning:

- Students are actively engaged in the learning process.
- Learning is viewed as relevant.
- Students have opportunities to learn from one another in cooperative settings. Discourse and reflection are encouraged, and the perspectives and opinions of others are considered and valued.
- Learning is based on real-world issues and meaningful problems that often are interdisciplinary or extradisciplinary.
- Higher-order thinking and problem solving are encouraged.
- The learning environment is dynamic and exciting. Often, the process of learning is as important as the content learned.
- Learning occurs in multiple settings that allow students to identify and to address problems in new contexts (transfer).
- Students are encouraged to take responsibility for monitoring and developing their own learning.
- Teachers' assessment of student learning occurs in multiple forms.
- Teachers employ a variety of appropriate teaching methods.

- Teachers often act as facilitators of student learning.
- An appreciation of students' diverse life contexts and prior experiences is considered fundamental to effective learning.

A primary goal of CTL in social studies is to have students address real problems in real contexts. This often requires students and teachers to explore issues and information that exist beyond the classroom. An important caveat is appropriate here. We recognize fully that teachers and students continually deal with real problems and real issues. On a daily basis in every school in the nation, teachers and children deal with a range of compelling social issues including teenage pregnancy, drugs, acquired immune deficiency syndrome (AIDS), dysfunctional families, racism, violence, crime, gangs, cults, and other similar serious concerns. Certainly schools, with their attendant problems and social issues, are also legitimate contexts worthy of serious inquiry. However, it is also true that a plethora of issues relevant to the lives of young people now and in the future exist beyond school boundaries.

Many critical issues should be explored by teachers and learners in social studies classrooms. At its best, the investigation of provocative issues involves students with multiple sources of information, including site visits, guest speakers, Internet and library research, and the findings of questionnaires, surveys, and interviews. A fundamental element in the CTL inquiry process is that students become actively engaged in assessing and regulating their own learning. For example, students working in research teams should learn to make decisions about work allocation and delegation, meeting deadlines, and continuously evaluating the quality of their own work and the work of others. Further, students should be fully involved in decisions about how and against what criteria their work should be assessed. Multiple forms of assessment also should be utilized (e.g., portfolios, formal written reports, oral presentations, case studies). Above all, CTL in social studies demands that students always actively engage in their own learning and assessment, discuss salient issues, defend positions taken, and respect the varying perspectives of others. These skills and experiences associated with CTL are particularly valuable for middle and high school students. We also recognize the explicit connection between the goals of CTL and the challenges of teaching middle and high school students in meaningful and engaging ways.

The core philosophy of CTL as explained above clearly also supports our efforts to demonstrate meaningfully how important methods of teaching fit within the context of well-designed instruction. Placing instruction on methods of teaching within units designed for middle and high school students demonstrates more clearly how effective methods support meaningful learning. Thus, each chapter has been used as a context to feature a specific method (e.g., decision making and problem solving are featured in Chapter 2, "Crisis at Blue Ridge Leather").

Three key CTL methods are featured throughout the book: cooperative learning, case-based learning, and authentic assessment. Each chapter includes elements of these methods. The material that follows offers a brief overview of these methods as they are used throughout *Real-World Investigations for Middle and High School Social Studies.*

COOPERATIVE LEARNING

Cooperative learning is commonly understood as both a teaching strategy and a student-group relationship established for learning. Many positive outcomes occur when teachers are skillful at organizing students into groups and providing opportunities for them to work together. Successful group work depends upon creating a positive climate in order for human relations to grow in the classroom. The teacher's role in establishing effective procedures for working together in groups is significant (Parker, 2001).

The following eight practices and procedures tend to decrease hostility in a classroom (Johnson, Johnson, Holubec, & Roy, 1984) and are helpful in establishing a positive classroom climate.

- Positive interdependence: Students understand that their success in reaching their learning goals depends on the success of others in the group.
- Positive statements by the teacher: Teachers establish friendly, professional communication with students.
- Recognition of and response to individual differences: Students are respected for their individual talents; teachers are sensitive to cultural, linguistic, cognitive, and affective differences.
- Relaxed, comfortable pace: Teachers are mindful of the needs of their students and maintain flexibility. Although they plan careful learning components, they are not driven by a schedule.
- Student involvement in planning and managing the class: Students have an active role in how their learning is planned and how their classroom is managed. A sense of community is created.
- Warm, friendly relationship between teacher and students: The teacher recognizes students' need

for love and affection. In the classroom, teachers are warm and friendly yet professional. Students should view their teacher as a caring member of the group.

- Many opportunities for pleasurable emotional experiences: Teachers should guide students in multiple modes of expression, which include speaking, writing, art, acting, and role playing.
- Rules about caring: Teachers help students to understand that rules exist as one expression of care about the group and that group members take care of themselves, other members of the group, and their common surroundings with respect and thoughtfulness.

Cooperative learning has many of the same elements as group work, although typically it is more specialized. Johnson and Johnson (1992) identify five elements of cooperative learning:

- clearly perceived positive interdependence;
- considerable promotive (face-to-face) interaction;
- clearly perceived individual accountability and personal responsibility for achieving the group's goals;
- frequent use of relevant interpersonal and small-group skills; and
- frequent and regular group processing of current functioning to improve the group's future effectiveness.

According to Johnson and Johnson (1998), people who work together in healthy relationships use these five elements.

Cooperative learning has been the subject of hundreds of research studies over the past 40 years. Recent reviews of the literature (Johnson, Johnson, & Stanne, 2000; Newmann & Thompson, 1987; Vermette, 1998) highlight several major methods of cooperative learning. Of these, Learning Together (LT) and Academic Controversy (AC) had the greatest effect on student achievement, although all methods were shown to be effective. The following brief descriptions provide an introduction to cooperative learning. For more information, see Vermette (1998).

STAD: Student-Teams-Achievement Divisions (Slavin, 1978, 1983, 1995). After being taught a lesson, students meet in small groups (with four or five members) to master the information presented. Individuals take a quiz, and scores are calculated on the basis of improvement over previous quizzes. Team scores are posted in a class newsletter each week.

TGT: Teams-Games Tournament (DeVries & Slavin, 1978). As with STAD, students work together to learn material after a lesson is taught. Students compete one-on-one with individuals from other teams who have similar achievements. Points are given on the basis of success against others. Team scores are calculated, and successful teams are recognized.

JIG: Jigsaw (Aronson, Blaney, Sikes, Stephan, & Snapp, 1978). Individual students on a team are given material to master on a topic the whole group is learning. Students with similar material form *expert groups* to enhance mastery of the information. Then students go back to their original teams and teach it to their peers. In Jigsaw II (Slavin, 1986), all of the students in the class are provided the same information, have experts teach specialized information, and take tests individually.

LT: Learning Together (Johnson & Johnson, 1987). Students work in groups on projects. The teacher develops a spirit of cooperation through positive interdependence, face-to-face interaction, individual accountability, use of social skills, and group processing. Students learn to assist one another and ask peers for help. Individual performance and group performance are assessed. Students do not compete with one another. Students are rewarded through praise, tokens, and privileges.

GI: Group Investigation (Sharan & Sharan, 1976). Students take on many responsibilities for their learning in small groups, which contributes to a larger group project. They decide what information is needed, how it should be organized, and how it should be shared with peers. Higher-order thinking is emphasized.

AC: Academic Controversy (Johnson & Johnson, 1989, 1995). Students engage in higher-order problem solving by conducting research on a controversial topic. Next, they prepare a position statement, present their position, counter opposing positions and rebut questions about their position, and come to a group consensus on which everyone can agree.

TAI: Teams-Assisted-Individualization (Slavin, Madden, & Leavey, 1984). Students belong to mixed-ability groups. They assist one another in studying their own materials. Students may help, encourage, explain, and evaluate each other's learning. Each team receives a score based on the team's average.

CIRC: Cooperative Integrated Reading and Composition (Stevens, Madden, Slavin, & Farnish, 1987). Students receive direct instruction and engage in cooperative team practice sessions through an integrated approach. Emphasis is placed on heterogeneous teams and literacy work.

CI: Complex Instruction (Cohen, 1994). Students are engaged in problem solving activities that require myriad abilities and talents. Especially pertinent to real-world experiences, this method helps students negotiate power structures in the classroom in order to complete tasks.

Teachers who have little experience with cooperative learning techniques often select one method and become familiar with its processes before trying it out in the classroom. For those just beginning to utilize cooperative learning, STAD or JIG may be good choices. When teacher and students become familiar with and experience success with initial forms of cooperative learning, they may move on to a more sophisticated model, such as AC. Each case described here lends itself to cooperative learning, which is essential to students' abilities to work fruitfully in groups and participate actively in society.

CASE-BASED LEARNING

Case-based learning is another key feature of every unit of instruction in this textbook. The "case approach to instruction usually involves brief narratives that focus on actual problems, situations, or issues" (Driscoll, 1995, p. 3). As a specific method of instruction, case study is utilized across disciplines, abilities, and students of various ages (Driscoll, 1995; Kagan, 1993; Koballa & Tippins, 2000). Case-based learning provides multiple opportunities for inquiry and examination of key concepts surrounding an issue. Cases are based on real-life experience and are typically of high interest to the learner. Case-based learning that emphasizes concepts, value conflicts, or controversial issues can provide powerful motivation for learning.

Case-based learning has long been a part of law, medicine, and business, where it is used to apply general principles to a specific context, problem, or issue. As early as 1871, in studies of law, cases initially advanced the *Langdell method*. It utilized original source materials and group investigation to solve problems and extract specific legal principles (Kagan, 1993). Cases soon were used in medical and business schools because of their applicability to real-world problems and solutions.

Our aim for teaching with the cases in *Real-World Investigations* is to give students the opportunity to work in cooperative groups; to provide motivational activities during which students can conduct research, solve problems, and make meaningful decisions in order to allow students to "live in the case" (Driscoll, 1995, p. 4); and to provide instructional opportunities that promote high-quality, authentic assessment of learning.

AUTHENTIC ASSESSMENT

Every teacher is faced with growing concern over accountability in the classroom. Parents and school administrators often expect and demand that teachers deliver, year after year, a full grade's growth in each subject for every student. Documentation of this growth is often tied to voluntary national standards and to state and local testing programs that measure the acquisition of a mandated curriculum's content knowledge and related key skills. These testing programs may or may not include elements of authentic assessment, but there is a trend toward making learning assessments evaluate more than students' ability to recall discrete facts. For this reason, each author in this textbook paid special attention to authentic assessment tasks in the design of these studies. Thus, teachers can be assured that just as national standards are being addressed in these case studies, the students' acquisition of these standards is also being assessed.

The term *authenticity* in learning and assessment refers to the quality of realism that is embedded in the tasks that students complete. For example, instead of simply asking students to write a few paragraphs describing a series of events, teachers may ask students to assume the role of a reporter and write an article for a classroom or school newspaper. In this way, students are given an authentic role and a purpose, which enhance the results. At other times, authenticity refers to the reality of the content under study. Rather than teaching map reading using created maps as examples, students are presented with real maps of real places to work with. Rather than using events and places from long ago and far away to illustrate intolerance or war or supply and demand, teachers offer examples from students' own community or experience.

The studies in this series, to the greatest extent possible, take an authentic approach to assessment by including multiple tasks throughout each study that will provide for ongoing performance-based evaluation of each student's progress. Not only is the subject matter of the studies taken from real life, the tasks students are asked to complete are ones most of us actually have to do. At the end of each study, there is also a culminating performance task, challenge, or activity that is intended to provide the teacher with documentation of students' learning. These tasks also mimic real-life challenges and deal with real-life situations and content.

These studies do not lend themselves to fixed-response testing (multiple choice, matching, and the like) because the emphasis is on the acquisition of broad-based knowledge and high-level skills rather than a compendium of facts and figures requiring low-level memorization and recall. Thus, student demonstrations of learning take the form of reports, presentations, speeches, and other student-generated exhibitions of knowledge and skill.

Procedures for carrying out assessment activities are carefully described and summarized in each set of lessons. The summary table that accompanies each study highlights assessment activities and points out that they occur almost daily.

SUMMARY

We believe that the methods of contextual teaching and learning are best learned through real-world implementation and reflection on classroom practice. The instructional materials offered here and in the following chapters demonstrate teaching methods to meaningfully engage middle and high school learners in issues-oriented inquiry, case-based instruction, cooperative learning, and authentic assessment. They also offer practical guidelines for handling controversial issues, teaching decision making and problem solving, improving geographic thinking skills, using interviewing, implementing character/values education, distinguishing fact from opinion, handling current events, achieving higher-order thinking goals, teaching children caught in poverty, and implementing service learning in middle and high school classrooms. These methods and the CTL approach to instruction are essential elements of meaningful education for today's classrooms and America's future citizens.

Is America United or Divided by Language?

by
Stuart J. Foster, David Clark, and B. Prentiss Woods

OVERVIEW

The beginning of the new millennium poses many challenges for the United States. Although the nation has never experienced complete homogeneity, for most of its history English generally has been accepted as the country's primary language. The 21st century, however, marks a dramatic shift in the demographic landscape of the United States. As a consequence, not all Americans accept English as the predominant language of the nation. The United States must now respond to a situation in which increasingly large numbers of citizens speak other languages and, perhaps more important, argue for the right to speak their languages in school, at work, and in other areas of civic life.

Debates over how the United States should respond to the language issue are rich and complex. In simple terms, however, the arguments may be divided into two opposing viewpoints. Some Americans believe that in order to unite and bring cohesion to an extremely diverse society, English should become the official language of the nation. Opposing this view, other Americans argue that the people of the United States should respect and celebrate the diversity of the nation by accommodating and welcoming the use of many different languages.

This investigation invites students to explore a variety of scenarios involving the use of English as the official language of the United States. Students investigate this contentious issue principally through group research and ultimately decide whether or not the United States should adopt a policy that makes English the official language of the nation. For the research component of the inquiry, students are divided into issue-focused research groups. These groups are challenged through the use of discussion questions, resources provided in the study packet, relevant Web sites, and presentation outlines to consider the complex arguments surrounding the issue of English as the official language of the United States. After the research part of the inquiry is completed, each group presents its findings to the class. Individuals are then required to make an informed and reasoned decision about whether or not English should be the official language of the United States. Students' final decisions are formally presented in an advisory position paper for consideration by the president of the United States.

CONNECTION TO NCSS THEME I: CULTURE

The study of non-English-speaking people and their role in the contemporary United States relates directly to the "Culture" theme of the NCSS standards. As members of an increasingly diverse society, especially in the use of language, many American citizens are becoming more and more conscious of their responsibility to develop an awareness and understanding of those whose native tongue is not English. Nevertheless, as the United States becomes more pluralistic, other Americans believe that the need for national unity, shared values, and a cohesive society is paramount. The debate over language, therefore, is fundamental to students' understanding of the complexity of culture and cultural diversity in contemporary U.S. society. Students' involvement in this study will help them understand a variety of important social education concepts. Among the most noteworthy are the significance of language to the identity and preservation of a people's culture; the considerable benefits but undeniable burdens associated with cultural and linguistic diversity; and the difficulties and doubts often associated with attempts to balance or resolve competing groups' claims to fundamental rights and elements of social and economic justice.

METHODS FOCUS: CONTROVERSIAL ISSUES IN A PLURALISTIC SOCIETY

The United States houses the most diverse ethnic, cultural, and linguistic school population on earth. In cities like Chicago, Los Angeles, Washington, D.C., New York, and San Francisco, half or more of public school students are persons of color. By 2026 the nonwhite and Hispanic student enrollment in U.S. schools will grow from 10 million (in 1976) to 45 million, comprising an astonishing 70 percent of the nation's students. Several large school districts are wrestling with the fact that over 100 languages are spoken by children attending school and that approximately 6 million children reside in homes where English is not the first language.

Contemporary schools are places where students from myriad different cultures congregate and interact. Reflecting the diversity of the larger society, students increasingly encounter people of their own age who hold different worldviews, opinions, and perspectives. For social studies teachers, this situation has enormous challenges and possibilities. Above all, it provides an opportunity for students and teachers to address issues of diversity in thoughtful, compassionate, and systematic ways. It also offers the potential to develop in young people the habits of responsible citizenship, which include tolerance, respect, and a willingness to learn from and listen to others. Indeed, some educators have argued that as the United States becomes increasingly diverse, asking students to memorize traditional bodies of knowledge is less important than having students appreciate the world from multiple perspectives (e.g., Hernandez and Metzger, 1996; Pugh & Garcia, 1996).

In a similar vein, other educators have argued that in order for students to become more informed about aspects of diversity, schools should directly address key issues head on (e.g., Gerzon, 1997; Ladson-Billings, 1996). Ladson-Billings contends, for example, that people in schools and in the larger society avoid talking about race because it is uncomfortable and raises "feelings of rancor and guilt" (p. 101). However, it is undeniable that issues of race affect all our daily lives and certainly are evident in public schools. Generations of citizens have, for example, argued over such divisive issues as segregation, busing, tracking, multicultural education, bilingual education, and Ebonics. The inquiry presented in this chapter adds to this tradition by focusing on the controversial issue of English as the official language of the United States. Yet, even though these are issues familiar to young people, few students have had the opportunity to investigate and discuss them in any considered, critical, and sustained way. Many educators argue, however, that because these issues are so central to modern life and because they offer the possibility of helping students appreciate differing perspectives in more informed and thoughtful ways, schools must embrace them in their curriculum. Above all, those who advocate the inclusion of multicultural issues in the classroom argue that in order to cultivate habits of democracy in a pluralistic society, schools must find ways to address these issues even though initially they may appear uncomfortable, contentious, and controversial.

Tackling controversial issues in the classroom, however, need not be confined to issues of language and race. Indeed, the advocacy of teaching controversial issues across a whole range of subjects has a long and rich tradition in the social studies. Before embracing controversial issues as an approach to teaching, however, educators must carefully consider a series of crucial questions. Specifically five questions stand out:

1. Why teach controversial issues?
2. What controversial issues should be explored?
3. What should be the role of the teacher?
4. What practical classroom issues should be considered?
5. What are the benefits of teaching controversial issues?

Why teach controversial issues?

Advocates of teaching controversial issues span the generations and include some of the most influential figures in the social studies profession. These include Dewey (1910), Griffin (1942), Hunt and Metcalf (1955, 1968), Oliver and Shaver (1966), Massialas and Cox (1966), Newmann and Oliver (1970), Engle and Ochoa (1988), and Evans and Saxe (1996). Each in his or her own individual and compelling way justified the teaching of controversial issues in the classroom. Although it would be erroneous to claim that these educators share identical positions, it is undeniable that they hold four positions in common.

First, these educators argue that controversial issues should be taught in classrooms because they provide opportunities to engage students in topics that appear relevant and interesting to them. Whether adults like it or not, in their daily lives students encounter a range of contentious issues. These include gun control, crime, TV violence, censorship, curfew laws, teenage pregnancy, abortion, drugs, school dropout, and myriad other equally crucial issues. Research tells us that little learning occurs if students remain unmotivated and uninterested in a particular subject. However, when students are engaged and interested, opportunities exist to tackle complex and sophisticated problems.

Second, advocates of controversial issues instruction argue that traditional teaching places too much emphasis on students' learning fixed, inert, and uncontested knowledge. They contend that requiring students to memorize factual material in isolation does not prepare them for responsible citizenship. They argue the need for students to research, investigate, and construct new knowledge. Students should appreciate that knowledge often is disputed and open to question; therefore, opportunities should be provided in school for deeper, more critical thinking. Indeed, some advocates argue that students should be encouraged to construct new knowledge that challenges established ways of thinking, a process that Engle and Ochoa (1988) called *countersocialization*.

Third, advocates state that controversial issues should be included across the school curriculum because most important issues do not easily fit within neat disciplinary boundaries. Issues are interdisciplinary, multidisciplinary, and extradisciplinary; typically, they involve aspects of life that contain social, political, cultural, economic, ethical, and scientific dimensions.

Finally, and arguably most important, advocates contend that throughout their lives, either directly or indirectly, students will face conflict and controversy. An essential condition of democratic life is that intelligent people will disagree on a range of issues. Accordingly, schools must model democracy and teachers must equip students with the necessary skills and dispositions to address controversy and to resolve difference in a rational, thoughtful, and sensitive manner.

As this overview suggests, many compelling rationales exist for teaching controversial issues in the classroom. However, before teachers engage in exploring such issues, it is vital that they construct their own rationales for so doing. It is not enough to teach controversial issues because they are sensational or fashionable, or appear as a desperate attempt to appease disgruntled students. Rather, teachers must be able to defend their decision to take on contested issues in an intellectually and academically responsible way. As James Shaver (1996) has written, "a carefully justified rationale is essential to teaching about controversy without being controversial" (p. 384). Ultimately, it is essential that teachers communicate their rationale to administrators, parents, and students. In some cases, it may even be useful to engage parents by asking for their comments and involvement.

What controversial issues should be explored?

Before addressing this question, consideration must be given to *who* decides on the choice of issue. Should students decide or should it be the responsibility of the teacher? Often an effective solution is for students and teachers to decide together. For example, teachers could ask students to brainstorm a list of issues or events that concern them (a) internationally (e.g., terrorism, pollution), (b) nationally (e.g., gun control, immigration), or (c) at a local or school level (e.g., the school dress code, drug abuse). In collaboration with the class, the teacher could examine commonalities and differences and discuss alternative proposals. The class and teacher could then make a collective decision (possibly by a vote) on what should be studied. In so doing, the class and teacher should consider the criteria by which an issue should be selected. For example, important criteria might be the following:

Time: Is enough time available for an in-depth investigation or is the issue too broad?

Resources: Do students have access to a range of sources necessary to acquire information on the issue (e.g., Internet access, media center, library facilities, resources in the community)?

Multiple perspectives: Is the issue one on which there are multiple, diverse, and competing perspectives or is it one on which most students are likely to agree?

Knowledge: Does the issue allow for the exploration of interdisciplinary and extradisciplinary knowledge or is it too narrowly conceived?

Practicality: Is the issue too inflammatory? Would it expose the school to unnecessary criticism?

Sensitivity: Is the issue one that the teacher and all students are comfortable discussing?

Enduring issues: Is the issue associated with dilemmas that have existed across the centuries (e.g., freedom of speech) or is it short-term?

Action: Might the issue lead to some useful end product and positive action or is it one that individual pupils feel they are powerless to affect or control?

Naturally, in such a discussion the teacher can offer alternative perspectives, play devil's advocate, and even try to influence the position taken by the students. Ultimately, however, the investigation into the selected controversial topic is more likely to succeed if students have some ownership of the subject matter.

What should be the role of the teacher?

When introducing controversial issues teachers must think very carefully about their own role in the classroom. Initially, it may appear easier for teachers to remain impartial. Adopting a stance that is neutral and noncommittal has obvious benefits. In particular, it avoids the accusation that the teacher is indoctrinating students or, at the very least, leading them to certain conclusions. Teachers must be aware, however, that students likely will ask for their views. Accordingly, it is very important that teachers consider their responses carefully. Some advocates argue that teachers should not be afraid to share their opinions with the class. In so doing, however, they should note three considerations. First, after expressing their opinions, teachers must be prepared to justify their argument with a logical explanation supported by evidence. Second, teachers must emphasize that their position is one of many and that students should know that this position may be challenged. Vitally important is that students learn to accept that intelligent people can disagree on a range of issues and still remain good friends and community members. By setting a positive example, skilful teachers act as excellent models of good democratic practice. Third, teachers should never introduce any controversial topic if they are not prepared to expose students to their own beliefs and values. Related to this consideration, teachers must feel comfortable with the students and believe that they have their respect and trust before tackling controversial issues. Knowing the background, developmental level, concerns, and interests of the students is crucial to the success of any lesson. Teachers will need to make judgments about the teaching approach that they believe is appropriate to the students they teach. In sum, teachers will have to make a variety of decisions that they believe are appropriate for their classrooms, but arguably the most important one is to consider how they will communicate their personal position to the class.

What practical classroom issues should be considered?

The greatest challenge to the teacher in dealing with controversial issues is to create a classroom atmosphere that is conducive to open, thoughtful, and sensitive discussion. For any meaningful and worthwhile classroom activity to take place, students must feel that their views are respected, taken seriously, and carefully considered. To achieve this aim, it is vital that teachers discuss with the class the ground rules for any discussion. Students may wish to create and prominently display a list of dos and don'ts for discussion. Ideally, these should include items such as the following: only one person speaks at a time; disrespectful behavior such as groans, gestures, and eye rolling is not permitted; people wishing to speak should raise their hands; all debates must have a moderator or chair; and so on.

Successful deliberation often causes individuals who hold a particular position to become passionate and excited. Although this enthusiasm should not be discouraged, it is important that students learn to interact in a civilized and democratic way. However, on occasion, teachers will need to diffuse tense and heated debates by employing a range of techniques (see, e.g., Onosko, 1996; Passe & Evans, 1996). For example, students who hold strong opinions may be asked to consider alternative perspectives (e.g., the teacher could say, "That's very interesting and you clearly feel strongly about this issue, but why do you think people might disagree with you? What arguments might they put forward?"). When students fiercely disagree, it is important that the teacher summarize the differences and explore with the class the logic of their positions in a calm way. Emphasis also must be placed on the notion that it is ideas that are being challenged, not persons. Humor can also be employed to great effect in tense situations. Above all, it is crucial that teachers acknowledge students' competing contributions and emphasize that holding strong but different views is an essential condition of democratic life. Furthermore, teachers should openly promote the idea that changing one's mind in the face of argument is a sign of thoughtfulness and consideration, not weakness and indecision.

Teachers should also seize the opportunity to use different formats for discussion. For example, some students often feel more comfortable in small-group settings. Small groups also allow students to identify particular arguments in the broader debate in more detail. In addition, they provide the opportunity to establish focused research teams. For example, Passe and Evans (1996) suggest 10 different formats for student deliberation including Socratic, Quaker, fishbowl, and panel discussion. Finally, after any period of deliberation, teachers must find ways to link together the essential points raised by the students to discussion of the central controversial issue.

Teaching controversial issues also has important implications for classroom assessment. Typically, no absolutely right or wrong answers exist concerning issues of social dispute. Instead, answers take on shades of correctness or goodness for certain purposes from certain perspectives. As a result, multiple-choice tests or other fact-based testing measures often are inappropriate. This does not mean, however, that arguments and viewpoints cannot be assessed. For example, students can be assessed on the way in which they evaluate competing arguments, select and deploy evidence to articulate a position, and draw thoughtful conclusions. In addition, performance-based activities such as role play, poster displays, multimedia presentations, or speeches often are more appropriate avenues for students to display their abilities than traditional paper-and-pencil tests.

What are the benefits of teaching controversial issues?

Carole Hahn's (1996) comprehensive review of research on issues-based education suggests that educators who employ controversial issues in the classroom are more likely to "find that their students become more interested in the political arena, develop a greater sense of political efficacy and confidence, and become more interested in the issues that they have studied as well as knowledgeable about them" (p. 37). The following chart also graphically illustrates the potential benefits of issues-based education versus traditional fact-based social studies:

In conclusion, those who advocate teaching controversial issues argue that if social studies education is designed to develop thoughtful, compassionate, rational, participatory, and responsible citizens, then issues-based education must be employed more extensively. This position arguably is especially compelling for a complex, modern, multicultural society like the United States.

COMMON CRITICISMS OF TRADITIONAL SOCIAL STUDIES	POTENTIAL BENEFITS OF TEACHING CONTROVERSIAL ISSUES
Learning is passive.	Learning is active. Student involvement is central.
Subject lacks relevance to students' lives.	Issues are selected that are of direct relevance to students' lives.
Knowledge and information are uncritically absorbed.	Information is critically examined.
Knowledge and information are absolute and static.	Knowledge is constructed, tentative, and open to examination.
Social studies is too compartmentalized into disciplines.	Controversial issues frequently are interdisciplinary.
Social studies courses cover too much, too quickly.	Controversial issues demand an in-depth focus.
Teaching is textbook-dominated.	Issues require a rich array of information sources.
Narrow perspectives are offered.	Multiple and diverse perspectives are encouraged.

Table 1.1 Lesson Overview for "Is America United or Divided by Language?"

	GOALS	ACTIVITIES	ASSESSMENTS
LESSON ONE	• Introduce students to the contentious issue of English as the official language of the United States. • Have students appreciate and understand different viewpoints in the controversy. • Encourage students to formulate and articulate initial opinions.	• Orient students to the issue of language in society through guided questions. • Have students read Handout 1.1. Use questions 1–7 to probe students' understandings. • Read Handout 1.2 with the class and discuss initial impressions. • Divide the class into groups and ask students to discuss guiding questions 1–5.	
LESSON TWO	• Research an identified issue related to the central controversy. • Develop students' skills of research, cooperation, organization, and planning. • Structure research findings into a coherent, accurate, and engaging class presentation. • Develop well-grounded positions on the central issue.	• Divide the class into four research groups and provide each group with one of four handouts (Handouts 1.3 to 1.6). • Ask the groups to read their handouts and discuss the questions provided. • Help the groups use relevant Web sites and other sources to investigate their topics. • Distribute copies of Handouts 1.7 and 1.8 to help students complete their research. • Work with the class to specify the requirements, rules, and criteria for presentations.	• Collect and examine the "Individual Research Task Completion Report" (Handout 1.8).
LESSON THREE	• Disseminate the research findings of each group. • Provide individual students with information necessary for them to reach an informed and reasoned decision on the central issue. • Develop effective communication skills and students' ability to identify, analyze, and synthesize relevant information so as to form a logical and coherent argument.	• Inform the class that they will be required to produce a two-page position statement following the presentations. • Have groups present their findings and ask students to record relevant information on Handout 1.9. • Following the presentations, summarize the central issue and record relevant arguments/points on the board. • Ask the class to vote on whether the United States should adopt English as its official language. • Require students to write down and defend their position on the central issue on Handout 1.10.	• Review and provide feedback to each group. Evaluate presentations against agreed-on criteria. • Collect and evaluate students' final position paper (Handout 1.10).

LESSON ONE: The Changing Face of America

Purpose This lesson introduces students to key issues surrounding the controversy over attempts to mandate English as the official language of the United States. Using two specific examples, students are challenged to think carefully about this controversy and about the wider issue of language in U.S. culture. Students are also encouraged to articulate their initial opinions on whether or not the United States should adopt English as the official language of the nation.

Duration Two class periods

Materials
Handout 1.1: People v. Superior Computers Inc.
Handout 1.2: A Tale of Two Languages

Procedures

1. Orient your class to the issue of language in society by asking students about their experience with other languages. Ideas for an opening question-and-answer session may include the following:

- Do they, or members of their family, speak another language?
- Is speaking another language beneficial? Why? Why not?
- Have they ever been in a situation in which they did not speak the language of those around them (e.g., in another part of the city or country or overseas)? How did it feel?
- What are people's attitudes toward those who speak languages other than English? Why?
- Would it be better if everyone in the United States spoke English? Why? Why not?

These questions are designed to draw on and expose students' own experiences and attitudes before engaging in the inquiry. The last question directly introduces students to the issue that they will try to resolve during the inquiry:

- Should the United States adopt English as the official language of the nation?

It is useful at this point to display this question prominently in the classroom and to leave it in open view for the duration of the inquiry. Explain to the class that the issue is complicated and impacts many aspects of society, as demonstrated by the examples that follow. Distribute Handout 1.1 and ask students to read about the controversy over English-only use in the workplace. The details presented in the handout are adapted from a real court case in California.

2. After the students have read Handout 1.1, use questions 1 and 2 to establish the different positions of the employer and the employees. It may be useful to write down the key points of disagreement on a chart, board, overhead projector screen, or computer display. Engage students in a preliminary discussion of the merits of each position.

3. Broaden understandings through a discussion of questions 3 to 6. These questions encourage students to think about the implications of the English-only policy beyond this particular case.

4. Discuss question 7 (the judge's decision) with the class. Encourage students to support their views with rational arguments.

5. Introduce a second example by distributing to the class Handout 1.2: A Tale of Two Languages. Read the handout with the class. Discuss with the class how the migration of Mexican workers has impacted the local community. Discuss the benefits that the workers brought to the community and why some people in the community objected to their arrival.

6. Divide the class into groups of four or five students. Ask them to read and discuss questions 1 to 5 on Handout 1.2 in their groups.

7. Once again, bring the class together in a whole-class discussion on the issue "Should the United States adopt English as the official language of the nation?" Clarify what *official* means. Note that an official policy would be embodied in law. Also point out that an official language would not prevent people from speaking their own language in their daily lives, but it could restrict the use of other languages in such formal settings as schools, workplaces, state and federal agencies, and other civic organizations. Students should also consider whether or not the United States needs an official language to unite its diverse population.

LESSON TWO: Should the United States Adopt English as the Official Language of the Nation?

Purpose This lesson requires students to research in more detail four major topics surrounding the issue of English as the official language of the United States. The intention is to broaden students' understanding of the complexity of debates over a national language. The lesson also challenges students to work cohesively as a team as they develop important research skills. Finally, the lesson acts as a springboard for the next lesson, in which students share their research findings in a presentation to the whole class.

Duration Three class periods

Materials
Handout 1.3: International Use of English as an Official Language
Handout 1.4: English-Only Workplaces
Handout 1.5: English as the Official Language at the State Level
Handout 1.6: Creating Multilingual Street Signs
Handout 1.7: General Web sites for Research Investigations
Handout 1.8: Individual Research Task Completion Report

Procedures

1. Divide the class into four research groups. Provide each group with one of four handouts (i.e., Handouts 1.3 to 1.6). Group one will research the international use of English as an official language. Group two will investigate further the use of English in the workplace. Group three will examine the implementation of English as the official language of states. Group four will explore the practicality of creating multilingual street signs.

2. Inform each group that their task is to work through the three components of their respective handouts:

- Read the information provided.
- Discuss the questions posed.
- Use their research findings to prepare a presentation to the class on their topic.

3. For the first component, require the members of each group to read the information quietly. For the second component, require the group to discuss each question carefully. Monitor each group's progress and engage in group discussion as appropriate.

4. For the third component, encourage the students in each group to divide up the responsibilities for researching their topic. For example, one individual may be assigned to investigate and report on a single aspect of the presentation or task, or students may be assigned responsibility for reading and reporting on a particular Web site. A research team coordinator who oversees the group's work may also be appointed or elected. Students should be asked to complete Handout 1.8 individually as a way of demonstrating the accomplishment of their work within their groups.

5. Provide access to the Internet sites identified in Handouts 1.3 to 1.7. Monitor each group's work with these resources and answer any questions students may have. Allow sufficient time for thoughtful consideration of these resources.

6. At an appropriate point, it is important to discuss with the whole class the requirements for the class presentation. Indeed, involving students in this process can increase their motivation and their sense of ownership. For example, students might decide that groups must

- limit presentations to an agreed-on time (e.g., 15 minutes);
- use visual aids to support their presentation;
- introduce the focus of their presentation;
- cover the three required components of the presentation guidelines;
- involve several different members of the team in the presentation.

7. During the time allocated for research, students may wish to secure additional resources from, for example, the media center.

8. Also, enough time should be provided for students to prepare well-thought-out, coherent, and engaging classroom presentations.

9. Finally, ensure that every student completes and hands in the Individual Research Task Completion Form (Handout 1.8).

LESSON THREE: Presentations and Decisions

Purpose This lesson brings together the research findings of all groups. Its primary goal is to provide students with enough information to allow them to make a reasoned and informed decision about the central issue of whether or not the United States should adopt English as its official language. The lesson also develops effective communication skills and students' ability to identify, analyze, and synthesize relevant information.

Duration Two class periods

Materials
Presentation resources (e.g., computer projection equipment, overhead projectors, posters)
Handout 1.9: Should the United States Adopt English as the Official Language of the Nation?
Handout 1.10: Final Position Statement

Procedures

1. Inform students that following the presentation sessions, they will be required to write a two-page position paper advising the president of the

United States whether or not to support a policy that makes English the official language of the United States. Accordingly, tell students that they are to listen carefully to each presentation in order to identify arguments and information relevant to making a decision about English as the official language. To help them evaluate the arguments, provide each student with Handout 1.9. Encourage students to make notes on the handout during the presentations.

2. Have each of the four groups present its findings in order. Groups should be given 15 minutes to present. After each group has presented, invite students to ask questions of the group; clarify points as appropriate and encourage open discussion. Also, require students to record relevant information on the handout.

3. Following all of the presentations, focus discussion on the larger issue of whether or not the United States should adopt an English-only policy in schools, the government, the workplace, and civic life. Throughout the discussion, ensure that students support their opinions with examples, evidence, and rational argument. It is also helpful to record key points on the board or on an overhead projector screen. Additionally, convert Handout 1.9 into an overhead transparency and illustrate and record key points on the handout. Conclude the discussion with a vote on the issue "Should the United States Adopt English as the Official Language of the Nation?"

4. Give the class the final assignment detailed in Handout 1.10. This writing assignment requires students to outline their arguments for or against the policy of English as the official language of the United States. Inform the class that they are to write down their arguments in a clear, cogent, and persuasive manner using information and evidence gathered from their research and the group presentations. Emphasize that the intended audience for their arguments is the president of the United States.

PEOPLE V. SUPERIOR COMPUTERS INC.

In an effort to make his workplace more efficient, Daniel Bailey, a plant manager for Superior Computers Inc., introduced a policy that made English the only language that his employees could speak while on the job. Located in the heart of San Francisco, California, the company's extremely diverse workforce speaks many different languages. When news of Mr. Bailey's new policy reached the employees, many of them were outraged.

Mr. Bailey and Superior Computers Inc. maintained that the measure was necessary. In a letter to his employees, Mr. Bailey wrote, "The English-only rule had been adopted to improve communication on the assembly line." He felt that Superior Computers Inc. was suffering from communication problems as a result of the many different languages that the workers spoke. The employees, however, protested that the languages they spoke did not interfere with their job performance. The issue became increasingly tense over the weeks that followed. The issue could not be resolved within the company. In late May 2000, 1 month after he initiated his English-only policy, Mr. Bailey and Superior Computers Inc. were taken to court by 12 of their Spanish-speaking employees and the Equal Employment Opportunity Commission (EEOC).

In their opening arguments, lawyers for the EEOC claimed that Superior Computers Inc. was "violating the civil rights of its employees when it arbitrarily penalized a single group based on their national origin." They went on to say that "blanket English-only policies, which require English at all times with no exceptions, are clearly unlawful." Superior Computers Inc. was quick to counter the EEOC, however, claiming that the English-only policy was essential to the success of the company. Mr. Bailey stated, "The company was having trouble with productivity and quality control because people weren't talking to each other. Regardless of this policy, we value diversity and the gifts it brings to our workplace." Both sides presented extremely convincing arguments, forcing the court to make a very difficult decision.

After much deliberation, U.S. District Judge Stan Learner decided in favor of the employees and the EEOC. In a lengthy explanation, Judge Learner reasoned that by prohibiting his workers from speaking their native language and forcing them to use English, Mr. Bailey was violating Title VII of the 1964 Civil Rights Act. In addition to ordering Superior Computers Inc. to eliminate the English-only policy, Judge Learner awarded the 12 Spanish-speaking workers $280,500 in damages.

GUIDING QUESTIONS

1. What arguments did Superior Computers Inc. put forward to justify their English-only policy?

2. Why did the EEOC and the workers object to this policy?

continued

Real-World Investigations for Social Studies
Hoge, Field, Foster, and Nickell

Handout 1.1 *continued*

3. What responsibility do immigrant workers have to learn the native language of their workplace?

4. What responsibility do employers have to provide language instruction to their workers?

5. What impact could the judge's decision have on the increasingly diverse workplaces of the future?

6. What impact might the decision have on venues other than the workplace?

7. Do you agree with the judge's decision? Why? Why not?

Real-World Investigations for Social Studies
Hoge, Field, Foster, and Nickell

A TALE OF TWO LANGUAGES

Nestled in the northeastern corner of Georgia, the community of Dalton has been renowned for decades as the center of American carpet production. The economic expansion of the 1990s, coupled with a lack of people able to work in the area, however, created a severe worker shortage in Dalton that demanded immediate attention. Community leaders, desperate to fuel the booming economy, considered many solutions. Finally, although some objected, a handful of businesspeople came up with the idea of importing workers from Mexico to fill the escalating demand for labor. Although the experiment solved the worker shortage, it also had many unforeseen effects on Dalton.

Initially, employers expected to import labor only on a limited basis. However, the number of Mexican workers in Dalton grew very quickly, and the community changed as a result. In many local schools, for example, the percentage of students who spoke Spanish as their first language exploded from approximately 5 percent in 1990 to nearly 50 percent in 2000. To accommodate the educational transformation, Dalton schools were forced to alter their tradi-tional English-only policy. No longer are classes taught or signs written only in English; bilingual teachers and notices have replaced their outdated English-only predecessors. The effects of the demographic shift also can be seen in other areas of the community. The local Catholic church, for instance, now offers services in both English and Spanish. Although Dalton seems to have handled the transformation well, the immigration of so many Spanish-speaking people brought with it inevitable controversy.

Outraged at the changes facing their community, many citizens of Dalton began a campaign to maintain the "purity" of the area. Critics of the immigration policy believed that the country was trading economic prosperity for the destruction of their culture and language. Although they were a minority, these critics went out of their way to make sure their views were heard. Some protesters even created shirts with the message "ENGLISH ONLY" to try to persuade others in the community that their culture and language were being destroyed. These arguments continue to this day.

GUIDING QUESTIONS

1. The Mexican workers were first employed during a time of economic prosperity, but what effect could a recession have on the relationship between the Spanish- and English-speaking people?

2. Dalton is located in a county of approximately 80,000 people. What effect might an equivalent migration of Spanish-speaking people have on a larger city such as Boston, Atlanta, or Detroit?

continued

Real-World Investigations for Social Studies
Hoge, Field, Foster, and Nickell

3. What other programs could Dalton initiate to ensure the long-term success of this multicultural community?

4. Do you think the schools were correct to adopt a bilingual approach to education? Why? Why not?

5. What other approaches might the schools have adopted to address the dramatic increase of non-English-speaking students?

GROUP ONE: INTERNATIONAL USE OF ENGLISH AS AN OFFICIAL LANGUAGE

Read the following information and the "Something to Think About" statements that follow.

With the United States acquiring increasing economic and political power, many formerly stable areas of the world are experiencing profound shifts. Many of the world's languages, for example, are facing daunting challenges as the 21st century progresses. In an effort to keep pace with the ever-expanding power of the United States and other English-speaking nations, many countries have neglected their own culture and language in recent years. Others, in the hope of preserving their own culture and language, have suffered drastic economic and political consequences by refusing to standardize and accept English. Some studies go as far as to claim that by the year 2050, more than 90 percent of the world's 6,000 languages will be extinct. Although the ultimate result of the English language expansion is uncertain, it poses many short-term problems for the smaller nations of the world.

Mauritania is a perfect example of a developing nation struggling with the problem of establishing English as the official language. Nestled in the center of northern Africa, Mauritania has traditionally been a country where Arabic languages and local dialects are predominantly spoken. The rapid global industrialization of the 21st century, however, places Mauritania in a troublesome predicament. Many of the nation's wealthier citizens have championed the adoption of English as the official language, claiming that it will provide the tools necessary to escape the centuries of poverty that have crippled the country. Furthermore, they claim that if English becomes the official language, Mauritania will be able to create many new and important political, economic, and military ties with nations in the West.

For other Mauritanians, adopting English as the official language would be the worst possible policy. Spearheaded by the religious groups within Mauritania, the critics claim that embracing English would, in effect, force out thousands of years of invaluable, unique, and irreplaceable Arabic culture. They also believe that welcoming English would not have the positive economic impact that its supporters claim it would. These critics are convinced that it would not stimulate the struggling economy, but would merely open it to increased exploitation by greedy American and other Western business people.

Something to Think About

Many countries, such as Zimbabwe, Liberia, Ecuador, Honduras, Singapore, and Fiji, where English is not a native language, have adopted English as one of their official languages.

continued

Handout 1.3 *continued*

Following years of controversy and internal strife, French-speaking Quebec unsuccessfully sought its independence from English-speaking Canada.

1. Having read the information above, discuss in your groups the following three questions:

    a. What positive impact would adopting a universal language, such as English, have on the world?

    b. What negative consequences would result from having a universal language such as English?

    c. In what ways does English influence countries that traditionally have not spoken English?

2. Working as a team, use the Web sites provided and any other relevant sources to present your findings to the rest of the class in a 15-minute presentation. Use the following guidelines for your presentation:

    Your presentation topic is "Should English Be the Official Language of the United States?: An International Perspective."

    a. Explain in your class presentation how English is increasingly used in many countries throughout the world. Explain why this is so. Provide examples to illustrate your points.

    b. Explain how and why a number of countries are (1) resisting the growth of English in their country and (2) accommodating the use of many languages.

    c. Tell the class what your group thinks about the increasing dominance of the English language in the world. Be sure to provide reasons and evidence to support your argument.

Real-World Investigations for Social Studies
Hoge, Field, Foster, and Nickell

To help with your research, a list of relevant Web sites is given below. In addition, Handout 1.7 provides a list of general Web sites useful for your research.

Key Web sites on International Language

http://iteslj.org/Articles/Kitao-WhyTeach.html
An excellent argument by a Japanese scholar explaining why learning English is so important in the 21st century.

www.cltr.uq.edu.au/alaa/proceed/brandle.html
Explores the growth of the use of the English language in Switzerland which has four official languages.

http://antonnews.com/gardencitylife/1999/12/17/opinion/
A brief editorial outlining the spread of English through Japanese culture and the possible adoption of it as a second official language.

www.globalvis.com/toubon.html
A site explaining the requirement of the French government that all consumer documents be in the French language. Also provides details about a lawsuit brought against the French campus of an American university which uses only English on its Web site.

http://www.newrules.org/journal/nrfallOOculture.html
Shows the extent to which countries have encouraged the creation of "national" arts so that English-oriented "Hollywood culture" will not take over their culture.

Handout 1.4

GROUP TWO: ENGLISH-ONLY WORKPLACES

Read the following information and the "Something to Think About" statements that follow.

As evidenced in the Superior Computers Inc. incident in San Francisco, the issue of English in the workplace is extremely volatile. In small towns and bustling cities all over the United States, local governments and employers are struggling over whether or not it is more prudent to promote a multilingual workplace or to force the universal adoption of English. No two towns or companies have approached the issue in the same way, and all have found different reactions to their policies within their respective communities.

Although much of the controversy centers on Spanish and its increasing prevalence in the United States, the recent growth in the populations of speakers of many other languages has spurred debate as well. In Seattle, Washington, for instance, many companies have large proportions of Asian employees. The recent immigration of thousands of East Asians to the American West Coast has introduced substantial diversity into the previously homogeneous population. The influx of Chinese, Japanese, and Korean workers, just to name a few, has forced many companies in the Seattle area to adapt their language policies to account for differences among their employees.

One company in Seattle has taken a new approach to this dilemma, much to the dismay of many other corporations in the area. Global Industries, a firm specializing in creating high-powered lasers, has begun to offer gradual pay increases for employees who become proficient in more than one of the high-demand languages. According to the new plan, a first-year laser technician at Global Industries, for example, receives a base salary of $40,000. The employee will earn a yearly bonus of $5,000 for each additional language spoken. A Chinese employee, for example, who also speaks Japanese and English fluently will earn $10,000 more per year than a worker who speaks only his or her native language.

Most of the employees of Global Industries praise this measure, as it encourages diversity and creates a sense of acceptance of other cultures. Furthermore, supporters claim the multilingual policy makes Global Industries more competitive in local, national, and international markets. The striking diversity within the company attracts the best job applicants within Seattle, while at the same time providing the people needed to excel in business deals with firms of many nationalities.

The critics of the policy, however, find many faults in the decision of Global Industries to promote multilingual employees. They complain that encouraging the use of languages other than English in the workplace creates communication barriers between employees. When workers are prompted, and sometimes even rewarded for, speaking multiple languages in the workplace, critics argue, misunderstandings inevitably appear following every major decision. Many critics also believe that by advocating a multilingual policy, employers are neglecting their

Real-World Investigations for Social Studies
Hoge, Field, Foster, and Nickell

responsibility to help develop conscientious American citizens. In other words, they feel that companies have at least partial responsibility for fostering a sense of pride in the English language, the United States, and the American way of life.

The debate between these two groups will linger as long as Seattle continues to diversify. With both groups adamantly opposed to compromise, companies such as Global Industries will remain controversial.

Something to Think About

People who have a first language other than English often want to use it with friends who also speak that language fluently. Would informal, friendly conversations in languages other than English create a cold and uninviting atmosphere in worksite break rooms where all workers have traditionally enjoyed the right to relax and converse freely?

1. Having read the information above, discuss in your groups the following five questions:

   a. What effect could the Global Industries policy have on other companies in the Seattle area?

   b. What options, other than offering pay incentives, could companies offer to encourage workers to become multilingual?

   c. On the other hand, what incentives could companies offer to their employees who speak other languages to gain proficiency in English?

   d. What are the arguments for and against encouraging workers to speak many languages?

   e. What do you think about the new policy at Global Industries? Do you agree with it? Why? Why not?

continued

Handout 1.4 *continued*

2. Working as a team, use the Web sites provided and any other relevant sources to present your findings to the rest of the class in a 15-minute presentation. Use the following guidelines for your presentation:

   Your presentation topic is: "Should English Be the Official Language of the United States?: A View from the Workplace."

   a. Explain in your class presentation how and why some businesses openly encourage employees to use languages other than English in the workplace. Provide examples to illustrate your points.

   b. Explain how and why some employees disagree with this practice and, instead, want to encourage the use of English alone in the workplace. Provide examples to illustrate your points.

   c. Tell the class what your group thinks about the English-only policy in the workplace. Be sure to provide reasons and evidence to support your arguments.

   To help with your research, a list of relevant Web sites is given below. In addition, Handout 1.7 provides a list of general Web sites useful for your research.

Key English-Only Workplace Web sites

www.english.gov.hk/main.htm
Deals with Hong Kong's attempt to mandate high English competency for its businesses so that Hong Kong can maintain its competitive edge as an international center of business, finance, and tourism. Click on the Campaign and The Benchmark of Workplace English standards icons to see Hong Kong's rationale and implementation procedures.

www.eeoc.gov/press/9-19-00.html
An EEOC press release concerning a lawsuit that determines that English-only rule in workplaces is unlawful.

www.saspc.com/art_117.htm
Deals with increasing legal challenges faced by English-only workplace rules.

Real-World Investigations for Social Studies
Hoge, Field, Foster, and Nickell

GROUP THREE: ENGLISH AS THE OFFICIAL LANGUAGE AT THE STATE LEVEL

Read the following information and the "Something to Think About" statements that follow.

Although most states have stayed away from the explosive issue of English as their official language, a few have decided to confront it head on. The approaches that different states have taken vary strikingly, from those that advocate the English-only policy to those that strongly support multilingual environments.

Many states in the mid-Atlantic region, for example, are faced with increasing numbers of non-English-speaking immigrants, forcing them to reevaluate many of their traditional governmental policies. In an effort to support a growing multicultural population, Holly Roper, a state senator from New Jersey, introduced a bill promoting the spread of languages other than English. Roper believed that the state government should play an essential role in the integration of new immigrants into American society. According to her bill, the government would publish all major documents in a minimum of two languages, English and Spanish, and attempt to find translations per request for all other documents. The bill also called for the state to provide Spanish-speaking social workers to assist the large Hispanic population. Champions of this bill believe that this would ease the transition of moving to the United States for many of New Jersey's immigrants. In addition, Roper argued that printing documents in numerous languages would prepare non-English-speaking people to become competent American citizens.

While Roper's arguments were strong, much opposition to her bill in New Jersey existed. John St. Hall, Roper's primary opponent, believed that incorporating a multilingual policy in New Jersey's government would be not only inefficient but also highly ineffective. St. Hall claimed that if New Jersey opens the door to Spanish, it would also be forced to print all state documents in every language spoken by its citizens. Furthermore, he maintained that if the state provided Spanish-speaking social workers, it would have to provide them for speakers of all other languages to avoid discrimination. Even if the state were able to achieve all of these changes, it would cost the taxpayers a great deal of money. St. Hall insisted there was no evidence that it would actually make a difference to the successful integration of non-English-speaking immigrants into U.S. society. Rather than instituting these drastic changes in New Jersey's government, St. Hall argued that the state would be served best if it fostered the further development of the English language. In other words, St. Hall wanted the government of New Jersey to provide classes for all of its non-English-speaking residents so that they can gain proficiency in the state's native language.

This issue remains contentious in many states throughout the United States.

continued

Real-World Investigations for Social Studies
Hoge, Field, Foster, and Nickell

Handout 1.5 *continued*

Something to Think About

During the Clinton presidency, the federal government considered many policies to support multilingualism in the United States.

Because immigrants usually seek the environment that is most favorable to them, the successful implementation of Roper's proposed policies might drastically change current migration patterns.

1. Having read the information above, discuss in your groups the following four questions:

   a. What are the benefits to states of having a standardized language?

   b. For places like New York City, where hundreds of languages are spoken, how would multilingual policies change the way local government is run?

   c. What are the problems of forcing people to adopt English as their primary language at the state or national level?

   d. Do you agree with Roper or St. Hall? Why?

2. Working as a team, use the Web sites in this handout and any other relevant sources to present your findings to the rest of the class in a 15-minute presentation. Use the following guidelines for your presentation:

   Your presentation topic is "Should English Be the Official Language of the United States?: The Perspective of the States."

   a. Explain in your class presentation why some politicians and their supporters believe that states should become more multilingual in their approach to society. Provide examples of the way they would change existing practice.

b. Explain how and why critics and other politicians oppose this view. Provide examples to illustrate your points.

c. Tell the class what your group thinks about plans to make government more responsive to multilingual populations. Be sure to provide reasons and evidence to support your arguments.

To help with your research, a list of relevant Web sites is given below. In addition, Handout 1.7 provides a list of general Web sites useful for your research.

Key Web sites for English as the Official Language at the State Level
www.midtesol.org/spc-page/second.htm
Explains how English-only policies at the state level would hurt students who speak other languages.

www.elandar.com/back/www-oct95/andar/voces/voces.htm
This webpage has as its focus the usefulness of English-only policies in successfully educating immigrant students.

www.ncte.org/positions/national.shtml
National Language Policy webpage that argues against English-only advocates by illustrating the rich cultural diversity of the United States. It powerfully makes the claim that English-only policies are a denial of basic civil rights.

www.pacificlegal.org/view_SearchDetail.asp?tid=Commentary&sField=CommentaryID&iID=32
Argues that English-only policies encourage assimilation of immigrants more readily than policies that encourage the accommodation of multiple language groups.

Handout 1.6

GROUP FOUR: CREATING MULTILINGUAL STREET SIGNS

Read the following information and the "Something to Think About" statements that follow.

The debate over the creation of multilingual street signs is not a new one. In fact, many European nations have been grappling with the issue for decades. Switzerland, for instance, began making all of its street signs in three languages midway through the 20th century in order to accommodate its extremely diverse population. Aware of the implications of ignoring diversity, many other countries in Europe followed the Swiss example and produced street signs in multiple languages.

Although the United States always has enjoyed diversity, not until recently has it been forced to examine the issue of multilingual street signs. Tucson, Arizona, for example, recently experienced intense debate over the issue of changing the street signs to both English and Spanish. Supporters of the idea cited an already large and growing Spanish population as the main reason. Not allowing such a large percentage of the population to read street signs is not only discriminatory, supporters believe, but also highly inefficient and dangerous. With more than half of its citizens of Spanish descent, Tucson has tens of thousands of drivers struggling to understand signs written in English. According to one backer of multilingual signs, "numerous accidents are inevitably caused every day by Spanish-speaking drivers taking their attention off the road to try to figure out where they are going."

Critics of multilingual signs in Tucson claim that transforming every street sign in the city would cost hundreds of millions of dollars that the city simply cannot afford. The city would not only have to foot the bill for the creation of new signs, but it would also have to devote countless hours of valuable workers' time to erecting the new markers.

Although opponents agree that having signs written only in English causes some delays for Spanish-speaking drivers, they strongly disagree with the idea that it causes accidents. Because most of the words on street signs can be easily interpreted by drivers of any language, detractors contest, there is no reason why Tucson should spend huge amounts of money to produce new signs. "There is absolutely no research to prove that Spanish-speaking drivers experience a higher number of accidents than those who speak only English," a critic said. "To assume this as truth and spend millions of dollars creating multilingual signs would be wasteful and irrational."

Something to Think About

Many people argue that there are more pressing social issues and concerns, such as homelessness, school reform, and crime prevention, that require more government funds and attention than the issue of multilingual street signs.

In many countries, signs in multiple languages are common. Supporters argue that these signs not only help people travel more efficiently, but also show respect for people's language and culture.

Real-World Investigations for Social Studies
Hoge, Field, Foster, and Nickell

1. Having read the information, discuss in your groups the following three questions:

   a. Do you feel that creating street signs in both English and Spanish would help solve the problem of language diversity in Tucson and the rest of the United States?

   b. What are the arguments for and against providing street signs in more than one language? What is your opinion?

   c. If the plan to create signs in both Spanish and English is adopted, which areas would be required to implement it? In other words, would every city in every state be forced to create multilingual signs or would only those areas with a certain percentage of Spanish speakers be obligated to do so?

2. Working as a team, use the Web sites provided and any other relevant sources to present your findings to the rest of the class in a 15-minute presentation. Use the following guidelines for your presentation:

   Your presentation topic is "Should English Be the Official Language of the United States?: A Sign of the Times."

   a. Explain in your class presentation the arguments that people in the United States and in other countries commonly make for having multilingual street signs. Provide examples to illustrate your points.

   b. Explain how and why some critics oppose multilingual street signs. Provide examples to illustrate your points.

continued

c. Tell the class what your group thinks about whether or not U.S. cities should adopt multilingual street signs. Be sure to provide reasons and evidence to support your arguments.

To help with your research, two relevant Web sites are given below. In addition, Handout 1.7 provides a list of general Web sites useful for your research.

Key Web sites on Multilingual Street Signs

www.dailyaztec.com/archive/1996/12/11/file004.html
A newspaper article that advocates English-only signs.

http://www.usdoj.gov/crt/lep/dotlep.htm
The official government Web site outlining the 2001 policy of the Department of Transportation to make U.S. travel multilingual. This includes all street signs, drivers' licenses, and other items associated with the Department of Transportation.

Real-World Investigations for Social Studies
Hoge, Field, Foster, and Nickell

GENERAL WEB SITES FOR RESEARCH INVESTIGATIONS

www.englishfirst.org
This is the official home page of English First, a national nonprofit lobbying organization whose goals are to make English America's official language, promote the learning of English by every child, and eliminate multilingual policies that are costly and ineffective. The site offers much information on the pros and cons of bilingualism/multilingualism. The "students/teachers" section provides resources for the study of this issue.

www.proenglish.org/
The home page of ProEnglish, an organization that promotes English only in the U.S. This easy to use site has many links to data, legislation and court cases useful in studying the issue.

http://www.aclu.org/congress/chen.html
This Web site provides the text of a speech delivered by Edward Chen before the U.S. House of Representatives. The speech outlines the position of the American Civil Liberties Union (ACLU).

http://ourworld.compuserve.com/homepages/JWCRAWFORD/langleg.htm
This is an excellent Web site dealing with language legislation in the United States.

archive.aclu.org/library/pbp6.html
An ACLU briefing paper archive on the issue of English-only policies. Has excellent answers to frequently asked questions section on the issue.

Handout 1.8

INDIVIDUAL RESEARCH TASK COMPLETION REPORT

Name: Date:

My group's assigned task was:

Working in my group, I did the following:

Here is what I found out:

Real-World Investigations for Social Studies
Hoge, Field, Foster, and Nickell

SHOULD THE UNITED STATES ADOPT ENGLISH AS THE OFFICIAL LANGUAGE OF THE NATION?

ARGUMENTS FOR	SUPPORTING EVIDENCE/EXAMPLES

ARGUMENTS AGAINST	SUPPORTING EVIDENCE/EXAMPLES

Real-World Investigations for Social Studies
Hoge, Field, Foster, and Nickell

Handout 1.10

FINAL POSITION STATEMENT

To: The President of the United States

From: _____

My Position:

I support/do not support* policies that require English as the official language of the United States in schools, the government, the workplace, and institutions of civic life.

My Argument:

_____

*Delete as appropriate.

Real-World Investigations for Social Studies
Hoge, Field, Foster, and Nickell

CHAPTER

2

Crisis at Blue Ridge Leather

The Intersection of One Life with Historical Social Structures

by
Ronald L. VanSickle

OVERVIEW

Educators want their students to understand how they are influenced by the physical, social, cultural, and historical contexts in which they live. Those larger contexts, whether they are ecological systems, economic systems, health care systems, religious traditions, atmospheric systems, or intellectual worldviews, create and destroy opportunities to live satisfying lives. Social studies educators particularly want students to understand how their lives are influenced by factors both nearby and faraway, both in the present and in the past. In order to make informed decisions about how to live, students must understand the changing social contexts that surround them. They need to understand how their lives intersect historical social structures and the consequences of those intersections. Through analysis of case studies, students can learn to interpret personal problems in the context of larger historical social forces and to make decisions that respond constructively to them.

The case study "Crisis at Blue Ridge Leather" provides students an opportunity to observe how historical social structures impinged on Alan Cantrell, the owner of a small business. In the first crisis, events distant in time and space threaten to run Blue Ridge Leather out of business. Those events include the Organization of Petroleum Exporting Countries (OPEC) oil crisis of the mid-1970s, the price of grain in the Midwest, 19th-century imperialism, the Industrial Revolution, and the developing economy of an Asian nation. At first, Alan Cantrell is bewildered by his inability to buy leather at a reasonable price, but eventually he understands why he is in trouble. Before learning what Alan chose to do, students engage in small-group and whole-group decision-making activities in an effort to devise a workable solution to the problems besetting Alan and his Blue Ridge Leather business. Even though Alan cannot change the larger social and historical contexts, his research of the problem provides valuable insights that lead to a successful business decision.

In the second crisis, Blue Ridge Leather is threatened again by the effects of social and historical forces that Alan Cantrell couldn't clearly foresee. A new shopping mall is coming to his town, Candlerville, and downtown businesses, including Blue Ridge Leather, are in jeopardy. Alan understands the commercial threat the mall poses for his business. However, he doesn't understand the interplay of historical and current social forces very well. Eventually, Alan begins to understand how his big problem, commercial centralization, was encouraged by a variety of historical events including the development of transportation systems within the state, the relocation of industry in the nation due to international competition, and the civil rights movement. Students again engage in decision-making activities to explore the problems facing Alan and to devise a productive solution to the threat of the new mall. Following their analysis and decision making, students learn how Alan and some of his friends, who also own downtown businesses, find hope for a brighter future in some of the same historical and social forces that caused their problem.

CONNECTION TO NCSS THEME II: TIME, CONTINUITY, AND CHANGE

The NCSS strongly recommends that social studies programs offer a substantial instructional program designed to develop deep understandings of history. The study of the crisis at Blue Ridge Leather helps

students achieve this goal by experiencing how a small-business owner who specialized in manufacturing and marketing high-quality hand-crafted leather goods made informed decisions that accommodated long-term shifts in global commerce and local changes in his downtown business community.

Students' involvement in this study will help them achieve a variety of valuable social education understandings. Among the most important is the realization that changes in the world economy can have substantial effects on American businesses; that the development of suburban shopping malls often has consequences for central city businesses; and finally, that there is real-world usefulness in clear-headed problem solving and strategic decision making.

METHODS FOCUS: DECISION MAKING AND PROBLEM SOLVING

The CTL that takes place in this chapter makes use of a range of familiar instructional methods (see "An Introduction to Contextual Teaching and Learning Methods"). In the present study, however, there is a clear emphasis on decision making and problem solving as intellectual skills that are brought to bear on one small business owner's economic woes.

Decision making and problem solving have long-established histories in the social studies literature (for example, the 1977 *Yearbook* of the NCSS, edited by Dana Kurfman, focused entirely on the development of decision-making skills). Engle (1960) argued that decision making should form the simple and singular emphasis of young citizens' social education. Senish (1968) also stressed the central use of problem solving as an instructional method for the learning of economics. More recently, Allen (2000) recounted the development and refinement of decision making and problem solving in the social studies and offered his own recommendations for the improvement of this important component of education for citizenship in a democracy.

At its simplest level, decision making may be thought of as a linear process that involves five steps:

1. becoming familiar with the nature of the decision occasion;
2. identifying available alternatives;
3. developing and clarifying criteria for making the decision;
4. using criteria to evaluate each alternative; and
5. making your decision.

In practice, however, decisions are often made without the benefit of such careful deliberation, and they are often influenced, as Allen demonstrates, by unrecognized emotional inputs and the vagaries of flawed or incomplete information.

What to do after the football game?	CRITERION 1: Not too expensive.	CRITERION 2: Stay out of trouble.	CRITERION 3: Have fun.	CRITERION 4: Be fit for work early Saturday.
ALTERNATIVE 1: Have a late date with girlfriend.	– –	+	+	–
ALTERNATIVE 2: Drive around with boys for an hour or so.	+	–	+	+
ALTERNATIVE 3: Go home to bed.	++	++	– –	++

Figure 2.1 Postgame activity decision-making grid

Despite these realities, the five-step model shown above remains a good starting point for beginning instruction on decision making. Importantly, the model should be introduced and frequently used within meaningful instructional contexts. In addition, students' exposure to a decision occasion and their use of the five steps of the model should employ metacognitive strategies that focus attention not only on the decision that is being made, but also on their use of the model and the quality of their thinking at each step. Accordingly, for example, the teacher should prompt students to reexamine whether they have fully understood the context of a decision occasion, developed sufficiently clear and necessary criteria, and envisioned an inclusive array of credible alternatives.

As a tool to support such activities, teachers may wish to have students develop decision grids where the various alternatives are clearly evaluated in terms of the specified criteria. Figure 2.1 shows such a grid for a decision occasion, identifying three alternatives and four criteria that, in this instance, are filled out with a teenager's alternatives and criteria related to a decision about what to do after a Friday night high school football game. Each cell in the grid could be filled with pluses or minuses to indicate how well each alternative met each criterion.

IMPORTANCE OF SHARED DECISION MAKING AND MEANINGFUL DIALOGUE

Of course, as Allen (2000) noted, decision making is seldom centered solely on a single individual, functioning without regard to others. In addition, decision making is hardly ever a simple linear process that results in a single clearly superior outcome or action. Even the most casual and fundamental decisions, upon examination, embody complexities and problems. It is easy to imagine, then, how difficult it is to make well-informed, carefully reasoned decisions about the more complex matters that confront us collectively as citizens of a modern multicultural democracy. Allen points out that a more realistic form of group-based decision making requires substantial dialogue and a willingness to share one another's meanings and interpretations of facts. This approach to decision making begins to approximate what many refer to as *problem solving*, and it follows the familiar patterns of *reflective inquiry* (Massialas & Cox, 1966) and *issues-based instruction* (see, e.g., Evans & Saxe, 1996; Newman & Oliver, 1970), and it requires, among other things, that students work collaboratively to thoroughly learn the rich contexts and meanings associated with real-world problems and the actions that have been taken or proposed to solve them.

This form of learning more closely approximates the kinds of problem solving and decision making that take place in business, government, and other social contexts. Engle and Ochoa (1988, pp. 72–76) offered their own interpretation of instruction designed to help students make decisions about public policy. They point out that whether or not students view something as a problem has a lot to do with their interests, goals, and values. To this we must add students' awareness and knowledge because these are often limited or entirely missing. Hence, the first phase of instruction aimed at skill development in real-world decision making or problem solving is to help students encounter the *question, problem, issue, or decision* (QPID) in a way that truly activates their desire to know more and engage in this learning. In essence, students must become motivated investigators who are positively driven to expose relationships, clarify meanings, and uncover data that relates to the QPID.

HOW TO HOOK STUDENTS INTO A QPID

The initial task of introducing a QPID may be accomplished by asking students to read conflicting-opinion editorials, listen to a dynamic guest presentation, or engage in a structured exploration of a well-designed Web site. As a concrete example, consider how these three strategies could be used to engage students in an investigation of their local waste management problems. This is a fertile topic for the practice of group-oriented decision making that has substantial economic and historical implications because virtually every community now faces a variety of waste management problems that range from simple efforts to promote recycling to looming shortages of sanitary landfill sites to severe problems with toxic wastes. Engaging students in QPIDs related to waste management can be as simple as clipping news, editorial, and countervailing citizen opinion articles from the local newspaper and asking students to read them carefully. Similarly, students could be introduced to the QPID by listening to well-informed speakers from local government or businesses involved in waste management who could come into your classroom to explain the local situation. Finally, students might profitably visit Web sites such as that of the Environmental Protection Agency's Explorer's Club (http://www.epa.gov/kids/) to examine many additional resources and aspects of waste management. Such introductory experiences should help students develop a thorough understanding of the QPID, reach agreement on the meaning of key terms, begin to locate sources of relevant and reliable information, and clarify important causal relationships that are implied by statements of the QPID. Basic questions that should drive students' exploration of these sources are: How are different types of waste handled in our community? Who pays for these services? What problems or issues are generated by the waste management policies and practices of our local government?

DEVELOPING DEEP UNDERSTANDING

When the students have become deeply involved in understanding the QPID, it is natural for them to turn to the question of alternative solutions, decisions, or policies. From an instructional standpoint, it is appropriate to encourage these speculations while at the same time beginning to turn students' attention to a consideration of the criteria by which we might judge the effectiveness of any given remedy or policy decision. Criteria might involve a consideration of the costs and benefits of each action, its legality, and its practicality. Engle and Ochoa (1988, p. 74) point out that it is necessary to consider, as a criterion, the values that one wishes to maximize by implementing any given solution or decision. It is also necessary to help students understand that maximizing one value often diminishes the degree to which some other value is promoted and, further, that groups often disagree on the importance or even the legitimacy of solutions based on value-centered criteria. At any rate, the delineation of criteria for assessing alternatives must include a consideration of the social values that are implicated in the QPID.

Following this initial work, considerable effort must be devoted to generating a comprehensive list of alternative solutions or answers to the QPID under consideration. Students should be challenged to look at prior attempts to address the QPID and to search across diverse cultures and history for relevant instances of action. Chains of probable cause and effect should be clearly specified and documented with evidence whenever possible. Assumptions, hunches, and formal hypotheses should be inspected and "tested" with expert opinion and data that may already exist. A concerted attempt must be made to predict the consequence of each alternative or action, as well as the likely consequences of taking no action. The long- and short-term consequences of alternatives must also be assessed because it is often the case that some actions have positive immediate results but may harbor negative consequences for the individual, subgroup, or society in the long run.

At some point, students will naturally begin to display signs that they are ready to endorse some decision or take some action that they feel is a justifiable response to the QPID. The class may fractionate and form advocacy groups around alternative responses. At this point, the teacher should help students focus on developing sound justifications for their positions and on helping them understand that decision making in a democracy often involves balancing conflicting interests and seeking compromises. In fact, every major piece of legislation or policy is the subject of substantial conflicts but ultimately is born in a spirit of compromise. Issue-oriented decision making and problem solving lie at the heart of our society's urgent need to build a cohesive consensus across the many areas of our shared lives. Middle and high school students need to see successful examples of these methods in action in addition to being engaged in practicing these high level skills themselves. "Crisis at Blue Ridge Leather" provides for both of these outcomes.

Table 2.1 Lesson Overview for "Crisis at Blue Ridge Leather"

	GOALS	ACTIVITIES	ASSESSMENTS
LESSON ONE	• Explain the past and present social forces influencing price rises and decide how to act in response to them.	• Read the first part of the case study (Handout 2.1) and check student comprehension. • Read the second part of the case study (Handout 2.2), check comprehension, and engage in small-group and whole-class decision making. Compare decisions with what happened in the third part (Handout 2.3).	• Write a paragraph comparing the strengths and weaknesses of your individual or group decision and the decision in the case study.
LESSON TWO	• Explain the past and present social forces that have brought the mall to town and decide how to act in response to them.	• Read the first part of the case study (Handout 2.4) and check student comprehension. • Read the second part of the case study (Handout 2.5), check comprehension, and engage in small-group and whole-class decision making. • Compare the decisions with what Alan did (Handout 2.6).	• Write a paragraph comparing the strengths and weaknesses of your individual or group decision and the decision in the case study.
LESSON THREE	• Research and analyze an existing business in your community.	• Prepare students to conduct their own case study of a local businessperson using Handouts 2.7 and 2.8. As a small-group project, students interview a local businessperson to learn about his or her business and key decisions he or she has made, and to identify historical and social factors creating problems or opportunities for the business.	• Write the case study and present it orally to the class. Focus on how historical social forces and events affected the business and how the businessperson made decisions about how to solve problems or benefit from opportunities.

LESSON ONE: The Great Leather Crisis

Purpose This lesson introduces students to Alan Cantrell and his Blue Ridge Leather Store. Students learn about the recent history of the business and about a crisis that threatens to destroy the business and Alan's way of life. They are challenged to begin exploring alternative solutions to Alan's problem.

Duration Two class periods

Materials
Handout 2.1: The Great 1970s Leather Crisis
Handout 2.2: The Bigger Picture
Handout 2.3: How Alan Solved His Problem

Procedures
1. Introduce the lesson by explaining that one of the valuable reasons to study history is to understand what has happened in the past that influences the problems and opportunities we experience in the present. By understanding the larger historical and social setting in which we live, we can sometimes make better decisions to achieve our goals more effectively and prevent or reduce problems. Explain that we are going to study a case study that will help us see how understanding the bigger picture can help us make better decisions.

2. Distribute Handout 2.1 to all students. Allow time for students to read the case study and then ask questions to check students' comprehension of the problem facing Alan Cantrell. Ask if anyone has a good idea about what Alan should do. Don't spend much time discussing the ideas at this point.

3. Distribute Handout 2.2 to all students. Ask students to read the handout and then check their

comprehension, with particular attention to the historical and social/economic factors influencing the situation facing Alan. Then divide students into small groups to use the decision-making process outlined in the handout. Conduct a whole-class discussion to compare and contrast the alternatives, criteria, and decisions of the small groups.

4. Either read Handout 2.3 to the whole class or distribute copies to the students so that they learn what Alan did and what happened. Compare and contrast what happened in the case study with students' alternatives and decisions. Focus students' attention on the historical and social contexts in which the case study problem and solution occurred.

5. For assessment, ask students to write a paragraph comparing the strengths and weaknesses of their individual or group decisions and the decision made and implemented in the case study.

LESSON TWO: The Shopping Mall

Purpose This lesson presents a problem Alan and his Blue Ridge Leather Store faced several years after the Great Leather Crisis. Students learn about the development of a major regional shopping mall on the outskirts of Candlerville and how the mall threatens Alan's business and many other businesses downtown. Using the same decision-making process, students investigate the reasons for Alan's problem and identify alternative solutions and criteria for evaluating those solutions.

Duration Two periods

Materials
Handout 2.4: The Shopping Mall
Handout 2.5: The Bigger Picture
Handout 2.6: How Alan Solved His Second Problem

Procedures
1. Introduce the lesson by reminding the class that one of the valuable reasons to study history is to understand what has happened in the past that influences the problems and opportunities we experience in the present. By understanding the larger historical and social settings in which we live, sometimes we can make better decisions to achieve our goals more effectively and prevent or reduce problems. Explain that we are going to study a case study that will help us see how understanding the bigger picture can help us make better decisions.

2. Distribute Handout 2.4 to all students. Allow time for students to read the case study and then ask questions to check students' comprehension of the problem facing Alan Cantrell. Ask if anyone has a good idea about what Alan should do. Don't spend much time discussing the ideas.

3. Distribute Handout 2.5 to all students. Ask them to read it and then check their comprehension, with particular attention to the historical and social/economic factors influencing the situation facing Alan. Then divide students into small groups to use the decision-making process outlined in the handout. Conduct a whole-class discussion to com-

pare and contrast the alternatives, criteria, and decisions of the small groups.

4. Either read Handout 2.6 to the whole class or distribute copies to the students so that they learn what Alan did and what happened. Compare and contrast what happened in the case study with students' alternatives and decisions. Focus students' attention on the historical and social contexts in which the case study problem and solution occurred.

5. For assessment, have students write a paragraph comparing the strengths and weaknesses of their individual or group decisions with those of the decision made and implemented in the case study.

6. If time permits, as an optional activity, have a volunteer read the following postscript to Alan's story:

The downtown development plan was successful, and Blue Ridge Leather continued to grow and prosper. The new civic center brought substantial numbers of people to Candlerville, and that helped all of the downtown businesses. The music scene blossomed, and Candlerville became known as a major popular music center in the nation. A few years later, after the shopping mall crisis, Alan decided to move his store across the street and more than doubled his display space. He bought the building and other property and further increased his financial resources. Life and business were going well for Alan.

Sometimes success creates its own problems. Some businesspeople believed that the development of the music scene had encouraged too many people to open downtown bars catering to Southeastern University's students. The university had grown, and there were many more students seeking entertainment in Candlerville. Some businesspeople feared that downtown would become a "Bourbon Street" like the one in New Orleans. They feared that many retail store owners would decide to close or move their businesses, because downtown was no longer the kind of place where they wanted to do business. The owners of the bars and clubs emphasized the benefits of their businesses for downtown and all of Candlerville. Of course, Alan was in the middle of all these worried and sometimes contentious discussions.

Society is always changing. Alan had learned this lesson from personal experience. He knew that historical, economic, social, and cultural forces would continue to shape life in Candlerville in new and unpredictable ways. Alan would contribute his business experience and wisdom to his community's efforts to identify alternatives for the future, evaluate those alternatives, and make decisions to promote not only the welfare of his business, but the welfare of all of Candlerville's citizens.

LESSON THREE: Business Case Study Project

Purpose This lesson enables students to move from studying a case of historical forces operating in an individual's life to investigating how history and the larger society have affected a local business and its owner. Students interview local businesspeople and prepare a case study to apply what they have learned about historical forces and decision making.

Duration Two class periods

Materials
Handout 2.7: Business Case Study Project
Handout 2.8: Sample Questions for the Business Case Study Interview

Procedures
Teacher preparation
- Check with your school administration to determine the need for a clearance or approval process for the students or the businesspeople before students begin this case study development assignment in your community.
- Prepare a letter of introduction that students can take with them when they initially talk with businesspeople about participating in the development of case studies about their businesses.
- Much time will be saved if you identify local businesses that will be receptive to students' inquiries; however, students should be allowed to contact other businesses if they wish.
- Assign students to small work groups for this project.

1. Explain that developing case studies in your local community can be an effective way to see how history and the larger society affect the opportunities and problems people experience. It can also demonstrate how people make decisions in response to historical events and events in contemporary society, and how we can make more effective decisions in our own lives.

2. Distribute Handout 2.7 and explain each part of the case study development task. Use the case study "Crisis at Blue Ridge Leather," that students have just studied, to illustrate points about the assignment. The case study materials in Lesson One or Lesson Two represent a good student project. Some students will need assistance along the way to limit the scope of the case study they develop.

3. Assist students in developing a set of questions to help them start their interviews. Distribute Handout 2.8 and add other questions that seem appropriate. For example, if students are studying late-20th-century U.S. history, you might want them to ask the businesspeople about specific historical events that might have influenced them in some way.

4. Present a time line for completing interim steps and the final product. A 2-week time period is suggested, but you will adjust it to fit your situation. Explain to students your requirements for producing a high-quality document and a class presentation and your criteria for evaluating their presentations and written case studies.

THE GREAT 1970S LEATHER CRISIS

Alan Cantrell made the big decision in 1975 and moved to Candlerville in order to open his own store, Blue Ridge Leather. He scraped together enough money to lease a small storefront downtown. It was so small that you could pass it in four steps, but it was a place to start. There was room for a small display area in front and a sales counter and workbench in the rear.

Alan enjoyed leatherwork and learned to make attractive leather clothing accessories while a college student. Leather items were popular in the early 1970s—he made countless belts, purses, bags, and head bands. He tooled popular designs including flowers, mushrooms, stars, crescent moons, and more abstract designs. His experience selling his leather products at festivals and in a popular resort area convinced him that he could make a living doing the craft he loved. However, he wanted a more stable lifestyle in an interesting place and he picked Candlerville, the home of Southeastern University, as the place to settle.

Things started well in Candlerville, and his store was becoming fairly popular with the university students as well as some local residents. He was making money—not much, but enough to live on. Now, however, his dream was in danger of dying just as it was beginning. For some reason, the price of leather was skyrocketing. His leather supplier in the state capital informed him that he should buy the remaining stock of leather now because the price was going to rise even higher. He would have to buy it very soon or it would be gone. Alan didn't have the money to buy a lot of leather. He went to the bank and learned that he could get a $10,000 loan to buy the less expensive leather that was still available.

Was this the solution? Alan wasn't sure. A big bank loan would have to be paid back out of the money he would make selling his leather goods. The monthly loan payment would start right away; it would be a big new bill each month. Also, he would have to charge higher prices for his products because the leather he could buy now was already more expensive than the leather he used to buy. The interest charges on the loan would force him to charge more, too. The amount of leather he would have to buy was huge for his small business. He couldn't use it all in a year, and he would have to store it somewhere else because his store had hardly any storage space. If he had to rent storage space, that would also force him to raise his prices a little more. How much would those college students spend in his store when they saw his new higher prices?

Alan went back to his leather supplier and asked if there was any other way to get less expensive leather. The supplier said that there was. He could buy imported beef hides from Argentina at a much lower price. That sounded good to Alan, but he had second thoughts when he examined samples of the Argentine leather. The price was low because the quality of the leather was much poorer than that of the leather from cattle grown in the United States. This "solution" would enable him to keep his prices low, but what would his customers think of his products made with the lower-quality leather?

What could Alan do? He reviewed his choices. He could take out a big loan, buy the U.S. leather, raise his prices, and hope for the best. He could buy the relatively inexpensive Argentine leather, keep his prices from rising, and hope for the best. What else could he do? He could go out of business. He could sell his remaining merchandise as quickly as possible, break his store lease, and minimize his losses. Of course, he would have to do something else for a living. What could that be? Perhaps he could enter a management-training program for a big discount department store chain. He didn't know what he would do if he sold out, but it was hard to imagine he would enjoy it half as much as owning and operating his own leather goods store.

Real-World Investigations for Social Studies
Hoge, Field, Foster, and Nickell

THE BIGGER PICTURE

Alan sat in his shop in the early evening after closing with his mind full of worry and uncertainty. His three solutions were all bad. He didn't want to choose between too much debt, poor-quality leather, and going out of business. He was afraid Blue Ridge Leather might go out of business anyway with too much debt and poor leather. Wasn't there another solution that would enable him to stay in business and do the work he loved? What caused the price of leather to go up anyway? He decided to investigate. If he had to go out of business, maybe at least he could understand why.

Alan talked to his leather supplier. The supplier told him that less American leather was being produced because cattle ranchers in the western states were taking fewer cattle to market. Fewer cattle meant fewer hides and less leather. Actually, the cattle ranchers had cut back on their production about 2 years ago, and the stock of leather in storage had decreased to its current low level. Because the ranchers were now producing smaller quantities of new beef and hides, the stock of leather wasn't increasing.

The supplier also explained to Alan that he was suffering from a double whammy. Not only was leather production down, but footwear companies in Italy and South Korea were buying huge quantities of the leather still available. International leather users were competing with U.S. companies for the available leather, and prices were going up as they bid against each other. The world's largest leather market was located in Boston. The U.S. cattle industry had produced large quantities of leather for many decades. Boston became the main leather market because American shoe companies had originated in New England and the port of Boston was the export center for American leather. As the giants competed for the leather in Boston, Alan's tiny leather business was in danger of being stomped out of existence.

Alan began to understand why he was in trouble, but he still had questions. It made sense to him that Italian shoe companies would

want to buy high-quality U.S. leather. Italy had long been a center of fashion in clothing, and Italian shoes had been popular for a long time. On the other hand, why was South Korea in the shoe business? Alan did a little reading and learned that South Korea, along with several other East Asian and South Asian nations, had been industrializing for several years. The footwear industry was one of the businesses that could benefit from the lower wage rates in South Korea, and it had grown greatly in the past few years. The South Korean companies were energetically exporting shoes at very attractive prices all over the world.

Alan remembered learning in history classes about the Industrial Revolution that began in the 18th-century. Industrialization created great wealth and spread slowly and then with increasing speed from England to other countries in Europe and to the United States. But it didn't stop in the United States; the peoples of many less developed nations wanted to industrialize, too. Now in 1977, South Korea and other nations were industrializing successfully with amazing speed.

Although Alan now could understand why the new additional demand for leather from other nations was forcing prices up, he still was confronted with a mystery. With all this demand for leather, why did the cattle ranchers cut back on production just when they could be making more money from the higher price for leather? If they produced more cattle, the price of leather might go up a little but it wouldn't skyrocket. This called for a little more research at the library.

It didn't take much searching to find out why cattle production was down. The cost of raising cattle had skyrocketed a couple of years earlier; consequently, many ranchers couldn't afford to raise as many cattle as before. And although their costs increased, prices didn't increase as quickly, so the ranchers cut back on the number of cattle they bought and raised. Alan noticed that his electricity bill had risen

continued

Real-World Investigations for Social Studies
Hoge, Field, Foster, and Nickell

over the past couple of years, and the price of gasoline had also gone up considerably. However, he hadn't seen the connection to cattle production because cattle don't use much electricity and oil out on the range. Cattle ranchers were quick to point out that you can't raise cattle for market without a lot of high-quality feed grain. Growing grain on midwestern farms takes a lot of energy. The cost of high-priced fuels and other forms of energy used by the farmers was passed on to the cattle ranchers in the form of high-priced cattle feeds. Consequently, numerous ranchers decided that it wasn't sufficiently profitable to raise so many cattle.

Alan knew from watching and reading the news that oil prices had increased because of OPEC. The OPEC members had agreed about 3 years earlier to cut back oil production and force buyers in Europe and the United States to pay more for each barrel of oil. The oil-importing nations including the United States didn't do much to reduce oil consumption, so they had to pay more and more to get the oil they wanted from the OPEC members. This was beginning to make a lot more sense to Alan.

He knew that the amount of oil underground in the OPEC nations was limited, and it would become harder and more expensive to pump out of the ground. That had already happened in the vast oil fields of Texas. He also knew that many of the OPEC members, such as Saudi Arabia, Iran, Iraq, Venezuela, Nigeria, and Mexico, had been exploited by the 19th-century and early-20th-century imperialist policies of several European nations and, to a lesser extent, the United States. Because oil was their big natural resource, those nations understandably wanted to get as much for it as they could. If the United States and European nations had to pay a lot for the oil, that seemed like justice to many people in the OPEC nations. The echoes of actions by corporations and governments decades earlier were helping to make life complicated for Alan and his little leather store.

Alan sat sipping hot coffee in his favorite restaurant, the Blue Jay Café, and mulling over his problem and the reasons for it. He realized that many of the reasons were located far away and long ago. He sat staring into space. Then a glimmer of an idea began to take shape. It grew and he began to tingle with excitement. Maybe there was something he could do to save his business. He left an extra big tip, paid for his coffee, and almost ran back to his shop. He needed to make some phone calls!

Does any of this historical background to Alan's problem prompt you to think of a new possible solution to his problem of high leather prices?

Decision-Making Activity

1. Alan has a serious problem with the price of leather. What do you think he should do? He identified three possible ways to solve his price problem. Can you think of any other potential solutions?
2. How can Alan decide which solution is best? What is important to Alan? What must happen for a solution to be a good one? List your answers to these questions. You can use these ideas as criteria or standards for judging the goodness of each potential solution.
3. Make a chart similar to the following one to outline Alan's possible solutions and criteria that might help him make a good choice from among the solutions.

Alternatives/Criteria	Criterion 1	Criterion 2	Criterion 3	Criterion X
Alternative 1				
Alternative 2				
Alternative 3				
Alternative X				

4. Discuss how well each solution satisfies each criterion. In the chart, put a plus in each box where a potential solution satisfies the criterion, put a minus where the solution doesn't satisfy the criterion very well, and put a question mark when you can't tell whether a solution will satisfy the criterion. If you wish, put two pluses or two minuses if a solution satisfies a criterion especially well or fails in a major way to satisfy a criterion.

5. Discuss your evaluation of Alan's alternatives and draw a conclusion about what you think he should do. You might feel uncertain about the best solution, but life often requires us to make decisions even when we don't know everything we want to know and are uncertain about the consequences. If Alan doesn't make any decision, his business is doomed. What do you think is his best choice?

Real-World Investigations for Social Studies
Hoge, Field, Foster, and Nickell

HOW ALAN SOLVED HIS PROBLEM

The next week, Alan was flying high above the Appalachian mountains on his way to Boston, the center of the world leather market. After his cup of coffee the week before, he had located and called several of the major leather companies in Boston. He asked if they ever had scraps and odd lots of leather left over after orders were filled for shipment. They did, and two companies said they would be willing to sell him small amounts of leather if he came to Boston to make arrangements for the purchase and paid his own shipping costs back to Candlerville.

Alan spent the next few days in Boston buying bits and pieces of leather. They were bits and pieces to the big companies that measured orders by the ton, but they were huge quantities for Alan. They would keep him working leather for a year. Actually, by buying up small amounts of leftover leather, Alan helped solve a problem for the companies that had to do something with the odds and ends not used in large orders. Consequently, they sold the leather to him at lower prices than he expected. While in Boston, Alan spent happy hours exploring historical sights from the time of the American Revolution, eating seafood and even Boston baked beans, and generally having a wonderful vacation.

While flying back home at the end of the week, Alan cheerfully mused over the turn of events. He now had a steady supply of the high-quality leather he wanted for his customers and for the craft he loved. He could buy the leather at prices even lower than those he had been paying the supplier in the state capital before leather prices skyrocketed. He had needed only a very small loan from the bank that he could soon repay. Because the trip to Boston was necessary for business, he was able to deduct most of his expenses from his taxes despite the fact that he had visited museums and had a good time. He also could look forward to annual business trips (and vacations) to New England for years to come. He would be able to keep his production costs and his prices from rising significantly, and he might even make larger profits than in the past. This business crisis had changed from a looming disaster to a wonderful business opportunity for Blue Ridge Leather.

Real-World Investigations for Social Studies
Hoge, Field, Foster, and Nickell

THE SHOPPING MALL

After Alan solved the leather crisis of 1977, Blue Ridge Leather prospered and Alan began to feel confident about the future. He thought he would do more business if he had more display space, so he rented a larger storefront and moved out of his hole-in-the-wall shop. He hired a salesperson for the store and hired a graduate student at the university as a part-time worker to help him with some of the easier leather work. He was right; business picked up a lot when he quadrupled his display space. He began making custom-made sandals and further increased his business. He enjoyed his business and made a good living doing it.

Downtown was the center of business, shopping, and entertainment in Candlerville. It had some major advantages that kept people shopping there. There was a good number and variety of restaurants, shops, and movie theaters. Several banks and many professional offices also were located there. Downtown shopping was anchored by four large, major department stores—Sears, JC Penney, Beauford's, and Darlington's. Also, along one edge of downtown was the Southeastern University campus. Downtown catered to the needs of all the citizens of Candlerville, including the 20,000 university students who lived within 1 or 2 miles of the city's center.

However, rumors began circulating among downtown businesspeople, and those rumors soon were confirmed as facts. A large real estate developer was planning to build a major shopping mall on the outskirts of the city near the intersection of a major highway and the city's bypass. The corporations owning the big downtown department stores were considering whether to lease space in the new shopping center that would open in less than 2 years. Owners of smaller stores were beginning to wonder if they, too, should lease space and move to the mall.

Many citizens of Candlerville were delighted to learn that their city would soon have a mall, to be named Magnolia Square Mall. They thought it was about time. Many drove over 60 miles several times a year to shop at the big malls scattered around the capital city. They liked the big city malls and wished one was closer to home. Among the downtown businesspeople, spirits were low and the emotional atmosphere was filled with sullen gray clouds. When the big department stores announced that they all would move to the new mall when construction was completed, many businesspeople, including Alan, didn't sleep very much because of worry and anxiety about the future.

The Magnolia Square Mall was a specter hovering over downtown. All the businesspeople had seen what the building of a bypass mall had done to many other downtowns. The big stores would move out and leave behind their huge empty buildings, with windows covered by old newspapers. The buildings would soon deteriorate due to neglect. Large numbers of customers would abandon downtown, and smaller stores would begin closing. Customers who did come downtown would be discouraged when they found fewer stores open. The downtown movie theaters wouldn't seem as attractive as the new multiplex cinema at Magnolia Square Mall and they, too, would close, leaving more empty buildings. The local government and the Chamber of Commerce might try to remodel and beautify downtown to make it more attractive for pedestrian traffic. That might help briefly, but with fewer reasons to shop there, downtown would begin to feel almost deserted. Soon, it would be the decaying, hollow core of the city.

Alan knew that another critical decision was looming for him and his business. What should he do about the imminent arrival of Magnolia Square Mall? What were his choices? He could lease space at the mall and move his business there. The mall developers had contacted him about the possibility of leasing space there. He reviewed the information with his accountant. The mall developers promised that the number of people seeing his store would be several

continued

Real-World Investigations for Social Studies
Hoge, Field, Foster, and Nickell

times greater than the current downtown pedestrian traffic passing his current store. However, the rent would be several times higher than his current rent, and he would have less space than he did now. He would have to sell a tremendous amount of merchandise to make a profit. Of course, the mall developers assured him that he would.

He could stay put, reduce expenses as much as possible, and hope enough customers would still come his way to keep him in business. That could work if the predictions of the collapse of downtown were exaggerated. If business shrank somewhat, he could lay off his part-time leather worker and his salesperson. Of course, he had gotten used to not having to be in the store every minute. Going back to a one-person business would mean more and harder work for possibly less money.

He could stay put, resign himself to going out of business in the next couple of years, and begin planning on a new way of life doing other work. He had faced this alternative during the leather price crisis a few years ago. He still liked doing leather work and owning his own business. There wasn't any other kind of work that especially appealed to him. He knew he could do other work, but it would just be work.

He could move and re-create his business in another university town. For example, he might move to Fredericksville, where Atlantic University was located. It had some of Candlerville's features, and people there might like his leather work as much as Candlerville people had. On the other hand, it would mean starting all over again. In Candlerville, he had many close friends and he knew well almost all the businesspeople, bankers, and government leaders.

Alan could stay downtown, invest even more energy and money in his business, and work with others to try to shape a new and prosperous future for downtown. Alan knew this was an optimistic alternative. Personally, he hadn't seen it work in other cities. However, downtown did have one advantage—the university along one edge of downtown wouldn't move to the mall. Downtown merchants appreciated student business, but most students didn't have a lot of money to spend. What could a bright future for downtown be?

Real-World Investigations for Social Studies
Hoge, Field, Foster, and Nickell

THE BIGGER PICTURE

Alan was not the only businessperson with mall nightmares. The local Chamber of Commerce scheduled a public meeting in May for everyone interested in discussing the future of downtown. After closing the store early in the evening, Alan walked in a light, warm rain toward the Southeastern University campus, where the meeting would be held. He noticed that the magnolia trees had begun to bloom, and their sweet scent mixed with the rain. He always had enjoyed the scent of magnolias, but now it just meant one thing—Magnolia Square Mall!

Alan's choices tumbled over and over in his mind; the right choice was not obvious. The room was nearly full when the meeting was called to order. The people represented various groups concerned with the city's welfare—many businesspeople, government representatives including the mayor and some members of the city council, several professors and university administrators, and numerous concerned citizens.

The meeting began with a series of brief presentations. Frank Collins, the current president of the Chamber of Commerce, reviewed some of the reasons Magnolia Square Mall was being built. The population of Candlerville and the immediate surrounding area had been growing rapidly in recent years and was expected to reach 100,000 in another decade. Mr. Collins described how roads in this part of the state had been improved steadily in recent years, and the mall developers expected to attract thousands of customers from surrounding counties who came to Candlerville only occasionally now.

Harold Wittrock, a business professor at Southeastern University, presented some maps that showed how roads had been improved in the state. Alan hadn't realized how many dirt roads had existed as recently as 25 years ago. Travel in the state certainly had speeded up. Dr. Wittrock described the state government's transportation plans, which included new four-lane highways linking Candlerville to other cities and to the interstate highways in this region of the state. He noted that Candlerville residents soon would be able to drive to malls in the state capital in about an hour. He also noted that commercial centralization for economic efficiency was not a new story. The business districts of many small towns in the area surrounding Candlerville had shriveled as people discovered they could travel to Candlerville more quickly than in the past and could find much greater choice and better prices. In the past, downtown Candlerville played the economic role of "the Mall" for other towns.

Evelyn Longstreet, a historian at the university, reviewed the troubled economic history of the state, including the Candlerville area, over the past century and the state's new optimism. The agricultural economy of the state did not provide a very high standard of living for many citizens. The state had long been among the poorer and less developed states in the nation. However, in the 1950s and early 1960s, important changes took place that provided the foundation for better economic times. Dr. Longstreet explained that city leaders in the state capital had worked very hard to make the city attractive to major corporations. The civil rights movement's success in ending racial segregation and the affirmative efforts of many state leaders to improve race relations made the social climate much more attractive to people in other parts of the nation. Alan had never thought of the civil rights movement as an important building block for business and prosperity. The energy crisis of the 1970s and foreign economic competition made the state even more attractive due to its mild weather and less expensive workforce. This was the Sun Belt factor. All these factors combined to encourage economic growth, the migration of people and business to the state from other parts of the country (particularly the Frost Belt), and the rapid growth of wealth in the region. Dr. Longstreet observed that Magnolia Square Mall was just one small part of this big historical process.

continued

Real-World Investigations for Social Studies
Hoge, Field, Foster, and Nickell

49

Handout 2.5 *continued*

Julian O'Hara, the mayor of Candlerville, described ideas people had mentioned to him about how to revitalize downtown. He described beautification projects, pedestrian malls, festivals, and other activities to encourage people to come downtown. Alan didn't put much confidence in those efforts to save downtown, but he was glad to hear that the city government wanted to work with businesspeople to keep downtown alive. Following the mayor's comments, there was a general discussion in which people expressed their anxieties, suggested ideas (a monorail transportation system like the one at Disney World to connect downtown and the mall raised many eyebrows), and made plans for a future meeting.

Alan and a couple of friends stopped at the Blue Jay Café for coffee and reviewed the meeting. The big problems seemed to be commercial centralization and the fact that downtown was no longer the desirable center for major retail stores and related services. Does any of this historical background prompt you to think of a new possible solution to Alan's choice about what to do with his business?

Decision-Making Activity

1. Alan has a serious problem because Magnolia Square Mall has persuaded the big department stores to move from downtown to the mall. What do you think he should do? He identified three possibilities to solve his price problem. Can you think of any other potential solutions?

2. How can Alan decide which solution is best? What is important to Alan? What must happen for a solution to be a good one? List your answers to these questions. You can use these ideas as criteria or standards for judging the goodness of each potential solution.

3. Make a chart similar to the following one to outline Alan's possible solutions and criteria that might help him make a good choice from among the solutions.

Alternatives/Criteria	Criterion 1	Criterion 2	Criterion 3	Criterion X
Alternative 1				
Alternative 2				
Alternative 3				
Alternative X				

4. Discuss how well each solution satisfies each criterion. In the chart, put a plus in each box where a potential solution satisfies the criterion, put a minus where the solution doesn't satisfy the criterion very well, and put a question mark when you can't tell whether a solution will satisfy the criterion. If you wish, put two pluses or two minuses if a solution satisfies a criterion especially well or fails in a major way to satisfy a criterion.

5. Discuss your evaluation of Alan's alternatives and draw a conclusion about what you think Alan should do. You might feel uncertain about the best solution, but life often requires us to make decisions even when we don't know everything we want to know and are uncertain about the consequences. If Alan doesn't make any decision, his business is doomed. What do you think is his best alternative?

Real-World Investigations for Social Studies
Hoge, Field, Foster, and Nickell

HOW ALAN SOLVED HIS SECOND PROBLEM

Alan and his friends sat in the Blue Jay Café pondering their fate. They talked about how things had changed for the better in many ways in Candlerville and this part of the state. They talked about commercial centralization, better roads and highways, people's greater mobility, and the growing general prosperity. They felt that they might be passed by in downtown Candlerville. On the other hand, the university wasn't going to move. There would still be more than 20,000 students walking around near downtown and several thousand university faculty and staff members coming near downtown 5 days a week. Also, 70,000 football fans would arrive in town several weekends each fall. Could downtown take advantage of centralization in some way even though centralization of retail shopping was moving to the mall?

At the next public meeting, several people including Alan began promoting the idea of transforming downtown into an entertainment, tourist, and conference center. Perhaps one of the big, empty department store buildings could be converted into a civic center. Perhaps another could be transformed into a new hotel. The exodus of the big stores and some other stores would free up business space and lower rents. That could make it affordable for new restaurants, some bars, music venues, and small specialty shops to open downtown.

The city government could support projects to make downtown more attractive, provide physical improvements to the streets, revise ordinances to allow sidewalk café seating in certain areas, and promote and regulate festivals to encourage people to think positively about downtown.

Alan made his choice. He decided to stay downtown and work with others to revitalize the old retail shopping area. The big department stores did move to Magnolia Square Mall, and other businesses closed or moved. However, a core of smaller stores stayed. A music scene grew downtown as new restaurants and music bars opened to cater to the younger population of the city. The restaurants, plus new and old shops, also drew university employees to downtown and provided services to the professional offices there. The idea of making downtown a conference center started slowly but made progress. The government organized citizens to consider a large civic center and auditorium, which were built a few years later. They established downtown as an important conference and cultural center in the state. Alan was in the middle of all these changes and became a prominent businessperson and community leader. Downtown changed a lot, but its future was bright, and Alan's store, Blue Ridge Leather, prospered with it.

Real-World Investigations for Social Studies
Hoge, Field, Foster, and Nickell

Handout 2.7

BUSINESS CASE STUDY PROJECT

1. Choose a business where you can interview an owner or manager. You need to interview someone who has decision-making authority. For this project, it will be best if the owner or manager has been with the business for several years so that he or she can tell you how things have changed over time.

2. Explain to the businessperson that you are working on a class project to develop a business case study for your social studies class. Emphasize that this is not a financial case study, and you will *not* ask questions about details of the business's finances.

3. Explain that you are especially interested in business decisions the owner or manager has made. Tell the businessperson that he or she may review the case study before you give it to your teacher.

4. Interview the businessperson at a convenient time about a broad range of topics. Your teacher will give you a list of questions to help you get started, but you are not limited to that list. Take good notes during the interview or make an audiotaped recording of the interview. Record the interview on an audiotape recorder only if the businessperson agrees. Some people don't like to be recorded. Review your interview records and your memory to identify one or more key decisions the businessperson has made.

5. Write the case study. Work to make your writing as interesting and engaging as possible. Try to include an element of drama that will show the reader that the businessperson (who is the central character) had a significant decision to make and that the outcomes had serious consequences for his or her life. The length of your case study depends on the complexity of the story and the amount of information needed by readers to visualize and understand the situation.

6. Include the following elements in the case study:
   a. Problem and setting: Describe the business and the central character (that is, the businessperson) so that readers have a mental picture of the business. Describe events, thoughts, and feelings that led to the problem about which a decision was made. Present the situation factually and descriptively.
   b. Identify the alternatives the businessperson considered. Identify other alternatives that the businessperson might have considered but didn't. Work them into the story as the character's thoughts or conversations.
   c. End the case study with an explanation of the decision the businessperson made and the good and bad results of that decision.

7. Finish the case study with a section that explains your views about how historical events and social processes operating in society affected the businessperson's opportunities, problems, and decisions.

Real-World Investigations for Social Studies
Hoge, Field, Foster, and Nickell

SAMPLE QUESTIONS FOR THE BUSINESS CASE STUDY INTERVIEW

- Who started your company? When?
- What previous experience did you/he/she/they have?
- What was your/their incentive, purpose, or motivation for going into business?
- What needs or wants of customers does your company try to satisfy?
- What does your company produce (goods or services)?
- What are the difficulties or challenges in producing your company's products?
- What businesses do you depend on to enable you to provide your products to customers?
- What effects do (or did) labor sources, taxes, the local community, and the environment have on your business?
- What factors influence customer demand for your company's product or products?
- Who are your company's competitors? How competitive is the business environment?
- What advantages or disadvantages does your business have compared to your competitors? Why do you have those advantages or disadvantages?
- How much change has there been in customer demand or in competition over the years? What caused that change?
- Have growth and expansion produced any problems for your company?
- How have business cycles, changing economic conditions, and technological changes affected your business?
- What effects have government actions at the local, state, and national levels had on your business?
- What major problems, opportunities, and decisions have you faced over the years? What have been the consequences of those problems, opportunities, and decisions?
- Have international relations or international economic conditions ever affected your business for better or worse?
- What factors affect the profitability of your business and businesses like it?

Real-World Investigations for Social Studies
Hoge, Field, Foster, and Nickell

3

The Lake Lanier Land Use Controversy

by
Geri Collins

OVERVIEW

Land use and development is an enduring public issue facing many communities. Growth-related land development places pressure on the environment as communities attempt to balance their need for more transportation, housing, shopping, industry, leisure, and recreation. Lake Lanier, a large artificial reservoir on the northern edge of metropolitan Atlanta, is currently the subject of an intense political struggle because the rapid development of areas surrounding it has affected the health and balance of this important ecosystem. Rapid population growth has surrounded the lake with many housing developments and dramatically increased lake-related recreational activities. These expanding uses of the lake and the surrounding land area affect animals and their habitats. As a result, many people are in conflict over how Lake Lanier should be used and managed. The lessons that follow in this chapter are based on the development of a new lakeside community; however, the lessons can be modified for any area that is experiencing growth that threatens existing ecosystems.

In this chapter, students are first introduced to the development scenario and to a collection of stakeholders who are involved in the lakeside development controversy. Students learn how these stakeholders feel about the use of the lake and the trade-offs that come with changing uses. Groups are then formed to represent each person's view, and they are instructed to find support for that view using a variety of Web sites, newspapers, interviews, and public opinion polls.

The information gathered by the groups is then organized into presentations given at a mock County Commissioners' meeting. Each group, representing the interests of one of the concerned people, presents its information to the Commissioners and listens to the decision that the Commissioners ultimately make. Students then discuss their part in the outcome of the meeting and explain how they feel about that outcome. Finally, students are asked to write a one-page assessment of the Commission meeting's outcome and its decision-making process.

CONNECTION TO NCSS THEME III: PEOPLE, PLACES, AND ENVIRONMENTS

A high-quality social studies program should include multiple learning experiences that provide for the study of people, places, and environments. This chapter helps students address this standard by involving them in a variety of activities that use geographic tools, data, and other resources to critically evaluate alternative uses of land and water resources in a lakeside community. Throughout their involvement in this experience, students are challenged to consider the competing needs of different citizens, analyze patterns of land and water use as these relate to ecosystem changes, and participate in the processes that citizens use to create places that reflect their cultural values and ideals as they build their communities.

METHODS FOCUS: GEOGRAPHIC SKILLS

The contextual teaching and learning that take place in this chapter make use of a wide range of familiar instructional methods. However, a clear emphasis exists on the way in which geography influences people's decisions about where they want to live, work, shop, worship, and play. Of course, making these decisions requires that answers be found to a wide variety of geographic questions.

The National Geography Standards (Geography Education Standards Project [GESP], 1994) lists five key skills that are considered essential for geographic literacy: asking geographic questions, acquiring geographic information, organizing geographic information, analyzing geographic information, and answering geographic questions (GESP, 1994, p. 30). According to the standards, a geographically informed person is someone "(1) who sees meaning in the arrangement of things in space; (2) who sees relations between people, places, and environments; (3) who uses geographic skills; and (4) who applies spatial and ecological perspectives to life situations" (GESP, 1994, p. 34). Furthermore, the standards recommend that students become geographically literate by thinking systematically about environmental and societal issues that directly relate to their communities.

This chapter gives students many opportunities to acquire and exercise their geographic skills. For example, Lesson One begins by asking students a number of context-setting questions that help them articulate their experiences in the kinds of places (lakes, new housing developments, small cities) involved in this unit. Students make use of maps, statistics, newspaper articles, government publications, and photographs in subsequent lessons to gain answers to questions they pose about the development around Lake Lanier.

The two most fundamental questions geographers ask are "Where is (something) located?" and "Why is it located there?" An object's location, as we know, can be given in either precise or relative terms. Its precise location is specified in the form of a grid coordinate system such as latitude and longitude or Universal Transverse Mercator (UTM) coordinates. Increasingly popular Global Positioning System (GPS) devices help people know where they are and plot courses to where they want to go by using satellites and map location data on the Earth's surface. However, although precise location is indeed useful, the numbers that characterize any specific point on the Earth's surface typically mean little to the average person. For example, who keeps in mind the fact that New Orleans, Louisiana, is located at about 30° north latitude and 90° west longitude? It would make better sense to most people to say where New Orleans is located by indicating its position relative to some other city, such as Pensacola, Florida, or to some region, such as the South. People also often specify the relative location of a place by stating how long it takes to get there by car, plane, or train and sometimes by specifying the general direction of travel, such as "It's about two hours north of here."

In this chapter, Lake Lanier's location, about 45 minutes (by car) northeast of metropolitan Atlanta, is critical to understanding why it is so heavily used for recreational water sports and why its development as a nearby vacation and resort area competes with other uses such as providing an attractive housing area for the cities of Gainesville, Buford, and Cumming, Georgia. Knowing its proximity to Atlanta, and knowing that Lake Lanier was created by damming the Chattahoochee River, also helps to answer the question "Why there?" The extension of interstate highways close to Lake Lanier and on to the northeast Georgia mountains also helps to explain some of the population growth and high land values in the area. Of course, the lack of other major lakes surrounding metropolitan Atlanta also has a major influence on the importance of Lake Lanier.

Helping students think about the questions "Where?" and "Why there?" requires some map study and some knowledge of how people use the land to satisfy their needs for employment, housing, education, shopping, worship, and recreation. A map of an area may not "speak" to the casual observer unless he or she needs to go somewhere in order to satisfy some need or desire. Answering questions about where you might be employed, what kind of neighborhood you can afford, how far you are able and willing to commute, and the presence of traffic congestion or mass transit is fundamental to most adults but often not on the minds of young people. Similarly, thinking about the attractiveness of certain housing locations and how different forms of housing and lifestyles influence one's everyday experiences in satisfying the need to eat and sleep may also escape the awareness of the young. Often, such awareness is developed only through observation of and interaction with one's parents.

Students must also be led to think about complex environmental issues and problems that are closely linked to people's use of the land. For example, Lake Lanier will remain an attractive place to live and play only if its water quality is maintained. Similarly, the wildlife that inhabit the lake and its surrounding areas can tolerate only a certain amount of habitat destruction and pollution. Fishing in Lake Lanier may become less and less attractive as fish populations dwindle and speed-boating becomes more popular. Living on the shoreline of Lake Lanier may become less attractive with increasing use of jet skis and other forms of noise pollution.

Teachers can help students acquire geographic thinking skills by using CTL materials such as those provided in this chapter. In using these materials, teachers must also help students draw on their own experiences (and those of their parents and relatives) to arrive at personal insights into problems related to population growth and development. Posing "what if" questions such as "What if Lake Lanier becomes very polluted?" can also be critical to developing students' thinking skills. In the end, there is no magic formula or recipe for developing geographic thinking skills. The best approach to this is the careful consideration of real-world events under the guidance of teachers who have learned to think geographically.

Table 3.1 Lesson Overview for "The Lake Lanier Land Use Controversy"

	GOALS	ACTIVITIES	ASSESSMENTS
LESSON ONE	• Identify the controversy. • Identify the citizen stakeholders' positions.	• Read the case study (Handouts 3.1 and 3.2). • Define the problem(s). • Clarify terms. • For homework, students should talk with a parent or neighbor about the point of view of their stakeholder.	• Assess student participation in identifying the problems discussed.
LESSON TWO	• Work in small groups. • Research the citizen stakeholders' perspectives.	• Research the stakeholders' positions (Handouts 3.3 to 3.6). • Design a survey for homework. • For homework, students conduct a survey of parents and/or neighbors about the case study and/or use the Internet or other sources to find support for their stakeholders' positions.	• Collect stakeholders' forms. • Review student work (Handout 3.3).
LESSON THREE	• Develop group presentations.	• Organize information. • Outline main points. • Create a speech. • Make illustrations. • Develop PowerPoint presentations (Handouts 3.7 and 3.8). • For homework, students should finish working on their presentations.	• Evaluate the presentation worksheet (Handouts 3.7 and 3.8).
LESSON FOUR	• Describe different citizen stakeholders' positions in a mock County Commissioners' meeting. • Analyze possible solutions to the controversy. • Describe further actions that could be taken.	• Give presentations at the mock County Commissioners' meeting. • Discuss the meeting's outcome. • Write an assessment paper. • For homework, students should finish the assessment paper.	• Presentation Assessment Rubric.

LESSON ONE: Local Access to Political Power

Purpose This lesson introduces students to the issue of growth and community development. In particular, students see how the development of a lakeside subdivision affects key stakeholders, the rest of the community, and the health of a nearby important resource: Lake Lanier.

Duration One class period

Materials
Handout 3.1: Development Difficulties
Handout 3.2: Stakeholder Profiles

Procedures
1. Begin this lesson by asking the students a few context-setting questions about their experiences with (a) fishing, water skiing, or swimming in a lake;

(b) new housing developments; and (c) small cities. For example, you might ask and accept several answers for questions such as "How many of you have ever done fishing, water skiing, or swimming in a lake?" "What kinds of businesses or government development activities do we typically find around a lake?" "What is life like around a suburban housing development?" "How does a developer go about getting permission to construct a new housing development?" "Why does most housing development happen in the suburbs?" "How should a local government respond to such requests?" Tell the students that in this unit they will learn about the difficulties that surround development around a lakeside community and that as they delve more deeply into this topic, they will see how important it is to "think geographically" about people's life activities.

2. Have students read Handout 3.1. When they are finished, brainstorm a list of the different problems (need for growth, employment, recreation, habitat for wildlife) that are presented by the scenario and list these on the board in the form of questions that must be answered. For example, "What will very likely happen to the lake as more and more development occurs?" "Does construction runoff damage fishing?" "Do local businesses need more customers?" "Is the existing sewage treatment plant big enough to handle more homes and businesses?"

Help the students refine their understanding of key terms such as *land use, zoning, infrastructure,* and *commissioner* so that everyone is working with the same ideas and frames of reference.

3. Explain that different members of a community are likely to feel differently about new development. Help the students imagine how a realtor, a builder, a Department of Natural Resources (DNR), a law enforcement officer, and a store manager might feel about a new lakeside housing development. Divide the students into research groups that will take the position of each citizen stakeholder. (You may wish to give the students some choice in their selections. For example, you could have them pick the stakeholder they like best or allow them to put down three choices in order of preference and then group them according to their choices.) Give each group a profile of their stakeholder (Handout 3.2) and allow them to discuss what this person might use as evidence to support his or her point of view.

4. As a homework assignment, tell the students to work with their parents to create a list of five problems or concerns that their stakeholder might encounter in daily life. Then they should try to imagine how these influence or contribute to their stakeholder's view of the development dilemma and state these concerns as questions that need to be answered.

LESSON TWO: Investigation of Positions

Purpose Students work in groups to determine the positions of the stakeholders they have chosen. Their investigation of what is most important to particular segments of the community helps reveal the positive and negative consequences of allowing more lakeside development.

Duration Two or three class periods

Materials
Handout 3.3: Stakeholder Worksheet
Handout 3.4: Lake Lanier Facts
Handout 3.5: Lake Lanier Zoning Restrictions
Handout 3.6: Newspaper Article Information

Procedures

1. Seat the students in their citizen stakeholder groups. Ask each group to share the results of their homework assignment and to reconsider the points presented by their stakeholder at the Commissioners' meeting. Distribute copies of the Stakeholder Worksheet (Handout 3.3) to each group and ask them to fill it out. You can help the students by giving them suggestions such as the following:

• Would your stakeholder be able to buy one of the new homes? Why or why not? How might

this simple fact influence his or her feelings about the development?

• What does your stakeholder's present and potential future employment depend on? How strongly is this employment picture related to continuing growth of the community?

• How do you think your stakeholder feels about the need to protect the environment? Why do you think this might be his or her view?

• What additional points might your stakeholder wish to make at the coming meeting of the County Commission?

• What outcome from the meeting will your stakeholder seek? How can this outcome be justified or supported?

2. Students will need to investigate their stakeholder's position and find points to present that will help them obtain the outcome they want. They can use the Internet, newspapers, interviews with people in the same situation, and information regarding local infrastructure and the growth of the county. You can provide some of this for the students, but most counties have Web sites that present a great deal of information about land use. They can also use the Lake Lanier Facts

(Handout 3.4) and Lake Lanier Zoning Restrictions (Handout 3.5). The history of Lake Lanier is available at the U.S. Army Corps of Engineers Web site: http://lanier.sam.usace.army.mil/history.htm

Note to teachers: Stakeholders on both sides of the development issue can use the information provided here. Students arguing for continuing the development can use the economic data, the recreational significance of the lake, and the statement that "Water quality in Lake Lanier is generally good." The other side of the argument has substantial data to support limited growth and standard enforcement. Helping groups to interpret the data is done easily as the teacher moves from group to group pointing out areas that lend support to each stakeholder's point of view.

3. Have the students read the Newspaper Article Information (Handout 3.6), a fictional account of Billy Parsons's violations of county building codes. Once the students have finished reading, ask some or all of the following questions that are designed to help students understand (a) the importance of a home's location, (b) the reasons for building codes, and (c) the motivations of builders and developers.

a. The importance of a home's location
- Why would Mr. Parsons want to build homes near the shoreline of Lake Lanier?
- Other things being equal, why is a home on the lakeshore more valuable than one across the street?
- Why is a home's location so important to homeowners?
- Why do people want to live near the places where they work, shop, and play?
- Does it make any difference what other structures (e.g., high-tension power lines, large freeways, a prison) and businesses (e.g., a stockyard, a rock quarry, a truck stop, a chicken farm) are close to a person's home? Why or why not?

b. Reasons for building codes
- What building codes did Mr. Parsons violate?
- When building near a lake, why is it important to spread hay over bare dirt, use silt fences (often made of heavy-duty black plastic strips about 2 feet high stapled to stakes that are driven into the ground every 4 or 5 feet; their purpose is to prevent runoff of topsoil into ditches, streets, streams, ponds, and lakes), and not grade slopes too steeply?
- Why do cities and counties attempt to prohibit construction within 25 feet of streams?
- Why do cities and counties attempt to prohibit the cutting of large trees?

c. Motivations of builders
- What is a builder ultimately attempting to do? (Answer: make a profit by building something that people want to buy.)
- Why would a builder sometimes need to take down trees?
- Why would a builder want to keep and not hurt trees?
- Why would a builder perhaps not pay close attention to building codes such as those that regulate runoff?
- What is a stop work order, and why is it very bad for a builder?
- Many homes are built to order, but others, often called spec homes, are built on the speculation that a buyer can be found if the home is built. The builder has to cover the cost of construction of a spec home and may do this with a bank loan that must be repaid when a buyer is found. Large housing developments and new subdivisions are often filled with spec homes.
- Why might builders who are engaged in large developments including spec homes cut corners (i.e., not do everything perfectly) compared to builders who are constructing built-to-order homes?

LESSON THREE: Developing Presentations

Purpose Using the information they have gathered in prior lessons, students create a presentation to achieve the outcome their stakeholders want.

Duration Two class periods

Materials Poster paper, markers, computer with projection system (optional)
Handout 3.7: Presentation Worksheet
Handout 3.8: Storyboard for PowerPoint Presentation (optional)

Procedures
1. Tell the stakeholder groups that they will have

to come before the Commission to advocate their position on the issue of whether to halt future shoreline development around Lake Lanier. Help the groups formulate a clear statement of their desired action and share these so that each group understands what the others will be asking for at the time of the Commission meeting. For example, Emily Burton's stakeholder group might ask the Commission to promote mixed-use development of the shoreline, interspersing low-, medium-, and high-priced housing developments with picnic and park areas that have designated fishing piers. Billy

Parsons's group might advocate unrestricted development of the shoreline, letting market forces determine the type and cost of housing that is built. Victor Sanchez's group might argue for a total ban on further shoreline development, and Sue Fletcher's group might support a proposal that would bring the greatest number of new homes to the market.

2. Now help the groups analyze and organize the information that they can use to support their point of view. Groups should be urged to prioritize their supporting information, offering their strongest evidence and tying it to desirable goals such as protection of the environment, managed growth, and historic preservation.

3. Distribute the Presentation Worksheet (Handout 3.7) and ask the student to complete it.

4. An illustration must be made for each presentation and can take many forms. Some suggestions are PowerPoint presentations (where available), a poster of action statement, a graph of statistical information, pictures of endangered habitats, or other forms (must be approved).

LESSON FOUR: Presentations

Purpose To give students an opportunity to present information and try to persuade an audience that their ideas are correct; to participate in a cooperative effort with many differing opinions that must be considered.

Duration One class period

Materials
Equipment for PowerPoint Presentation (optional)

Procedures
1. Arrange the classroom so that a group of Commissioners is seated at the front. You may have one group of five or seven students that become the Commissioners or you may invite parents, teachers, local government administrators, clerks, or other adults to serve as Commission members.

2. Determine the order for the presentations and begin the Commission meeting. Have each group give their presentation and allow the Commissioners to ask questions if they desire to do so. Use the Presentation Assessment Rubric to help evaluate each group's presentation.

3. Have the Commissioners vote on which of the four stakeholder positions they most strongly support, and have them announce their reasons for this choice.

4. Conclude this lesson by discussing the decision made by the Commissioners. Do the students think it was the best alternative? What changes will likely happen as a result of the Commission's decision? What else can be done to help achieve the goals that were neglected as a result of the Commission's decision?

Presentation Assessment Rubric

Content: Did the information given support the stakeholder's point of view, and were accurate facts presented?

Points 25:_____

Illustration: Was the illustration neat and eye-catching? Did it represent the information that was being presented?

Points 25:_____

Participation: Did all the members of the group participate in the presentation, either in the speech or by finding the facts given to support the speech?

Points 25:_____

Total Points 75:_____

Grade:_____

DEVELOPMENT DIFFICULTIES

As the dim light of morning filtered softly through the pine trees, Alex and Emily Burton performed a familiar ritual. The fishing tackle was already in the car, and bait worms were waiting in the old back porch refrigerator. Alex examined the worms to make sure that they were still alive. Emily poured coffee into her thermos and packed a small cooler with sandwiches and fruit. Fishing was a family tradition that Alex and his mom, Emily, had used at almost every opportunity since he was a young boy. Now that middle school was almost over, Alex thought that his frequent family fishing trips might soon come to an end.

As Alex and his mom drove to their favorite fishing spot, he thought about the many times he had taken this familiar path. He had played along the shoreline of the cove with his best friend during the summers, exploring the different habitats of the animals that lived there. He wondered if the beaver dam he had discovered last fall was still there. He was anxious to see if there were new baby turtles, and he wanted to see if the owl had returned for its summertime visit.

As Alex and his mom approached the cove, they heard the sounds of large earth-moving machines at work. Rounding the last curve, they saw a temporary 2 by 4 inch post and a plywood sign announcing the development of a new lakeside community. Beyond the sign, the road to their favorite fishing cove was blocked by uprooted trees. Huge yellow machines had leveled the ground and shaped a swarm of the new streets for the housing development. Noise, clouds of yellowish dust, and the odor of diesel fuel filled the air.

Looking at his mother, Alex remarked, "Well there goes our fishing cove. Guess there'll be no fishing from there anymore. Where else are we going to go, Mom? And what's going to happen to all the animals that lived here? The developers are going to ruin everything. Where can we go this summer to fish, and where will the turtles, beavers, and owls go?"

Emily said, "I don't know, but I know what I can do about it!"

Casting an exasperated look her way, Alex said, "You can't do anything about this. You know those people can do anything they want. They have the money and they have the power. All you are is one person against the whole bunch of them."

"You're wrong, son," she said. "There's many people who feel like us, and there's a County Commissioners' meeting next week and I intend to be there. I know several other people who are upset about this kind of development, and we've begun talking about what we can do. Now I can see there is no time to lose, so I'm going back home and start making some phone calls. It won't be easy, but if we can find enough interested people, there will be more than just my one small voice opposing this development, and that's real power."

"I think it's a waste of time," Alex said. "I don't understand how going to some silly old Commissioners' meeting will help this situation. What can they do?"

"Alex, they are the ones who decide what gets built because they are the ones who give the permits to the builders," Emily said. "But they have to listen to the public because it's the public that puts them in office, and my friends and I are the public. Remember last November when I went to vote? That's when the present Commissioners were voted into office. I'll tell you what; you come with me to the Commissioners' meeting and see how things work. This is the best way to get involved in government, and you can observe how government impacts all our lives."

"Oh, brother," Alex complained. "Now I've done it. You did this on purpose, didn't you? You knew about this new housing development before today, didn't you?"

"No, honey," his mom said. "I didn't, but it's time for you to learn how the local government works. You need to learn how things happen so

continued

Real-World Investigations for Social Studies
Hoge, Field, Foster, and Nickell

you can be involved in your own community when you are old enough to vote. Even if you can't vote now, your opinion is valuable, and you have every right to let the County Commissioners know how you feel. If people like you and me want a say in things, we must make the effort to get involved. Now let's turn this car around and get started."

The First Commissioners' Meeting

The County Commissioners' meeting was packed. Emily's group had received permission to speak regarding the new lakeside housing development and the plan for land use around the lake. She introduced her concerns about the need for shoreline fishing facilities, low-cost lakeside recreation spaces, maintaining the high water quality of the lake, the lack of infrastructure to support so much new development in the county, and whether or not the commissioners' land use plan adequately protected the environment.

After Emily spoke, Billy Parsons, the builder of the development, asked to speak. He acknowledged Emily's concerns but said that they were unfounded and that the building industry was under government mandate to follow U.S. Environmental Protection Agency (EPA) regulations that limited environmental damage. He also stated that the Commissioners would not have granted the building permit if they didn't think the infrastructure could support the new development. He said, "Why, that's my brother on the Commission, and he's an honest man. He's not going to do anything wrong. You can trust him."

Mr. Parsons's comments sparked some exchanges and questions among the Commissioners and people in the audience. Next, Victor Sanchez, the head of the local environmental watchdog club, spoke. He presented evidence of several previous violations of environmental regulations by builders. He stated that regulations were often overlooked and that overbuilding throughout the county was seriously stressing the welfare of the ecosystem and much of its wildlife. Mr. Sanchez concluded, "I suggest a halt on all building permits until these concerns that are before the Commission can be resolved. It's only fair."

Mr. Parsons stood and replied, "You can't do that. You're going to take away the jobs of all those people working on the new development that the Commission already approved. They have families to feed and bills to pay. What about all of them?"

"Now, wait a minute," Emily said. "We're not asking you to stop homes that are already being built, but don't you think it is reasonable to slow down new growth, try to balance the public's right to use the lake for low-cost recreation, and examine the impact of all this development on the environment?"

"Now let's talk about growth," said Sue Fletcher, a local real estate broker. "If you make it so hard on the builders, then the real estate market is going to be hurt. The growth in this county is at an all-time high, and slowing down the builders is only going to make people build somewhere else. You are asking our Commissioners to stand in the way of progress. If we don't allow building in this county, then some other county will, and we will have lost out on a great opportunity. You are asking too much."

Alex was amazed that the meeting had held his attention. An hour had passed and he had hardly noticed. Sitting there, he began wondering who was right. He saw his mother's point and wanted her to win. But he also understood that the other side had legitimate concerns. He was glad he was not on the Commission and wondered how an equitable solution could be found.

The rap of the Commission President's gavel brought Alex back to the reality of the meeting. The President spoke: "It's almost ten o'clock, and I promised when I became the Commission President that we would keep civilized hours for our work. The question before us is not whether Mr. Parsons will be allowed to continue developing the Blue Gill Bay subdivision. He has already received the proper permits for doing that. What we need to decide is whether we want to halt future developments around Lake Lanier's shoreline. We'll meet again in two weeks to take up this question."

Real-World Investigations for Social Studies
Hoge, Field, Foster, and Nickell

Handout 3.2

STAKEHOLDER PROFILES

Emily Burton

Age: 37

Occupation: Store manager at a local outlet mall

Income: $32,000

Goal: Protect the lake for shoreline fishing and other forms of low-cost recreation

Emily Burton's family has lived in this area for over 50 years, and she wants to make sure that the lake remains healthy for shoreline fishing and other forms of low-cost recreation such as picnicking and bird watching. She especially does not want to see the fishing ruined by the construction of lakeside housing developments. She is concerned for herself, Alex, and her potential future grandchildren. Ms. Burton is a single parent and lives in a modest two-bedroom home with her middle school–age son, Alex.

Billy Parsons

Age: 33

Occupation: Residential home builder

Income: $100,000

Goal: Keep building homes, stay employed, and keep making money

Mr. Parsons has his own company, has worked hard to make it profitable, and wants to keep it that way. He has invested large amounts of time and money in getting this project started and stands to lose a great deal if it is stopped or even slowed down. The Commission has approved Phase I of the project, which includes 30 homes located on 1/2-acre lots. Phase II, which will double the size of the development, has not yet been approved. Mr. Parsons's development plan calls for completion of the 30 homes by the end of the year. In order to meet this goal, he will have to employ almost 50 carpenters, plumbers, electricians, roofers, and other skilled workers. The expected price range for the homes he is building will be between $200,000 and $250,000.

Victor Sanchez

Age: 46

Occupation: DNR law enforcement officer

Income: $45,000

Goal: Preserve the environment and stop growth throughout the county

Victor Sanchez is very concerned about the wildlife of the county and maintenance of a healthy ecosystem for the lake. He knows that growth-spurred construction will cause more pollution of the lake and further destruction of animal habitats. He has statistics that show a decrease in both land and water animals and the decline of water quality in the lake. He feels that all construction must be stopped and that no more should be allowed in order to save the lake.

Sue Fletcher

Age: 27

Occupation: Real estate broker

Income: $150,000 (average)

Goal: Keep building lakeside houses to promote upscale growth of the community and help guarantee her excellent annual income.

Sue Fletcher has become one of the top salespersons of her company. She is working to become the number one salesperson of the year. She believes that this new development will provide her with many opportunities to increase her sales for the year. In fact, she has signed an agreement with Mr. Parsons to list the first 10 homes in his development. She can see no visual damage to the lake and uses the lake as a selling point when talking to prospective customers. If the project is stopped or if Phase II is not approved, she believes that growth will occur in other nearby counties, businesses will move out of her area, and she will lose many customers.

Real-World Investigations for Social Studies
Hoge, Field, Foster, and Nickell

STAKEHOLDER WORKSHEET

Stakeholder's Name

Position

What actions does your stakeholder want from the Commissioners?

What actions might your stakeholder be willing to perform to help achieve his or her goal?

Real-World Investigations for Social Studies
Hoge, Field, Foster, and Nickell

Handout 3.4

LAKE LANIER FACTS[1]

The facts presented below were condensed and adapted from a report on Lake Lanier written for the state Environmental Protection Division (EPD) under the U.S. Environmental Protection Agency's Clean Lakes program. You will want to consider the following questions as you read this material:

1. How will this information help your stakeholder convince the Commissioners to accept his or her proposal?
2. What facts about the lake development support your stakeholder's position?
3. What facts and figures make your stakeholder's ideas the best solution to the problem presented to the Commissioners?

Lake Lanier's Location

Lake Lanier, a reservoir completed in 1959 by the Army Corps of Engineers, lies in the uppermost part of the Chattahoochee River Basin. Buford Dam, located 48 miles upstream from Atlanta, forms the lower bound of Lake Lanier. From that point, Lake Lanier continues 44 miles north along the Chattahoochee River and 19 miles up the Chestatee River.

Each river contributes substantially to Lake Lanier's water; the Chattahoochee provides approximately 45 percent of Lake Lanier's water while the Chestatee contributes approximately 28 percent. At surface level, Lake Lanier has an area of 38,000 acres, a volume of 1,917,000 acre-feet, and approximately 540 miles of shoreline. Lake Lanier is one of the biggest and busiest lakes in the South. It is the most frequently visited of all of the Army Corps of Engineers lakes nationally and provides numerous game fish, especially various types of bass (http://lanier.sam.usace.army.mil/Default.htm).

Georgia has designated Lake Lanier as a recreational area. Much of its shoreline is developed with housing and marinas, with development continuing at a rapid pace. Lake Lanier lies within Hall, Lumpkin, Gwinnett, Forsyth, and Dawson counties. Other counties in the basin include White, Habersham, Union, Towns, and Cherokee. The population of these counties has grown tremendously in recent years; Forsyth, Henry, and Paulding counties rank among the ten fastest-growing counties in the nation (U.S. Census, 2002). The following table contains the 1990 and 1996 population, percent growth, and annual rate of growth for the 10 counties identified in the Lake Lanier area. Those counties immediately surrounding Lake Lanier have seen some of the largest population growth in the state; each county's annual rate of population change exceed[ed] the figure for Georgia [as a whole,] and several counties [had] more than double the rate of growth in Georgia. Four of the five remaining counties also have growth rates that exceed the state average.

Lake Lanier's Economic Significance

Lake Lanier's contribution to the regional economy is substantial. Boaters alone spent an estimated $213 million during their trips to Lake Lanier. The value of Lake Lanier to the economy is estimated to exceed one billion dollars per year.

---

[1]The full report can be found at http://www.cviog.uga.edu/projects/lanier

Real-World Investigations for Social Studies
Hoge, Field, Foster, and Nickell

Population of Counties in the Lake Lanier Area, 1990 and 1996

	1990 POPULATION	1996 POPULATION	PERCENTAGE CHANGE, 1990–1996	ANNUAL RATE OF CHANGE
Counties Immediately Surrounding Lake Lanier				
Dawson	9,543	13,016	36.39	5.31
Forsyth	44,766	69,127	54.42	7.51
Gwinnett	356,596	478,001	34.05	5.00
Hall	96,000	113,033	17.74	2.76
Lumpkin	14,697	17,286	17.62	2.74
Remaining Counties in the Lake Lanier Area				
Cherokee	91,391	121,496	32.94	3.86
Habersham	27,740	30,794	11.01	1.76
Towns	6,772	7,990	17.99	2.79
Union	12,072	14,293	23.62	3.60
White	13,093	16,140	23.27	3.55
State Average			13.01	2.06*

*Source: http://www.cviog.uga.edu./projects/lanier/chapter7.htm/ Heading 7

Threats to Water Quality at Lake Lanier

Nonpoint (areas of land that are not on the lake but [that contain] activit[ies] affect[ing] the water . . . that eventually enters the lake) pollution sources represent the greatest threat to water quality in Lake Lanier. Specifically, bacteria, nutrients such as phosphorus and nitrogen (waste product from animal waste, crop production, and crop fertilization), chlorophyll a (from wastewater treatment plants, agricultural runoff, and leakage from faulty septic tanks), and sedimentation (from soil erosion increased by logging, farming, mining, and land development activities) are listed as threats to Lake Lanier's water quality. This study and others have provided information that substantiates the claims that while water quality in Lake Lanier is generally good, nonpoint sources [of pollution] remain a threat to water quality.

The Chattahoochee River Basin Management Plan (RBMP) identifies five threats to Lake Lanier: metals, fecal coliform, erosion and sedimentation, nutrients, and water quantity. The threats from metals derive from water pollution control plant discharges and nonpoint sources and consist of lead, copper, zinc, and mercury. The data in this report indicate that metals concentrations are low; lead and mercury in tributary streams, however, may pose a problem. The next iteration of the Chattahoochee RBMP process will include the collection of additional metals data.

Fecal coliform enters streams from numerous sources, including urban runoff, septic systems, sewer overflows, rural nonpoint [sources,] and animal wastes. Since the sources of fecal coliform are so widespread, the RBMP process resulted in separate strategies to deal with urban and rural uses.

Recommendations for Protection of Lake Lanier

In order to manage urban sources of fecal coliform, local governments will continue to operate and maintain sewer systems and wastewater treatment plants,

continued

Real-World Investigations for Social Studies
Hoge, Field, Foster, and Nickell

develop stormwater management programs, and implement zoning and land use planning. EPD will also require municipal permit applicants ([for] new or expanding plants) to include in their applications plans for dealing with non-point sources of pollution, thus compelling municipalities to consider future growth plans. Finally, as part of the approach to control urban sources of fecal coliform, EPD will encourage greater involvement with Adopt-A-Stream programs. In rural areas, EPD will rely more on voluntary compliance and implementation of best management practices, especially those that the Georgia Soil and Water Conservation Commission (GSWCC), local Soil and Water Conservation Districts (SWCDs), and Resource Conservation and Development (RC&D) councils implement. Local governments in rural areas will need to enforce septic system requirements and utilize land use planning.

Construction runoff, unpaved rural roads, silviculture, and agriculture contribute sediment to bodies of water. To control sediment discharges into Lake Lanier, GSSWC, local SWCDs, RD&C Councils, the Georgia Forestry Commission (GFC), and the United States Forest Service (USFS) will need to encourage and implement best management practices. Local governments will need to enforce erosion controls in construction and promote greater involvement with Adopt-A-Stream programs.

Nutrients also pose a threat to the waters of Lake Lanier, [entering] the water from pollution control plant discharges and agricultural and urban nonpoint sources. Since the transmission of nutrients into the Lake is similar to that of sediment, proposals for managing nutrient loads follow the same procedures proposed for sediment.

Information is adopted from *Diagnostic/Feasibility Study of Lake Sidney Lanier*, Carl Vinson Institute of Government, University of Georgia, 1998. Used by permission.

Real-World Investigations for Social Studies
Hoge, Field, Foster, and Nickell

LAKE LANIER ZONING RESTRICTIONS

The Army Corp of Engineers shoreline management plan for Lake Lanier establishes the following shoreline zoning categories and restrictions.

Limited Development

Construction for private use such as docks and other structures is permitted along the shoreline. Permits for construction of any floating or nonfloating structures must be obtained from the shoreline management organization (Army Corps of Engineers).

Authorized structures on private property are the responsibility of the owner and are subject to trespassing laws regarding private use. Public access to the shoreline cannot be restricted. The limited development areas of Lake Lanier comprise approximately 46 percent of the total shoreline.

Public Recreation

These areas are set aside for the development of recreational facilities including, but not limited to, campgrounds, day-use parks, primitive or natural areas, lands leased to public groups and local, state, or federal agencies for recreational use or development, and marine services. Public recreation areas cannot include private shoreline use facilities, and no commercial activity is allowed without a permit. Public recreation areas comprise approximately 29 percent of the total shoreline.

Protected Shoreline

Due to rapid urban development, specific areas are designated as protected to preserve the scenic appeal of the lake. Protected areas also secure habitats for fish, wildlife, and species classified as endangered. These regions also include areas of historical, cultural, and archaeological significance. Navigational channels and areas that pose a navigational difficulty, because of winds or shallow waters, are restricted from development.

Public boating and pedestrian traffic are permitted as long as no environmental, historical, or natural resources are damaged. No private use facilities are authorized at these locations. Protected shoreline comprises approximately 25 percent of the total shoreline.

Prohibited Access

These areas are so classified to protect recreational visitors and project operation sites. Restricted visitation is allowed, but no shoreline use permits are issued. The areas are in the vicinity of powerhouse intakes, dams, saddledikes, spillways, tailraces, and the Army Corps of Engineers marine yard. Less than 1 mile of the shoreline is prohibited from access.

For more information, contact Lake Lanier, Army Corps of Engineers, P.O. Box 567, Buford, GA 30515-0567, call 770-945-9531, or visit http://lanier.sam. usace.army.mil/Default.htm

Real-World Investigations for Social Studies
Hoge, Field, Foster, and Nickell

Handout 3.6

NEWSPAPER ARTICLE INFORMATION[1]

Gainesville, GA—The County Building Code Enforcement Authority cited Billy Parsons, a local subdivision developer, for repeatedly violating the county's soil erosion laws at the new Blue Gill Bay subdivision located on the shoreline of Lake Lanier southwest of Gainesville.

Lt. James Marlin, who issued the court summons and a Stop Work Order, said the violations included not having groundcover (such as hay) spread over the bare dirt, not keeping mandatory silt fences in good repair, grading the lot slopes too steeply, violating the 25-foot stream-buffer law, ignoring the county's tree-protection ordinance, and not having construction entrances properly designed to keep mud from being tracked into the street. Mr. Parsons, who could not be reached for comment, is scheduled to appear in the County Court at 2:30 P.M. on July 12 to answer the charges.

"Mr. Parsons has been pushing his luck for quite some time, and we finally just got fed up with his conduct," said Lt. Marlin. "We usually cut developers quite a bit of slack, but this case was just too far gone for us to ignore. Maybe Mr. Parsons will respond to a Stop Work Order and a court summons."

---

[1]This is a fictional account using pseudonyms, but it is based on similar stories that have been reported in newspapers.

Real-World Investigations for Social Studies
Hoge, Field, Foster, and Nickell

PRESENTATION WORKSHEET

A. State the action that your stakeholder group wants the Commission to take regarding whether to halt further development around Lake Lanier's shoreline.

B. Give three supporting reasons that your recommended action should be taken.

C. Conclusion: Restate the action wanted and thank the Commissioners for the opportunity to state your position.

Illustration: (required for each group)

Suggestions: PowerPoint Presentation (if available), poster of action statement, graph of statistical information, pictures of endangered habitats, others (must be approved)

Real-World Investigations for Social Studies
Hoge, Field, Foster, and Nickell

Handout 3.8

STORYBOARD FOR POWERPOINT PRESENTATION

4

C H A P T E R

Getting a Job and Keeping It

Expectations in the Workplace

by
Sherry L. Field and Pat Nickell

OVERVIEW

The school-to-work movement provides ample evidence that middle and secondary students need a variety of opportunities to explore the world of work (Borko & Putnam, 1998; Steinberg, 1997). Although field trips, job shadowing, apprenticeships, and youth-run enterprises inform youngsters about the variety of careers and job opportunities that are available, it is also important that students consider the expectations that exist when one becomes an employee. Work environments are enhanced when employees exhibit behaviors and attitudes that enable them to work well with and show respect for others, show initiative, take pride in their work, and promote honesty, fairness, and goodwill among other workers.

Middle and high school students can benefit from an introduction to what employers look for in job candidates, what citizenship skills are valued among workers, and hour those skills are measured by supervisors when workers receive evaluations. In their extensive look at the role of society in preparing youth for the world of work and how teens respond to it, Csikszentmihalyi and Schneider (2000) note that "A positive work ethic seems to be necessary to socialize children into adulthood.

Without it we might expect an increasingly inefficient, demoralized, and passive population unable to exploit opportunities" (p. 11).

Employers repeatedly note that the workers they seek must be reliable, work effectively with others, exhibit strong leadership and communication skills, and have the know-how and the common sense to carry out required tasks. They attempt to identify such workers through the application and interview processes. Once workers are hired, such skills and qualities continue to be measures of their effectiveness, appearing in instruments and processes used to evaluate their performance. Students will quickly recognize that the skills expected of them in school and in most homes are mirrored in workplace values. Thus, a very realistic school-to-work[1] connection becomes apparent through this inquiry.

CONNECTION TO NCSS THEME IV: INDIVIDUAL DEVELOPMENT AND IDENTITY

The NCSS encourages teachers to provide learning experiences that powerfully demonstrate how personal identity is shaped by one's culture, by groups, and by institutional influences such as those encountered in the workplace. In addition, Standard IV promotes deep understanding of personal relationships and influences on them. At the same time, students who are well versed in individual development and identity understand human growth, identity, and sense of self, as well as "the interactions of ethnic, national, or cultural influences in specific situations or events" (NCSS, 1994, p. 37). In this case, examining the relationships between social norms, employment expectations, and a young person's emerging individual identity can provide a powerful platform for the growth of positive values and life expectations. This chapter on workplace expectations directly addresses this important NCSS theme.

METHODS FOCUS: CHARACTER/VALUES EDUCATION AND INTERVIEWING

The CTL that takes place in this chapter builds strongly on the elements of cooperative learning and case study. Within key learning sequences, however, character/values education and interviewing are emphasized. Powerful aspects of prior knowledge, life skills, and attitudinal elements

come into focus in this chapter as students consider the workplace, its many human relations dimensions, how learning takes place on the job, and how employees are motivated.

Character/Values Education

Values education plays a prominent role in the American schooling experience. The general public considers broad-based democratic values such as individual rights, the common good, diversity, justice, and responsibility to be important. Democratic values are viewed as an intrinsic part of the nation's historic documents, such as the Declaration of Independence and the Constitution. As Parker (2001) suggests, these general values can be promoted by classroom activities that stress care and consideration for others, historical studies about the development of the country and the ideals of its founders, biography study, analyses of documents, cross-cultural studies, and study of law and the justice system. Although it is generally recognized that the responsibility for values education lies in the home, schools traditionally have promoted values education.

The question of teaching values in schools is one with which all teachers grapple, especially when they must make decisions about which values to promote and how they are to be taught. According to Chapin, it is important to "think about your own values as you become a teacher. Your values will influence your planning and teaching based upon what you consider important for students to learn" (Chapin, 2003, p. 22). Various approaches to teaching values, particularly in the form of character traits or virtues, exist. Especially in elementary and middle schools, the most prominent approach is character education. Increased public attention resulting in character education programs is not new to education. In the 1920s and 1930s, programs devoted to the development of good character were widespread. Almost all schools in the United States had adopted a formal character education curriculum, and many were based on various objectives, activities, and character traits to be emphasized (Field & Nickell, 2000).

Many similarities to the programs of the 1920s and 1930s exist in contemporary character education programs. Today, most states have mandated some form of character education, which typically includes a focus on traits such as honesty, trustworthiness, kindness, responsibility, courage, and fairness. In the early grades, this education may take the form of defining terms, hearing and writing stories about

---

[1]Allen, Hogan, and Steinberg (2000) suggest that the term *school-to-career* is preferable to *school-to-work* because "the key to self-sufficiency in the labor market is the ability to advance in a career, not simply get a job. Also, the term school-to-work can misleadingly suggest a one-time transition to employment and be associated with entry-level work rather than career advancement" (p. 85).

people who exhibit desirable character traits, and finding ways to act on the development of personal and group virtues. For older students, character education may include taking important responsibilities in the school, neighborhood, and community. Moving toward and engaging in social action is a desirable outcome of character education. [2]

Interviewing

Several of the lessons in this chapter require that students learn by conducting interviews. Planning, conducting, analyzing, and reporting on an interview are valuable learning experiences for students because they are required to learn by doing and to develop higher-order thinking skills. Students should be well prepared in advance in order to complete the interview process successfully. The principles and guidelines for interviewing presented in this section provide meaningful prior experiences that students need to maximize the unit's benefits.

Viewed as a major form of inquiry, the interview is an excellent tool for gaining primary source data. Much has been written about the interview, especially as it relates to oral history investigations and learning how to do the work of a historian, psychologist, or sociologist. For social scientists, interviews may be major data sources during research. Kvale writes about interviewing as a "mode to understanding" and a way to gain knowledge about the "lived world of the subjects" (Kvale, 1996). Classroom teacher Paula Rogovin wants her students to ask "questions, questions, and more questions!" [3] Local oral historians learn to follow several steps during the interview process. The following steps drawn from oral history are pertinent to most short interviews as well (Baum, 1995):

1. Contact the narrator or interviewee.
2. Explain the purpose of the interview.
3. Prepare the interview outline and questions.
4. Practice questions beforehand.
5. Arrive at the appointed time; check equipment if using a tape or video recorder.
6. Start the interview and establish rapport.
7. Take accurate notes.
8. Ask questions that were not anticipated.
9. Close the interview.
10. Analyze the responses to the questions.
11. Record your interpretation of the interview.

Teachers should allot time for preparation, including development of questions, practice with classmates, discussion of how to extend a line of examples interview, modeling how to establish rapport, showing results, and critiquing the interview process. Valerie Yow (1994, p. 79) has developed a Checklist for Critiquing Interview Skills:

A. Positives (Add 10 points for each item checked)

1. Indicated empathy when appropriate
2. Showed appreciation for narrator's help
3. Listened carefully
4. Followed narrator's pacing
5. Explained reason for changes in topic
6. Used a two-sentence format when introducing line of questions
7. Probed when appropriate
8. Used a follow-up question when more information was needed
9. Asked a challenge question in a sensitive manner
10. Requested clarification when needed

B. Negatives (Subtract 10 points from the score above for each item checked)

1. Interrupted the narrator
2. Kept repeating what the narrator had just said
3. Inferred something the narrator had not said
4. Failed to pick up on a topic the narrator suggested was important
5. Made irrelevant, distracting comments
6. Ignored narrator's feelings and failed to give empathetic response
7. Failed to check the sound on the recorder
8. Let the narrator sidetrack the conversation with a long monologue on an irrelevant topic
9. Asked a leading question
10. Asked several questions at the same time

Helping students attend to the details listed above prior to the interview will likely yield rich information during the interview and contribute to the success of guided in-class discussion following the interview. After the interviews have been completed and discussed in class, the teacher and students may use Yow's checklist to critique their work.

Often middle and secondary students will have an opportunity to conduct in-depth interviews on topics related to social studies, such as the Depression, World War II, space exploration, the Vietnam War, the Cold War, and the technology boom. On such occasions, students will not only probe for historical

---

[2]For more information on social action and community service learning, see Wade and Saxe (1996).

[3]Rogovin's (1998) account of her first-grade students' experiences doing research by interviewing suggests that no student is too young to use interviewing as a key investigative tool.

understanding during interviews, but will also learn about sociocultural contexts that shape the interviewee's understanding. Most important, students' experiences in conducting interviews will contribute greatly to their understanding of multiple perspectives and points of view.

This chapter is an investigation allowing students to learn the concepts of workplace values, expectations, and the work ethic in an effort to introduce them to the expectations of employers in the world of work. Lesson One engages students in a dialogue in which employers reveal a number of common issues, concerns, and/or problems they face in dealing with their respective workforces. Issues of communication, anger, staying on task, and others are raised as employers air their concerns. The term *work ethic* is introduced in the dialogue, and students are asked, based on the reading, to use the context to develop a definition. Students learn more about workplace expectations by interviewing adults they know about the jobs they hold and what their employers expect.

During Lesson Two, students graph the frequency with which various expectations are identified in the interviews to develop a better picture of general workplace values. In addition, through second interviews, they learn from employees about the application and interview processes and the employer expectations these processes reveal. Lesson Three continues to focus on the application process to identify common workplace expectations. In this lesson, students analyze an actual application for a job and draw conclusions from it about expectations that apply to all applicants, as well as discussing other expectations that might be more specific to particular jobs. In Lesson Four, students begin to think about what is expected once an employee has been on the job for a period of time. In this lesson, they examine a variety of work evaluation instruments and make generalizations about expectations related to employee performance.

Lesson Five is designed to help students summarize and use what they have learned. First, based on their study of the application and performance evaluation processes, they generate a list of the qualities that appear to be expected of employees in most situations, both as applicants and as members of the workforce. Second, they specify those qualities that would be necessary for a person to be effective in a particular work role (e.g., teacher, coach, parent).

Table 4.1 Lesson Overview for "Getting a Job and Keeping It: Expectations in the Workplace"

	GOALS	ACTIVITIES	ASSESSMENTS
LESSON ONE	• Investigate a situation that includes a number of problems related to workplace values and ethics; identify the issues.	• Read the investigation springboard story (Handout 4.1) • Review the facts of the case and identify the values and expectations of these three employers. • Review Handout 4.2 prior to dismissal.	• Write a summary of the findings from interviews with parents related to workplace expectations and prepare to share them with the class.
LESSON TWO	• Use real-life experiences of adults to develop a working definition of the work ethic. • Consider relationship issues in the workplace arising from differing values.	• Discuss homework findings. • Create visual representation of common workplace expectations. • Discuss the work ethic (Handout 4.3). • Create interview questions to learn about adults' job application experiences.	• Create a role play or skit involving a job interview in which the employer wishes to discover applicants' views on the importance of, for example, "going the extra mile."
LESSON THREE	• Learn from adults' experiences about the job application process. • Examine job applications from a variety of sources to identify values of employers.	• Discuss the experiences of workers and the job application process. • In small groups, examine a job application form (Handout 4.4) using Handout 4.5.	• Assume the role of an employer and evaluate the job application completed in terms of the impression it would make. • Make comments in the margin, as the employer might.
LESSON FOUR	• Consider how employees are evaluated in the workplace. • Identify work ethic issues and concerns.	• Discuss the completion of the job application form and the questions that arose. • In pairs, scrutinize and compare performance review forms (handouts will vary). • Complete the performance review form assessment (Handout 4.6).	
LESSON FIVE	• Apply what has been learned about assessing the workplace values of job applicants and workers.	• Generate a list of traits that are valued by the employers studied. • Individually or in pairs, create an application form that focuses on an appropriate work ethic and desirable values for a particular role or job.	(May serve as a summative assessment)

LESSON ONE: Expectations in the Workplace

Purpose   This lesson is an introduction to expectations that employers have of workers in the real world. Students explore the concept of work ethic and develop an understanding of the values and expectations that exist in various work settings.

Duration   One class period

Materials
Handout 4.1: An Informal Conversation among Human Resources Administrators
Handout 4.2: Workplace Expectations Interview Guide

Procedures
   1. Have students read the scenario (Handout 4.1). Ask them to list words or phrases that they would like to understand better. Following their reading and after explaining unfamiliar terms, ask students to read the scenario again, this time underlining words and phrases that identify the values and expectations of employers regarding work performance, attitudes, and behaviors.

   2. Guide the class discussion in which students enumerate the work performance, attitude, and behavior expectations they identified. These should be recorded for future reference.

   3. Homework assignment: Distribute Handout 4.2, the Workplace Expectations Interview Guide, and review the instructions with students.

   4. Assessment option: Have students write a summary of their findings from interviews with parents and share it with the class.

LESSON TWO: An Investigation of the Work Ethic

Purpose This lesson follows up students' homework from Lesson One, helping students expand their understanding of the term *work ethic*.

Duration One class period

Materials
Handout 4.3: What Is the Work Ethic?

Procedures
   1. Discuss homework findings and, using the data students gathered for question 7 of Handout 4.2, list common workplace expectations on the overhead projector. You may wish to have students develop a bar graph depicting the frequency of expectations identified, thus creating a visual representation of this important information.

   2. Refresh students' recollection of the use of the term work ethic in Handout 4.1. Guide a discussion of the term using the questions provided in Handout 4.3.

   3. Spend a few minutes helping students create interview questions for use with an adult to learn about his or her job application experiences.

Students should write their interview questions and use them as a template for their homework assignment: to interview an adult about how he or she applied for a job and whatever else the application and interview processes entailed. They should pay particular attention to how the adult learned about the expectations and values of the workplace involved. Students should be encouraged to practice the interviewing process with a classmate.

   4. Assessment Option: Have students, individually or in pairs, create a role play or skit involving a job interview in which the employer wishes to discover applicants' views on the importance of something they have identified as a workplace expectation or value—for example, "going the extra mile."

Note: If this activity is to serve as an assessment, the teacher should observe pairs at work, ensuring that both students are participating, contributing, and self-evaluating. The process itself should be a reflection of one workplace value: teamwork!

LESSON THREE: Looking at a Job Application

Purpose This lesson builds on Lesson Two by emphasizing what can be learned about workers' expectations from the job applications process. It enables students to identify from job applications some of the values of potential employees.

Duration One class period

Materials
Handout 4.4: Employment Application
Handout 4.5: Job Applications: What Does the Employer Value?

Procedures
   1. Using interview data from the previous homework assignment, guide students to discuss the experiences and comments of workers interviewed.

   2. Divide students into small groups (no more than three or four per group) and provide each group with a copy of the job application (use Handout 4.4 or one or more job applications that come from local employers). Give each group one copy of Handout 4.5. Ask students to examine these applications to identify the values and expectations of the businesses and agencies they represent and write responses on Handout 4.5.

3. For homework, have students practice the job application process by completing a job application. Distribute applications and tell students to fill them out to the best of their ability.

4. Assessment Option: Following completion of their job applications, have students assume the role of an employer and evaluate the job application in terms of the impression it makes. Students should be instructed to make comments in the margins, as the employer might, and turn the application in to you. Your assessment should include both the completion of the application and the comments made by the "employer."

LESSON FOUR: Looking at Performance Reviews

Purpose Continuing a careful examination of the job application process and the values and expectations that become apparent from it, students discuss completion of the job application and any questions that arose. Students also begin to examine performance review forms to increase their understanding of values and expectations in the workplace once workers are employed.

Duration One class period

Materials
Performance review forms (to be obtained from local businesses)
Handout 4.6: Analyzing Performance Review Forms

Procedures
1. Review each part of the application form with students. Did anyone leave anything blank? Students will benefit from any guidance teachers can provide regarding the completion of application forms. For example, teachers should explain that when persons apply for a job, it is important to be honest and fill out every part of the form completely. If it is a first job, then there will be no job experience, but after the person holds several jobs, each one must be named. Employers will want to know what applicants were doing during times when they did not appear to have a job.

2. Teachers may also wish to explain that if job applicants have a police record (and students should be cautioned that arrests do not disappear from the police record just because a sentence is served or a fine is paid), it is better to be honest about it than to let the employer find out in performing a background check. In the latter case, not only does the applicant have a record, he or she lied about it.

3. Collect performance review forms from various workplaces in the community. These might include a restaurant, bank, factory, school district office, or fire department. Additional performance review forms may be found online. Divide students into pairs and provide each pair with one copy of the various performance review forms. Using Handout 4.6, give students ample time to scrutinize and evaluate the performance review form in order to identify additional values and expectations revealed in job performance assessments. Have them note their conclusions.

4. Students share findings and compare them to identify similarities and differences across workplaces.

LESSON FIVE: Creating Values for the Workplace

Purpose In this final lesson, students demonstrate their ability to recognize values shared by various workplaces and their ability to generate a job application form that reflects many of these values.

Duration One class period

Materials
None required

Procedures
1. Students individually generate a list of valued traits, attitudes, and behaviors frequently sought by employers studied and named by the adults with whom they have spoken during their homework assignments.

2. Assessment Option: Individually or in pairs, students create an application form that focuses on an appropriate work ethic and desirable characteristics for a particular role or job (e.g., teacher, coach, fast-food manager, pool lifeguard, bank teller).

3. Assessment Option: Engage students in a discussion of the following:

- Why is it difficult to create an application form that reveals the characteristics you feel are important?
- Why did the application form you completed ask for different information from that sought in the performance evaluation forms you examined?
- Should application and evaluation forms seek to establish the same information? Can they?

Handout 4.1

AN INFORMAL CONVERSATION AMONG HUMAN RESOURCES ADMINISTRATORS

The Chamber of Commerce meeting was adjourned. Bill and Marilyn, human resources directors for two large companies, had sat next to one another and, after the meeting, began to share concerns about recent applicants and new employees.

"Bill, tell me if I'm being old-fashioned. This young man came in the day before yesterday to fill out an application to work with us, and you wouldn't believe what he had on," complained Marilyn. "His jeans had holes in them, and he had on a t-shirt that had a rock band's logo and some offensive lyrics across the back. It seems so odd to me that a young person would really expect to get hired when he comes in looking like that. Do you ever have to deal with that?"

"Oh, sure. It happens all the time, but I don't hire them unless they apologize and explain why they are dressed inappropriately. One girl recently came in wearing overalls to fill out an application, but she immediately explained that she didn't realize she would come in contact with a potential employer. She thought she would just be completing the application and hoping for a call. She said she had been babysitting, and overalls were the most appropriate attire. I had to agree. And she did end up getting the job and has been very professional in her dress from day one! Wish all my employees were as professional as Keisha has turned out to be. A woman in our printing department is just the opposite. She's managed to hurt everyone's feelings in the department one way or another. She is just mean-spirited and doesn't care what she does to people—just tromps all over their emotions and walks away grinning. I'm going to have to help her supervisor deal with it in her performance evaluation next week."

Mark, overhearing this conversation, chimed in. "Let me tell you what happened over at my place yesterday. There were these two guys loading one of our trucks, and one of 'em, Reggie, slipped off the ramp into the other guy, Jeff. Jeff went off—shoved Reggie back against the ramp, accusing him of jumping him for no reason. A couple of other guys saw what was happening and grabbed Jeff before he hurt himself or Reg, thank goodness. His supervisor called me, of course, and I had to run down there and try and sort things out. I was really tempted to let him go on the spot, but he's usually a pretty good worker, so I told him that if there is one more outburst like that, he's gone. I just hope he cools down and doesn't come to work still angry today. He was just out of control! It's crazy how people lose control on the job!"

"Did you check his references before you hired him?" asked Marilyn.

"Yeah, we checked. It looked clean, but if he ever asks me for a reference, it might be a different story," replied Mark.

Bill sympathized. "Yep, been there. Think Reggie will be okay with him still around?"

"Reggie's a really cool guy—he'll handle it. He's shown some real leadership qualities in the past," responded Mark, "but then I'm also worried about another guy in that department. See if this sounds familiar: Andrew arrives at work late about half the time, takes more than his share of breaks to go talk to his girlfriend over in Shipping, and leaves the security doors open so that he doesn't have to ring himself back through. And if you say anything to him about it, he sulks like a kid and threatens to quit."

"So let him quit," Marilyn offered.

Mark rolled his eyes. "Yeah, right. Like I can just go find a replacement in thirty minutes. The last guy we hired to replace a quitter was Jeff! C'mon, Marilyn, you know how hard it is to find good, hard workers. I'm better off putting up with this goof-off than trying to find someone to replace him. At least he does half a day's work most days, which is better than an empty spot."

"Yeah, I've got the same issues. Where's that old thing called a work ethic?" Bill mused, looking at the ceiling as if searching for answers written there. "But you know," he continued, "I've got several folks who just watch this kind of behavior by their coworkers

Real-World Investigations for Social Studies
Hoge, Field, Foster, and Nickell

in disbelief. I've got one woman who has had perfect attendance for twelve years, gets to work ten minutes early every morning of the week, never has to be reminded to do something twice, and everyone is just crazy about her!"

"Oh, sure," added Marilyn. "I've got some of those as well. They just love their work, are really productive, and get along with everyone. We started this new program last year called the 110 percent Award, and it ups the person's salary by 10 percent—hence the 110 percent business. We had a really hard time choosing who to give the first one to, we had so many deserving people. It was refreshing to go through that selection process; it reminded all of us how many good folks we really do have."

"I like that 110 percent idea, Marilyn," Mark said. "I think I'll take that idea back to our place. Maybe it would spark some others to start demonstrating that good work ethic Bill mentioned."

Handout 4.2

WORKPLACE EXPECTATIONS INTERVIEW GUIDE

Identify one or more adults whom you would like to interview and about whose job you would like to know more. Please use the following guide to focus your interview. Feel free to supply additional questions of your choosing.

1. Where do you work?
2. How long have you worked there?
3. What is your position?
4. How long have you held the position?
5. What attracted you to your company originally?
6. How did you learn about what your supervisor expects of you?
7. What are some of the things your supervisor expects you to do?
8. How does he or she indicate to you how you are doing or if changes need to be made?
9. If you were giving advice to a new employee about how to succeed at the company or institution, what would it be?
10. Did anyone give you advice when you began working there? What was it? Who offered advice? Did any fellow workers offer any advice? What?
11. Is there anything else you would like to add about your employer's expectations of you?

Real-World Investigations for Social Studies
Hoge, Field, Foster, and Nickell

WHAT IS THE WORK ETHIC?

1. Sometimes people are said to have a "good work ethic" or a "poor work ethic." How do you think a person with a good work ethic might act? What about one with a poor work ethic?
2. In school, what might a good work ethic on the part of a student consist of? (Make a list of the traits mentioned and put it on a poster for future reference.)
3. How would you describe a teacher with a good work ethic?
4. Think of someone you know who has a good work ethic in a particular situation. Who would like to tell us about the person you're thinking of?
5. There are several ways in which the accounts in Handout 4.1 illustrate a poor work ethic. Can you name them?
6. Why was Mark reluctant to fire the person who came to work late and took too many breaks? What would you do if you were Mark?
7. Is it fair to keep a person who abuses the work schedule when others do not? How do you think people in the workplace would feel about such a person?
8. Think of five reasons why employees consider it important that their employees have a good work ethic.

Handout 4.4

EMPLOYMENT APPLICATION

Please complete this application carefully. Answer all questions. Print legibly and use blue or black ink.

I. Personal Information

1. Name _____
2. Street Address _____
3. City, State, Zip Code _____
4. E-mail Address _____
5. Home Phone_____ Cell Phone_____
6. Business Phone _____

II. Job Sought

1. Position Applied For _____
2. Preferred Hours _____
3. Special Needs/Requirements _____

III. Education, Work Experience

Please List Your Educational Experiences (Schools Attended)
Name _____
City _____ State_____
From _____ To _____
Grade Level Completed _____

IV. List All Work Experience Below

From_____ To _____
Company _____
Phone _____
Supervisor _____
Position _____
Reason for Leaving _____

V. Professional References (List three professional references who may be contacted regarding your employment history.)

Name_____
Company_____
Title_____ Phone_____
Relationship to Employee_____

VI. Employment Questions

1. Why do you want to work for this company/firm? _____
2. What qualifications do you have for the position? _____
3. What are your strengths? Weaknesses? _____
4. Have you ever been terminated from a position? If yes, why? _____
5. Have you ever been convicted of a crime? If yes, what was the crime and when were you convicted? _____
6. What would you like your future employer to know about you? _____

Real-World Investigations for Social Studies
Hoge, Field, Foster, and Nickell

84

JOB APPLICATIONS: WHAT DOES THE EMPLOYER VALUE?

You have been given a job application form for a particular company or agency. Of course, they want all the important information that will enable them to identify you, such as your name, address, and phone number. But what else do they ask? What do they want to know about potential employees? Often there are far more applicants for a position than there are positions to fill. In this case, employers decide which applicants look best on paper and interview only these few. How might the information on the application form you have completed help employers decide whom they might want to bring in for an interview?

1. What information does the application ask for besides personal identification data?

2. What information is asked about first? Second? Third, and so on?

3. What might this indicate?

4. Can you identify several values on which the company may rank applicants?

5. What responses on the application form do you think the human resources person might ask about in an interview?

6. Does the prospective employee have any opportunity to state why he or she wants to perform this type of work? Why he or she feels he or she would be good at this job?

7. Do any questions on the application form seem unusual or unfair to you?

8. Were any of the questions a surprise to you? Why or why not?

9. Have you ever had to fill out an application form for anything (e.g., camps, athletic teams, ballet lessons)? In what ways were you careful about how you completed the application form?

Handout 4.6

ANALYZING PERFORMANCE REVIEW FORMS

Every workplace uses some type of assessment to let employees know what kind of job they are doing and if they are meeting, not meeting, or exceeding the expectations of the supervisor. Use this form to evaluate the performance review forms you have received. First, read the company's assessment form and think carefully about what each item means. Next, answer the following questions:

1. What information does the performance review form give the employee?

2. What seems to be valued at this company or institution?

3. What types of ratings are possible?

4. Are there ways other than ratings in which the supervisor provides information to the employee?

5. Does the employee have an opportunity to express an opinion about how well she or he is performing? If so, where is this indicated on the performance review form?

6. Do any questions on the performance review form seem unusual or unfair to you?

7. What should be asked but was not found on the performance review form?

8. Were any of the questions surprising to you? Why or why not?

9. How are you assessed at school? What does this kind of assessment tell you about what the school values?

Real-World Investigations for Social Studies
Hoge, Field, Foster, and Nickell

CHAPTER

5

Defusing Hate

With Malice Toward None, with Charity for All

by
Pamela S. Roach

OVERVIEW

This chapter is about intolerance and its often disastrous results. Intolerance and its dangerous offspring, organized hate, have occurred for a very long time, not only in American society but also throughout the world. This chapter examines intolerance, hate, and organized violence in a variety of settings, from Ku Klux Klan activities to the 1957 integration of Little Rock Central High School in Arkansas to recent incidents of school violence in Paducah, Kentucky, and Littleton, Colorado. It illus-

trates the complexities of hate issues to children and prepares them to develop a plan to reduce hatred in their own surroundings.

Students begin this chapter by considering why hate occurs, its origins, and group demonstrations of hate by analyzing a photo of a toddler dressed in a Ku Klux Klan outfit who is marching in a demonstration that, ironically, is guarded by African-American state patrolmen. After this introduction, students analyze primary source documents and oral histories from the integration of Little Rock

Central to determine what happened that led to violence and if hate played a role. Students then apply their beliefs and principles developed using past events to more recent instances of school violence, and analyze newspaper accounts to determine what led to the violence in these situations and how it could have been prevented. The purpose of this case is to help students examine incidents of hate; identify intolerance as a common, misguided, and dangerous wellspring of hatred; and encourage them to reject violence as an inevitable resolution to the problem of hate.

CONNECTION TO NCSS THEME V: INDIVIDUALS, GROUPS, AND INSTITUTIONS

The NCSS recommends that social studies programs include multiple learning experiences through which students develop an understanding of how individuals, groups, and institutions interact and influence one another. This study of intolerance, and the hatred and violence that can result, will help students come face to face with one of the most fundamental questions related to human and group interaction: How do we and, more important, how should we deal with difference?

This chapter helps students analyze how institutions such as government agencies, schools, and families have dealt with hate issues in the past. Beyond this analysis, students are asked to weigh the costs and benefits of local, state, and federal governments' attempts to reduce intolerance and to control hatred and intergroup violence. Students also examine the tensions that exist between policies and laws that a society establishes versus the private beliefs of persons within that society. Finally, students develop a school plan for minimizing intolerance.

METHODS FOCUS: ANALYSIS OF HISTORICAL DATA SOURCES

The teaching methods used in this chapter rely heavily on student analysis of historical data sources. Students begin by analyzing a historical photograph that illustrates the irony of the police protecting people from harm so that they can demonstrate their hatred toward people just like their protectors. After this introduction, students' investigation of hatred moves on to an examination of other photographs, facsimiles of historic documents, and secondary source accounts that detail instances of hatred in the United States. Carefully developed questions guide students through these documents in order to generate important insights

and deep understanding of history. These analysis lessons conclude with reflection assignments that help students synthesize and organize their thoughts and conclusions, committing them to paper. To end the study, students are asked to apply what they have learned by developing a plan to address any hatred or intolerance that may exist in their own school. This activity provides a positive ending to the series of serious and disturbing historical events with which students have been dealing.

Deep analysis of historical documents is an important skill that lies at the core of extracting meaning from new information, whether in the classroom, on the job, or in a testing situation. To increase student engagement, the data sources and information students will analyze in this study are (a) interesting, (b) authentic, (c) relevant to the lives of middle and high school students, and (d) straightforward yet complex enough to be challenging. The material and lesson structures provided in this chapter are intended to develop students' skills in critical thinking, logical reasoning, and metacognition. As a result, students will be better prepared to attempt other tasks requiring these skills.

Historical investigation is the central methodology used in this chapter. Students have opportunities to play the role of historian through the analysis and interpretation of historical documents. However, a note of caution is warranted. When these techniques are used, it is important to caution students not to draw sweeping conclusions from limited samples of documents or photos because these may not be representative of the time period or event under investigation. However, historical investigation is a useful research tool that allows students to increase their understanding of the past and to deal with real-world events.

Fraenkel and Wallen (2003) offer a concise summary of the key concepts and strategies of historical research. They point out that all documents (e.g., historical photographs, diaries, news articles, government records) should be subjected to both external and internal criticism. Thus, both primary sources (i.e., firsthand accounts prepared by individuals who participated in or directly witnessed the events in question) and secondary sources (i.e., accounts written by individuals who have secondhand knowledge of an event) should be equally questioned for their authenticity and accuracy. Further, it should be clear that the document writer's perspective, bias, and communication purpose play a role in both types of sources and that the accuracy of accounts rendered by primary sources does not necessarily exceed that of well-researched secondary source documents.

The question of authenticity is the focus of external criticism. Accordingly, when a primary or secondary source document is first encountered, a student should attempt to establish who wrote the document, when, and for what purpose. Furthermore, the student should attempt to become familiar with both the immediate (site-specific) and larger (social, economic, political) conditions under which the document was written. Such knowledge can greatly enhance understanding of the meanings the document was intended to convey. Of course, students should also consider the remote possibility that the document is a forgery and/or that it was composed to purposely mislead readers.

The question of accuracy is the focus of internal criticism. Once authenticity questions have been answered, the historian turns to a careful examination of the facts and conclusions presented in the document. The questions that must be answered include: Was the author clearly in a position (physically, mentally, socially) to know what he or she claims? Can the author's version of events be corroborated or refuted by other evidence? What do we know about the author's life that might have caused him or her to intentionally or unintentionally alter the account of events? What motives or duties gave rise to the production of the document, and how might these have influenced its content?

Although this type of historical document analysis is crucial to understand much of the information we encounter, a special subset of skills is needed to conduct the historic photograph analysis that is used as an integral part of this chapter. In order to build students' understanding of a historic photograph, prior knowledge and visual detective work are important. Photographic analysis helps students to think like historians by asking them to interpret contextual clues and build evidence to substantiate their insights. Students should be asked to "speculate, infer, and hypothesize" about the photos (Foster, Hoge, & Rosch, 1999). General questions that can facilitate these processes and serve as a starting point for the analysis include the following sample questions.

Sample Discussion Questions for Photo Analysis

I. Content and Context Analysis

Tell me what you see in this photograph.
    Probe: Do you see anything else?
What do you think these people are doing?
Who do you think these people are?
Where are these people?
    Probe: Why do you think that?
When do you think the photograph was taken?
Who took the photograph?
What message, if any, was the photographer trying to convey?
How does the photographer convey this message?

II. Photographer and Camera Analysis

Where do you think the photographer was positioned?
Do you think the photograph was staged or taken spontaneously?
How would the staging of a photograph make a difference to the type of picture created?
What type of camera technology do you think the photographer used?
How has age affected the details in the photograph?
Do you think the photographer knew the people in the photograph?
    Probe: Why do you think that?
Why do you think this photograph was taken?
    Probe: What tells you that it was _____ ?
What does this photograph tell you about this person's life?
    Probe: Why do you say that?

III. Summary and Validation Analysis

What are other possible interpretations of this photograph?

To what extent does this photograph provide a representative image of the times?

How can the message of the photograph be corroborated by other sources?

How reliable and accurate is this photograph?

If a historian wanted to find out about life at this time, what are the problems of using just this one photograph?

What more would you like to know about this photograph?

   Probe: Anything else?

How useful is this photograph to the historian?

(Questions excerpted from Foster, Hoge, & Rosch, 1999, p. 207)

Detailed sample discussion questions regarding specific photos are provided within the relevant lessons.

Table 5.1 Lesson Overview for "Defusing Hate"

	GOALS	ACTIVITIES	ASSESSMENTS
LESSON ONE	• Introduce the case and get students to start thinking about hate issues.	• Examine the Ku Klux Klan toddler photo (Handout 5.1). • Brainstorm a list of instances of hate and discuss whether organized groups should be able to express their ideas. • Discuss freedom of expression, assembly, and hate.	• Write a paragraph about how you would handle hate if it was directed at you or how you dealt with hate when you experienced it.
LESSON TWO	• Demonstrate the complexity of one hate situation and think about the origins of hate. • Illustrate the interpretive nature of history and encourage students to think about preventing hate.	• Read the Elizabeth Eckford story (Handout 5.2) and examine her photograph. • Begin analysis of the Little Rock Nine crisis scenarios (Handout 5.3) and primary sources (Handouts 5.4 to 5.8). • Prepare (use Handouts 5.9 and 5.10) and give presentations for stakeholder groups. • Conduct a discussion of the presentations.	• Think about the Little Rock Nine; how would you handle hate if it were directed at you? • Students develop antihate principles and reflect on how they could prevent similar events from happening in their school or community.
LESSON THREE	• Become aware of current problems. • Develop a hate prevention plan.	• Groups analyze the Paducah, Kentucky, school violence newspaper account (Handouts 5.11 and 5.12), research on violence prevention (Handout 5.13), and students' responses to school violence (Handout 5.14). • Groups share results and problem-solve using the article analysis model. • Groups develop and share hate prevention plans (Handout 5.15).	• Begin writing a hate prevention plan using the article analysis model and the hate prevention plan handouts. • Present the plan to the school.

LESSON ONE: Do I Hate You? Why?

Purpose This lesson serves as an introduction to group hate and its origins through the analysis and discussion of a poignant photo taken at a Ku Klux Klan rally. Students are asked to consider issues of freedom of expression, assembly, and protectors versus protected in instances that have erupted in violence.

Duration One class period

Materials
Handout 5.1: Ku Klux Klan Toddler

Procedures

1. Display Ku Klux Klan toddler picture (Handout 5.1). Ask students to examine the picture for a minute. Students should not share ideas yet.

2. Have students individually write five statements about the picture.

3. Lead the class in a photo analysis. Suggested questions include the following:
   - Where was this photo taken?
   - Why are the police officers standing there? What are they wearing (riot gear)? Why?
   - What is going on here? What is the toddler doing?
   - Explain the toddler's clothing.
   - What do the toddler's clothes symbolize?
   - What is the child looking at?
   - What differences does the child recognize between him/herself and the police officers?
   - Does the child hate anyone?
   - What is the Ku Klux Klan?
   - What does the Ku Klux Klan believe?
   - What is the role of the police?
   - What might the police officer be thinking?
   - How would you feel if you were the white police officer? The black police officer? Examine the different perspectives of each police officer.
   - What is the woman doing there?
   - Assume that the woman is the child's mother; what will she tell her child?
   - What is the irony in this picture?
   - What does it say about authority?
   - Who has the power? Are you sure? (No right or wrong, but consider both perspectives.)
   - When do you believe this picture was taken? (1994)

4. Continue the lesson by moving on to a discussion of hate.
   a. Suggested discussion questions
      - What is hate?
      - Why is it difficult to define hate?
      - Describe hate. Where does it come from? What might cause one person to hate another?
      - For what reasons do people hate other people?
      - Is there anything in this photo that represents hate?
   b. Have students brainstorm examples of hate. Record these; they will be used in the last lesson.
   c. Ask the students to identify similarities and differences between the items on the list. Help the students see that some items are examples of group hate, whereas others represent individual hate.
   d. Categorize instances of hate that students have brainstormed and ask students to consider these questions:
      - Are there any examples of group hate?
      - Why wear something that represents hate if you do not hate?

5. Talk about group hatred; refer to the photo.
   - Is the activity in the photo okay? Are the brainstormed example of hate correct? Why or why not?
   - Might the child in the photo hate someone in a few years?
   - What are two things that can cause us to hate? (Direct experience and being taught to hate.) Which one is more powerful? Which is the more common cause of organized hate?
   - Should organized groups be allowed to display their ideas publicly if the ideas have to do with hate?
   - What is the most effective way to stop hate—by silencing it or by allowing it?
   - Discuss freedom of expression, freedom of assembly, and freedom to express hatred.

6. Describe how you or someone else would have felt if it were you in the picture as one of the police officers, the child, or the woman.

Suggested Homework Assignment

Write a paragraph about how you would handle hate if it were directed at you. Alternatively, have you ever experienced hate? How did you deal with it?

Internet Resources

The Ku Klux Klan toddler photo is available online at two Web sites:

http://www.splcenter.org/teachingtolerance/tt-index.html

The Southern Poverty Law Center Web site. Click on "Ten Ways to Fight Hate"; the photo is found on p. 31 of the pdf file.

http://www.tolerance.org/10_ways/index.html

A Web project of the Southern Poverty Law Center. Click on "Download a printable version of 10 Ways to Fight Hate."

LESSON TWO: Integration at Little Rock—A Lesson in Getting Along?

Purpose This lesson further develops students' understanding of how hate can erupt into violence by examining the integration of Little Rock Central High School. The students develop a set of principles dealing with the causes of violence that they will use in the future. This lesson also illustrates the interpretive nature of history as students work as historians to explain events from varying perspectives.

Duration Two class periods

Materials
Handout 5.2: Elizabeth Eckford Story
Handout 5.3: Little Rock Nine
Handout 5.4: White Students and School Administrators
Handout 5.5: Journalists
Handout 5.6: Governor Faubus
Handout 5.7: President Eisenhower and His Aides
Handout 5.8: Arkansas National Guard
Handout 5.9: Guidelines for Evaluating the Authenticity of Documents
Handout 5.10: Little Rock Central Concept Web

Procedures

1. Introduce Little Rock Central by telling the story of Elizabeth Eckford (Handout 5.2) and showing the photograph of her located online. The photograph can also be found in *Witnesses to Freedom: Young People Who Fought for Civil Rights* by Belinda Rochelle (New York: Puffin-Penguin, 1997), which your media center may have. Ask students what they believe is happening in the photo. Is Elizabeth being bullied? What does Hazel Bryan (the woman to Eckford's left) seem to think of Elizabeth Eckford?

2. Provide students with background information on Little Rock Central and explain that many different accounts of Little Rock Central exist.

In 1957, the U.S. Supreme Court decision in *Brown v. Board of Education* declaring segregation unconstitutional was tested as Governor Orval Faubus of Arkansas, a populist with a progressive record on integration issues, called out National Guard troops supposedly to prevent violence. This pretext kept nine African-American students from integrating Little Rock Central High School, located in a working-class neighborhood. Faubus would soon attempt to run for a third term. Segregationists showed up at Central High in droves from all over the United States to protest in the hope of containing integration there.

Little Rock Nine—The nine African-American students who had been selected to integrate Little Rock Central High School in 1957. There was one senior, Ernest Green, and eight others including Melba Pattillo, Elizabeth Eckford, Minnijean Brown, Jefferson Thomas, Carlotta Walls, Gloria Ray, Terrance Roberts, and Thelma Mothershed.

Other Students—The white students attending Central had mixed feelings about the Little Rock Nine.

School Administrators—The school board's plan for integration (the Blossom plan, named after the school superintendent) took effect the same year that a new high school, Hall High School, opened. The way the district lines were drawn sent most of the school board members' children to Hall High School, where integration would not take place.

Journalists—The *Arkansas Gazette* was much more sympathetic to and supportive of integration than the *Arkansas Democrat*. These two papers merged in 1991 and are now published as the *Arkansas Democrat Gazette*. The student media group will have the important role of writing the Little Rock Crisis story based on information provided by both newspapers.

Parents—Many wanted segregation, whereas others supported integration.

Politicians: Faubus and Eisenhower—represented many different viewpoints. Ironically, Faubus was very progressive on integration issues but was likely to face a staunch segregationist in his reelection bid for a third term as governor. He did not have a career outside of public service.

Arkansas National Guard—charged with keeping order. All units were federalized to keep Faubus from using any of the troops for his own purposes. The troops who had been assigned to Little Rock Central under Faubus were not mobilized to serve there under Eisenhower. Instead, they reported daily to their home armories. Many members of the Guard were students in high school or college or taught school. Most of these men were excused from duty in Little Rock with a hardship release after approximately 2 weeks of service so that they could return to school or teaching. They still had to report to their local armory.

For additional information about Little Rock Central, consult the books or Web sites listed under Resources.

3. Group students into the following teams and assign roles: Little Rock Nine, white students and administration, parents and journalists, politicians and the Arkansas National Guard. Background information is provided above, along with a short description of each stakeholder and group.

4. Pass out primary sources (Handouts 5.4 to 5.8) to each group as indicated. Ask students to read their group's sources, analyze them (Handout 5.9), and fill out a concept web (Handout 5.10) explaining what led to the crisis and what resolved it (students may not be able to answer both questions, depending on which actor they are assigned). Tell students that in this incident, hatred came to influence people's actions. Ask students what role their group played in that situation. What should/could their group have done? Each group should prepare to present their findings to the class and to answer the reporters' questions.

5. Each group should give a short presentation of their findings, and the reporters should ask questions to clarify their stories and eliminate inconsistencies while compiling their findings.

6. After the presentations, students should be asked which account they believe and then focus on analyzing the veracity and believability of their sources. Ask them if they think their account should be edited in order to resolve any discrepancies with the accounts of other groups.

7. Ask students what they believe caused the crisis and what resolved it.

8. Conclude this phase with a discussion of how history is written and affected by human interpretation and perception. Students should realize that historical accounts change as new discoveries are made.

9. Ask students if they believe that Elizabeth Eckford and Hazel Bryan could ever be friends. Hazel apologized to Elizabeth by telephone in 1962, but they met for the first time only at the 40th anniversary of the school's integration. Together, they attended a workshop on racial healing and put the past behind them, becoming friends. See the press release for Will Counts's book to read short quotes from Counts about their reunion at http://www.indiana.edu/~iupress/books/0-253-33637-6pr.html or read the book, *A Life Is More Than a Moment: The Desegregation of Little Rock's Central High* by Will Counts (Bloomington: Indiana University Press, 1999).

10. For homework.
- End of Day 1: Think about the Little Rock Nine. How would you react if someone hated you? Write a paragraph describing how you would respond.
- End of Day 2: Students should reflect on the previous lessons in a paper discussing what they believe they could do in their school to prevent something similar from happening.

Resources

Arkansas Gazette. (1959). Crisis in the South: The Little Rock Story. Little Rock: *Arkansas Gazette.*
Editorials published at the time of the crisis printed in chronological order.

Bates, D. (1987). *The long shadow of Little Rock.* Fayetteville: University of Arkansas Press.
Memoir of Daisy Bates, a local leader in the National Association for the Advancement of Colored People (NAACP), who, together with her husband, championed civil rights in their weekly newspaper, the *Arkansas State Press*, and organized and supported the Little Rock Nine.

Beals, M. P. (1994). *Warriors don't cry: A searing memoir of the battle to integrate Little Rock's Central High.* New York: Pocket Books.
This book describes how Beals felt about Central and her beliefs about her fellow students, the school administration, the army (both the 101st Paratroopers and the Arkansas National Guard), and the NAACP. It has a perspective that any teenager could relate to and understand. The passage describing how she becomes a warrior (Danny, Grandma, and Gandhi) illustrates how teens can make a difference in their world and deal with violence.

Chappell, D. L. (Ed.). (1997). Special issue: 40th anniversary of the Little Rock school crisis. *Arkansas Historical Quarterly, LVI,* 257–333.
Several articles discuss the Little Rock crisis from different perspectives.

Hampton, T., & Fayer, S. (1990). *Voices of freedom: An oral history of the civil rights movement from the 1950's through the 1980's.* New York: Bantam Books.
A companion book to the *Eyes on the Prize* video series that presents more than 1,000 oral histories of those involved in the civil rights movement.

Huckaby, E. (1980). *Crisis at Central High: Little Rock, 1957–1958.* Baton Rouge: Louisiana State University Press.

Elizabeth Huckaby's experiences as Dean of Girls and English teacher is presented in Chapter 4. This reading is very important because it shows a different perspective from that of the administration. Huckaby describes the same events as Beals, and the reader is left wondering about the situation. Huckaby illustrates how the administration dealt with pressure from various groups, including the NAACP and the Mothers' League of Central High.

Record, W., & Record, J. C. (Eds.). (1960). *Little Rock, U.S.A.: Materials for analysis.* San Francisco: Chandler.

This book contains primary source documents that provide a chronological description of the crisis and instructions on how to write a research paper.

Rochelle, B. (1993). *Witnesses to freedom: Young people who fought for civil rights.* New York: Puffin Books.

This brief book describes Elizabeth Eckford's experiences in dealing with the crowd and the Arkansas National Guard, which was charged with keeping the Little Rock Nine out of the school. Eckford's feelings, as expressed in the famous photograph of her, are explained in this passage.

See the following for more information:

Eckford, E. (1997). The first day of school in Little Rock. In R. Finkenbine (Ed.), *Sources of the African-American past: Primary sources in American history.* (pp. 167–169). New York: Longman.

Elizabeth Eckford's personal account of the first day of school at Central High School in Little Rock. The book is a collection of primary sources covering key themes in the African-American experience from West Africa to the present, chronologically organized.

Eckford, E., with Bates, D. (1981). The first day: Little Rock, 1957. In C. Mayfield (Ed.)., *Growing up southern: Southern exposure looks at childhood, then and now* (pp. 257–261). New York: Pantheon Books.

Another first-person account by Elizabeth Eckford of her first day of school at Central High School. This primary source book captures the lives of southern children from all walks of life.

Internet Resources

www:ardemgaz.com/prev/central/counts.html

Additional photographs of Elizabeth Eckford's first day at school can be found at this Web site featuring historic photographs taken by former Arkansas Democrat staff photographer Will Counts.

http://www.centralhigh57.org/

This Web site commemorates the 40th anniversary of the integration of Central High. It includes links to the student newspaper *The Tiger*, a here-and-now account of the Little Rock Nine, the *Arkansas Democrat* Central High Web site, and the dedication of the Central High Museum Visitor's Center. It also has a very good narrative of the crisis and descriptions of the anniversary activities.

http://www.ardemgaz.com/prev/central/

This *Arkansas Democrat* Web site has a timeline of events at Little Rock Central's integration, a "who's who" identifying key figures, photos from the integration, selected editorials and opinion columns from 1957–1958 and 1997, and newspaper articles from the 1997 40th anniversary of the school's integration. Complete texts of the editorials in Handout 5.5 and other editorials from this period can also be obtained from this site. Select the editorials and opinion columns or go directly to them at http://www.ardemgaz.com/prev/central/CHSEdit.html

http://www.pbs.org/newshour/bb/race_relations/july-dec97/rock_9-25a.html

An interview from *PBS Newshour*, with historians and the Little Rock Nine describing their feelings in 1957 and during the 40th anniversary of the crisis in 1997.

http://www.unbrokencircle.org

Oral histories and narratives produced by the Southern Regional Council for radio from five cities: Atlanta, Georgia; Little Rock, Arkansas; Montgomery, Alabama; Jackson, Mississippi; and Columbia, South Carolina. You can read the programs and listen to some accounts of civil rights activists. But screen these before using them with a class, as some accounts are graphic.

LESSON THREE: Why Do Terrible Things Happen?

Purpose Students apply what they have learned from evaluating Little Rock Central to contemporary situations such as Paducah, Kentucky and Littleton, Colorado. Students investigate non-racial situations of hate in order to better assess the origins of hate. Students are asked how they could prevent similar things from happening in their hometowns. In order to do this they must examine the causes of hate such as fear, revenge, lack of knowledge, and inaction.

Duration Two class periods

Materials

Handout 5.11: Paducah, Kentucky, Incident: Teen Pleads Guilty But Mentally Ill in School Shootings

Handout 5.12: Article Analysis Worksheet

Handout 5.13: Knowledge Leads to Prevention

Handout 5.14: Student Responses to School Violence

Handout 5.15: Hate Prevention Plan

Book: Bunting, E. (1993). *Terrible things: An allegory of the Holocaust.* Philadelphia: Jewish Publication Society. (Optional)

Procedures

1. Divide students into three groups. One group will study newspaper and Web site accounts of school violence (Handout 5.11); the second group will examine a research report on violence (Handout 5.13); and the third group will search for Web sites on students' responses to violence (Handout 5.14). The first group should also use the Article Analysis Worksheet (Handout 5.12). This worksheet will assist this group in contributing to the development of antihate plans.

2. Ask the groups to appoint a spokesperson. After analysis, the spokesperson for each group should present a summary of the material the group examined. Record these summaries.

3. Following this discussion, ask students what all these events have in common: the toddler picture, the Little Rock Central High School crisis, and the incident in Paducah. What does this tell us about all these situations?

4. Have students refer back to their brainstormed list (from Lesson One) and ask if they know of anything they want to add to it now (if not mentioned, help students to identify bullying, teasing, or other instances that turn to hate).

5. If possible, read *Terrible Things* to class. Ask students what aspects of this account they could apply to their own lives.

6. Ask students how they could prevent these instances of hate (refer to the brainstormed list) from happening at their own school.

7. Have students return to their groups and develop a plan for dealing with organized hate in a community and on an individual basis that focuses on its causes. Assign each group a different aspect of the causes of hate and violence, drawing from their earlier group work if possible (see Procedure 2). If their work identifies very similar causes of hate and violence, include other causes such as hate language, violence, visual images promoted by the media, class prejudices, social prejudices, or hate groups. Use Handout 5.15 as a guide for the groups in developing their plans.

8. Combine group plans into a class plan and present it to the school (if desired). Students may wish to develop a training program to teach younger students how to deal with hate.

Resources

Allen, R. F. (1996). The Engle-Ochoa decision making model for citizenship education. In R. W. Evans & D. W. Saxe (Eds.), *Handbook on teaching social issues* (pp. 51–58). Washington, DC: National Council for the Social Studies.

This article describes one approach to teaching with the problem-solving or decision-making model and provides examples and sample questions.

Bunting, E. (1993). *Terrible things: An allegory of the Holocaust.* Philadelphia: Jewish Publication Society. Slowly but surely, all the animals who live in a clearing are carried away, one species after another, by the Terrible Things. The last species taken away, the rabbits, learn that if they had bonded together with the other animals and not looked the other way, then perhaps terrible things would not have happened.

Grossman, D., & DeGaetano, G. (1999). *Stop teaching our kids to kill: A call to action against TV, movie, and video game violence.* New York: Crown.

The authors of this book use empirical evidence to document the effects of television, movies, and video games on children. They argue that these sources are not only conditioning children to violence but also teaching them how to kill. If you cannot find the book, search for the articles written by Grossman.

Internet Resources

http://www.splcenter.org/teachingtolerance/tt-index.html

The Southern Poverty Law Center's Web site on teaching tolerance has multiple resources. Click on "Responding to Hate at School" for many ideas and resources including "Ten Ways to Fight Hate" at http://www.tolerance.org/10_ways/index.html

http://www.stopthehate.org/

The Web site of Stop The Hate, a Student Civil Rights Project of Massachusetts. The site is designed to receive reports of hate incidents and provide information and resources to students, educators, law enforcement officers, and communities to help combat prejudice and hatred in schools.

Handout 5.1

KU KLUX KLAN TODDLER

Photograph courtesy of Todd Robinson.

ELIZABETH ECKFORD STORY

Elizabeth Eckford glanced at her reflection in the mirror. The dress that her mother had made for this special day was beautiful. It was her first day at a new high school and she was nervous. She looked at the clock. It was almost time to meet her friends.

Elizabeth nervously set off for school. When she stepped off the bus, she faced a large, angry crowd of white people and hundreds of soldiers.

Because the United States Supreme Court had prohibited segregation, many schools were forced to admit black students. Some schools obeyed the federal order and desegregated immediately, allowing black students to attend previously all-white schools. But in cities, officials refused to comply with the federal order. Arkansas and Texas were the only two states in the South that tried to obey the Supreme Court decision.

School officials in Little Rock, Arkansas, planned to desegregate the local high school in 1957 by admitting a small number of black students to Central, the school for white students. Originally, seventy-five black students registered to attend. After a review by the Little Rock school board, only nine students were allowed to enroll, including Elizabeth Eckford, Jefferson Thomas, Gloria Ray, Thelma Mothershed, Melba Pattillo, Terrance Roberts, Carlotta Wall, Ernest Green, and Minniejean Brown. These nine students became known as the "Little Rock Nine."

Daisy Bates, the president of the Arkansas NAACP and the editor of a local newspaper, served as an advisor to the black students.

Local officials tried to plan a smooth transition, but the governor of Arkansas, Orval Faubus, refused to cooperate. He did not approve of integration and promised to place the National Guard, a state military force, at the school to keep out all black students.

Many people supported the governor. On the first day of school, hundreds of people gathered outside of the school to prevent the Little Rock Nine from entering Central.

Elizabeth faced the angry crowd alone. She did not see the other black students because Daisy Bates had decided to take them to school on their first day. She had told the students and their families to meet at her house before going to Central High School, but she had been unable to get in touch with Elizabeth because the Eckfords didn't have a telephone.

When Elizabeth tried to walk to the main entrance of the school, the angry crowd followed her. Some people spat at her. She walked toward the National Guardsmen, thinking the soldiers would help her get into the school, but the guardsmen blocked her from entering.

From *WITNESSES TO FREEDOM* by Belinda Rochelle, copyright 1993 by Belinda Rochelle. Used by permission of Lodestar Books, an affiliate of Dutton Children's Books, an imprint of Penguin Putnam Books for Young Readers, a division of Penguin Putnam, Inc. All rights reserved.

Handout 5.3

LITTLE ROCK NINE

NAACP lawyer Wiley Branton had filed suit on behalf of thirty-three black children and their parents in Little Rock to speed the integration process and to broaden it to include all school grades. In the summer of 1957, he watched the city begin to back away even from the token high school integration it had proposed. (p. 40)

Wiley Branton

In 1957, Faubus was in his second term of office, and the term at that time was only two years, and only one governor in the history of the state had ever been elected for a third term. Faubus was not a lawyer; he was not much of a businessman, he had nothing to fall back on other than to be governor, hopefully, and when he saw what [Governor] Marvin Griffin was doing in Georgia and some of the other places, somebody told him, "If you can whip up this thing and holler loud enough, you can be elected for a third term." So much of what he did was due to his own political desires to have something to retain him in office. And it worked. (p. 41)

> In the memories of the nine black children who lived it, the real battle at Little Rock Central was fought out of range of news cameras, and it lasted for a full school year. The school itself was an integral part of the drama, a structure so large [that] thousands could riot at one end of its campus and not be heard at the other. (p. 36)

Ernest Green

In early August, the newspapers ran the names of the nine of us who were going to Central. And I'll never forget what happened when I went to work the next day. This young guy, he was about my age, his folks were members of the Jewish country club where I worked as a towel boy, and he came up to me and said, "How could you do it?" I said, "What do you mean, how could I do it?" He said, "You seem like such a nice fellow. Why is it you want to go to Central? Why do you want to destroy our relationship?" For the first time it began to hit me that going there was not going to be as simple as I had thought when I signed up. I was still committed to go, but it made me know at that time that it was going to mean a lot to a lot of people in that city. Particularly to white folks. From then on, events started to cascade. (pp. 38–39)

Melba Pattillo Beals

I wanted to go to Central High School because they had more privileges. They had more equipment, they had five floors of opportunities. I understood education before I understood anything else. From the time I was two, my mother said, "You will go to college. Education is your key to survival," and I understood that. It was a kind of curiosity, not an overwhelming desire to go to this school and integrate this school and change history. Oh no, there was none of that. I just thought it'd be fun to go to this school I ride by every day. I want to know what's in there. I don't necessarily want to be with those people; I assumed that being with those people would be no different than being with people I was already with. My getting into Central High School was somewhat of an accident. I simply raised my hand one day when they said, "Who of you lives in the area of Central High School?" That was two years before, in 1955.

Real World Investigations for Social Studies
Hoge, Field, Foster, and Nickell

And they said, Who had good grades? and I had excellent grades. It was an accident of fate. (pp. 39–40)

On the first day of school, the school board asked that black students stay away from Central "until this dilemma is legally resolved." Within hours, a federal judge ordered Little Rock to proceed with integration. There would be no breathing space. The black students were to be admitted the next day, September 4. (p. 42)

Ernest Green

The morning that we went to school, Daisy [Bates] had called us all up to meet at her house. And eight of us showed up. Elizabeth had missed the call—she didn't have a phone, I think—so she wasn't there. . . . So that morning, we went by car to Central. We got to school. We were at one end of the school, Fourteenth Street, and Elizabeth was at the other end, Sixteenth Street, neither group knowing where the other was. Because it's a big place. Two blocks separating it. And we just made a cursory kind of attempt to enter school, but we were denied access. Elizabeth attempted to go through the guards and have the mobs behind her. It had to be the most frightening thing, because she had a crowd of a hundred, two hundred, white people threatening to kill her. She had nobody. I mean, there was not a black face in sight anywhere. Nobody that she could turn to as a friend except this white woman, Grace Lorch, came out of a crowd and guided her through the mob and onto the bus and got her home safely. None of us knew that until we met at Daisy's house. Elizabeth was there; she was in tears. The rest of us had not experienced anything like that. (pp. 42–43)

The mobs at Central High School became an international story. On September 14, Governor Faubus met with President Eisenhower at the summer White House in Newport, Rhode Island. Ike was cordial but refused the governor's request to help delay the federal court order to integrate. Instead, the president wanted Faubus to use the Arkansas guard to protect the black students.

The governor had a different plan. A week later, he went on television to announce his removal of the troops from Central. The following Monday, September 23, the guard was gone. So was Faubus, who had left for a governors' conference in Georgia. But the mob had returned.

The nine black students, who still had not taken their classroom seats, were scheduled to enter the school under police escort. (p. 44)

Melba Pattillo Beals

The first day I was able to enter Central High School, what I felt inside was terrible, wrenching, awful fear. On the car radio I could hear that there was a mob. I knew what a mob meant and I knew that the sounds that came from the crowd were very angry. So we entered the side of the building, very, very fast. . . . I'd only been in the school a couple of hours and by that time it was apparent that the mob was just overrunning the school. Policemen were throwing down their badges and the mob was getting past the wooden sawhorses because the police would no longer fight their own in order to protect us. So we were all called into the principal's office, and there was great fear that we would not get out of this building. We were trapped. And I thought, Okay, so I'm going to die here, in school. And I remember thinking back to what I'd been told, to understand the realities of where you are and pray. Even the adults, the school officials, were panicked, feeling like there was no protection. A couple of kids, the black kids,

continued

that were with me were crying. . . . And we were taken to the basement of this place. And we were put into two cars, grayish blue Fords. And a man instructed the drivers, he said, "Once you start driving, do not stop." And he told us to put our heads down. This guy revved up his engine and he came up out of the bowels of this building, and as he came up, I could just see hands reaching across this car, I could hear the yelling, I could see guns, and he was told not to stop. "If you hit somebody, you keep rolling, 'cause the kids are dead." And he did just that, and he didn't hit anybody, but he certainly was forceful and aggressive in the way he exited this driveway, because people tried to stop him and he didn't stop. He dropped me off at home. And I remember saying, "Thank you for the ride," and I should've said, "Thank you for my life." (pp. 45–46)

> With the 101st Airborne protecting them and the Arkansas National Guard federalized, the Little Rock Nine went to school on September 25. (p. 47)

Ernest Green

There was more military hardware than I'd ever seen. We went to school in an army station wagon, and I think if anything stays on my mind as long as I live, this does. The colonel in charge of the detail escorting us to school was from South Carolina. And that seemed, from what I knew about southerners, so incongruous—that this guy with this deep southern accent was going to provide us with our protection. When we got into the station wagon, the convoy that went from Mrs. Bates's house to the school had a jeep in front, a jeep behind, they both had machine gun mounts, and there were soldiers with rifles. Then when we got to the front of the school, the whole school was ringed with paratroopers and helicopters hovering around, and we marched up the steps with this circle of soldiers with bayonets drawn. Walking up the steps that day was probably one of the biggest feelings I've ever had. I figured I had finally cracked it. (p. 48)

Melba Pattillo Beals

I went in not through the side doors, but up the front stairs, and there was a feeling of pride and hope that yes, this is the United States; yes, there is a reason I salute the flag; and it's going to be okay.

The troops were wonderful. There was some fear that they were dating the girls in high school, but I don't care what they were doing: they were wonderful, they were disciplined, they were attentive, they were caring. They didn't baby us, but they were there. So for the first time I began to feel like there is this slight buffer zone between me and this hell on the other side of this wall. They couldn't be with us everywhere. They couldn't be with us, for example, in the ladies' bathroom, they couldn't be with us in gym. We'd be showering in gym and someone would turn your shower into scalding. You'd be walking out to the volleyball court and someone would break a bottle and trip you on the bottle. I have scars on my right knee from that. After a while, I started saying to myself, Am I less than human? Why did they do this to me? What's wrong with me? And so you go through stages even as a child. First you're in pain, then you're angry, then you try to fight back, and then you just don't care. You just, you can't care; you hope you do die. You hope that there's an end. And then you just mellow out and you just realize that survival is day to day and you start to grasp your own spirit, you start to grasp the depth of the human spirit and you start to understand your own ability to cope no matter what. That is the greatest lesson I learned. (pp. 48–49)

Thelma Mothershed Wair

We would meet at Daisy Bates's house every morning, then we'd go back there in the evening for our parents to pick us up. That's when we gained our support from each other—who had done what and what had happened to who and this sort of thing.

Most of the faculty were helpful, but there were a few that weren't. My homeroom teacher was kind of strange. She just did little strange things. I remember that when we were absent, we'd have to go to the office and get a readmittance slip. When I would come in to give her my readmittance slip, she wouldn't take it. So I would just put it down on the desk, and then she would sign it and put it in the book and slide it back across to me. Now, that was really strange. I guess she had to do something to show her class that she wasn't particularly happy about me being in there. And then she—well, they set us in alphabetical order and in the row where I was, there were about two seats behind me—and she started the next person at the front seat in the next row, because she knew nobody wanted to sit behind me. She just kept those two chairs empty. So she did little strange, subtle things—subtle as a ton of bricks. (pp. 49–50)

Ernest Green

The interesting thing about graduation was, being the only senior, I'd given up all the graduation activity that had gone on in the black high school—the school play and the prom and all of those kinds of things. Sometimes because of not having that activity, I would really feel isolated, because I wasn't going to Central High School's prom, and I wasn't going to be invited to be in the school play at Central. But all of the black students at Horace Mann, which was the school that I would have graduated from, invited me to all the activities, included me in all of it, really made me feel a super part of it. So that I had the best of both worlds. I had cracked this white institution and still had all of my friends who were supersupportive of what I was trying to do.

At the graduation ceremony, one of the guests was Martin Luther King. He was speaking in Pine Bluff, Arkansas, at the black college there. And he came up to sit with my mother and Mrs. Bates and a couple of other friends in the audience. I figured all I had to do was walk across that big huge stage, which looked the length of a football field. I'm sure it was very small, but that night before I had to walk up and receive my diploma, it looked very imposing. I kept telling myself I just can't trip, with all those cameras watching me. But I knew that once I got as far as that principal and received that diploma, that I had cracked the wall. (p. 51)

In September 1958, three months after the first black student graduated from Central High, Orval Faubus closed all the public high schools in Little Rock; they were not to reopen until August 12, 1959, after the U.S. Supreme Court ruled the closing unconstitutional and called the action to prevent integration an "evasive scheme."

Not all Americans agreed with the Court's position. In December 1958, Faubus was named one of the ten most admired men in the world, according to a Gallup poll. Others on the list were President Eisenhower, Sir Winston Churchill, Dr. Albert Schweitzer, General Douglas MacArthur, and Dr. Jonas Salk. (p. 52)

From *VOICES OF FREEDOM* by Henry Hampton and Steve Fayer, copyright © 1990 by Blackside, Inc. Used by permission of Bantam Books, a division of Random House, Inc.

Handout 5.4

WHITE STUDENTS AND SCHOOL ADMINISTRATORS

Harold Engstrom (president and youngest member of the Little Rock School Board)

Little Rock was certainly not a dedicated southern city, like in Alabama or Mississippi. On the other hand, we in Little Rock were not as liberal as some of the other parts of the state—like the northwestern part of the state, which had always been a little more closely tied to Missouri and to the Midwest. Little Rock was in between. We had a moderate, median attitude about things.

When we got the interpretation of what the integration decision was, the key words were "with all deliberate speed." And we could understand that that was a contradiction. We could understand that there probably was a lot of compromise, within the Supreme Court, on the ruling, and that there were no precedents for what "all deliberate speed" was and was not. So we had to come up with our interpretation, and we felt, like anyone in our position, that it would be related to our problems in our community.

As we approached the first day of school in 1957, there were certain anxieties about having everything in order for the plan to start smoothly. The key point was what would the police do, what would the governor do? Or the dissidents, the ones that did not agree with us. The NAACP was not at all satisfied with our construction of what deliberate speed was. The people who were against integration, especially integration on a voluntary basis, were saying it wasn't necessary. So we needed some help from the officials—the state officials, the county, the city—and primarily from Governor Faubus, as to what he told the people, whether it was the law or not. Could we get him to say that regardless of what his opinion was, it was the law of the land? The governor of North Carolina had done that. So we delegated Mr. Virgil Blossom, our superintendent of schools, to make direct communication with Governor Faubus. And it was done on an informal basis, at the mansion, in the afternoon, just visiting one-on-one. And whenever Mr. Blossom could get an appointment, why, they'd continue the discussions. It felt like there'd been a dozen such meetings. And each time Mr. Blossom would come back and report to us. Blossom was confident that in the end Governor Faubus would come down with a statement more or less to the effect that integration was the law of the land. And that the deliberate speed that we had construed was reasonable, and that integrating under a controlled situation, instead of a forced situation, would be satisfactory for our particular community. He wouldn't have to say it for the whole state, just for our particular community. But as the world all knows, it went the other way. The last thirty days [before school was to open], Governor Faubus began to get much stronger pressures from other people, a lot of them outside the community. And he finally came down with his decision that he would not publicly take the position to support us. But we did not get any information that he would forcefully prevent it, either. And we were in a meeting—we met morning, noon, and night—we were in a night meeting and saw on television Faubus calling out the guard and the pictures of the guard being put around Central High. And so we failed in our objective of getting support from the governor. (pp. 37–38)

Real World Investigations for Social Studies
Hoge, Field, Foster, and Nickell

Craig Rains (a white senior and an officer in student council)

There really wasn't anything like Central High anywhere in the country, back in 1957. When the building itself was built in 1928 it was named the most beautiful high school in America. The facilities were unlike anything in this part of the country. We were unique in that we had two or three thousand students going to one school. Central was like a small city.

I don't remember exactly when I first realized that the school was going to be integrated, but I do remember that one of the things that bothered me was that we were being told to do something that we might or might not want to do. I was a student of the Civil War, and Robert E. Lee was, and still is, one of my ideals, and he was a man that believed equally in local government having a closer knowledge and awareness of what the people wanted, as opposed to the federal government. So my first thought was not that we were going to have to go to school with blacks, that didn't bother me, but that we were being told by the federal government to do something and we didn't have any say-so in that.

One of my jobs as an officer in the student council was to raise the flags outside. That gave me an opportunity to see what was going on outside the school, to see the anger. You could cut it with a knife, the tension outside the school, with these people who had come in from other parts of the state, other states. There were license plates from out of state. Very few people from Little Rock were there causing these problems, that I could see. But it was an ugly attitude. Especially when Elizabeth Eckford came to try to get into school. And the crowd began to heckle her, and cheer and shout, as she walked along. I was just dumbfounded.

I had my camera at the time; I ran up and took a picture of it. And then as she went on I thought, Well, I can't believe people would actually be this way to other people. I began to change from being somebody who was a moderate, who, if I had my way, would have said, "Let's don't integrate, because it's the state's right to decide," to someone who felt a real sense of compassion for these students. I also developed a real dislike for the people that were out there that were causing problems. It was very unsettling to me. (pp. 43–44)

Marcia Webb Lecky (secretary of the senior class)

You would see the soldiers in the hall. You would see them at cheerleader practice, or gym, or football games, but they never bothered us, and we thought they were there because Faubus was causing problems, and I think most of us were glad when the resolution came with President Eisenhower taking charge.

I didn't see much of the black kids. If you didn't have any classes with any of the nine, one really didn't know if they were in the building or not. And the school is so large. Occasionally I would see Ernie Green. He is the only one of the Little Rock Nine who was a senior, and in my class, and the one that I knew by name. I would say, "Hi, Ernie," but that was it. One didn't have time to stand around the hall and talk to anyone. But it would be the smile, and the "Hi." Now I can see it from their perspective, not knowing what was going on in the minds of the other students, and yet we did not go enough out of our way to seek them out. I'm sure those students had some teachers that they felt comfortable with, and I know that Mrs. Bates offered a lot of support for them, but there were a lot of us who could have helped, and I wish we had. (pp. 50–51)

Real World Investigations for Social Studies
Hoge, Field, Foster, and Nickell

Handout 5.5

JOURNALISTS

The following are excerpts from editorials that appeared in Little Rock newspapers at the time of the crisis. The title of each piece is listed at the beginning and the date it was published is listed at the end of each excerpt.

A Time of Testing

In his clear and forthright ruling in the Little Rock School case Federal Judge Ronald N. Davies has swept away the legal confusion generated by the apparent conflict between state and federal laws.

This means that on Tuesday some 15 Negro children will be enrolled at Little Rock Central High School along with more than 2,000 whites. There are those who have suggested that this cannot be done without inciting the populace of this city to violence. They have, we believe, too little faith in the respect of our people for law and order.

We are confident that the citizens of Little Rock will demonstrate on Tuesday for the world to see that we are a law-abiding people.

September 1, 1957

The Crisis Mr. Faubus Made

Thus the issue is no longer segregation vs. integration. The question has now become the supremacy of the government of the United States in all matters of law. And clearly the federal government cannot let this issue remain unsolved, no matter what the cost to this community.

Until last Thursday the matter of gradual, limited integration in the Little Rock schools was a local problem which had been well and wisely handled by responsible local officials who have had—and we believe still have—the support of a majority of the people of this city. On that day Mr. Faubus appeared in Chancery Court on behalf of a small but militant minority and chose to make it a state problem. On Monday night he called out the National Guard and made it a national problem.

It is one he must now live with, and the rest of us must suffer under. If Mr. Faubus in fact has no intention of defying federal authority now is the time for him to call a halt to the resistance which is preventing the carrying out of a duly entered court order. And certainly he should do so before his own actions become the cause of the violence he professes to fear.

September 4, 1957

The Case for Orval E. Faubus

Governor Faubus added very little to his own case in his television address last night. He simply reiterated the position that he has taken from the beginning—that school integration is possible at Little Rock if only it had been conducted on a time schedule devised privately by the governor and never yet revealed to the public school officials charged by a federal court with admitting nine Negro students at this term.

The governor, indeed, sounded very much like an integrationist himself—particularly when he once again went out of his way to point out that his own son is now attending a state college which has been integrated with his support and approval.

The only significance of this latest exercise in double-talk lies in what the governor did not say.

September 27, 1957

Now Tell Us Who Are "My People"

Governor Faubus dodged the basic question of whether he had reneged on the language of truce terms with the White House when he said in his Wednesday press conference:

"They want me to take troops and put bayonets in the backs of the students of my state and bludgeon and bayonet my people."

Nobody, of course, wants the governor to do anything of the kind, but it would be interesting if he would attempt to identify "my people."

The mob at Central High School never numbered more than 1,000 persons at the largest, many of them the idle curious and others drawn not only from the corners of the state, but from out-of-state as well. Does "my people" include the more than 100,000 people of Little Rock who have never been in the crowd in front of Central High School at any time?

And who are the "students of my state" for whose safety from bayoneting the governor professes to be so mightily fearful? Are these the fewer than 75 students who rashly walked away yesterday morning from their opportunity for a free public education?

Does the governor's select company include the youngster who boasted Wednesday that he was engaged in a conspiracy to physically harass the Negro students in defiance of a federal court order? Or should we—and the governor—be more concerned about the more than 1,500 students who by their conduct throughout the mess created by their elders have continued to demonstrate that they, at least, have read their civics texts?

October 4, 1957

The Moderates vs. The Extremists

Perhaps the only terms that now have any real validity are "extremists" and "moderates." An extremist is one who would defy the law and use force if necessary to prevent the entry of Negroes to any school heretofore reserved for whites. A "moderate" is one who will obey the law, no matter how distasteful it may be to him personally—and who under no circumstances will condone violence against any person for any reason.

If we divide the population of the state on this basis—as ultimately we will have to do—we believe the extremists would account for only a small minority.

October 20, 1957

Governor Faubus Mounts the Stump

Governor Faubus's speech to the county judges the other night can only be regarded as the formal announcement of his campaign for a third term as governor—the campaign for which he has been callously laying the groundwork in the recent weeks of school crisis in Little Rock.

Back on familiar ground and uninhibited by the peering lenses of national television cameras, the governor aimed his pitch straight to the homefolks. It was an address distinguished by some remarkable untruths.

The governor also came up with another one of those remarkable private pieces of information, source unidentified, which he delights in dropping into the political pot when it shows signs of simmering down. This one had to do with an alleged plot by the publisher of the *Gazette* to plant a psychiatrist at one of the governor's press conferences and have him write his findings "in the form of a news release to be used by this paper." The plan, the governor alleged, didn't come to full flower — although he didn't say why.

The reason, of course, is that there never was any such plot. Although a few of our readers have suggested in letters to the editor that Mr. Faubus may be suffering from some aberrations, this newspaper has never been that charitable in its own view.

We believe Mr. Faubus knows exactly what he is doing—and we suspect we have earned his wrath because through accurately reporting his devious course step by step, we have shown precisely where he is taking the people of his state in the furtherance of his political ambitions, and the terrible price all of us are going to have to pay as a result.

October 25, 1957

All excerpts reprinted by permission of the publisher from "Editorials," *The Arkansas Gazette.* © 1957 by *The Arkansas Democrat Gazette.*

Handout 5.6

GOVERNOR FAUBUS

September 4, 1957 Governor Orval Faubus's Telegram to President Eisenhower and all Governors

President Eisenhower,

The question in issue at Little Rock at this moment is not Integration vs. Segregation. Peaceful integration has been accomplished for some time in the University of Arkansas, State-supported colleges, and a number of public schools including three more of our largest: Fort Smith, Van Buren, & Ozark. The Supreme Court recognized that conditions in each community must be considered and I have interpreted your public statements to indicate that you are in agreement with this premise.

The question now is whether or not the head of a sovereign state can exercise his constitutional powers and discretion in maintaining peace and good order within his jurisdiction, being accountable to his own conscience and to his own people.

Certain units of the National Guard have been placed on duty to preserve the peace and good order of this community. You, as a military man, know that the commander must have the authority and the discretion to take the necessary steps warranted by the situation with which he must deal.

Excerpted from "Faubus telegram sent to President Eisenhower and every Governor on September 4, 1957, 9:54 p.m." The Orval Faubus Collection, Series 14, Subseries 3 (496:9), Special Collections, University of Arkansas Libraries, Fayetteville.

President Eisenhower and Governor Faubus met September 14, 1957 in Newport, Rhode Island. The following statements were issued after their meeting.

Statement by President Eisenhower

In the matter of the high schools of Little Rock, the Governor stated his intention to respect the decisions of the United States District Court and to give his full cooperation in carrying out his responsibilities in respect to those decisions. I am sure it is the desire of the Governor not only to observe the supreme law of the land but to use the influence of his office in orderly progress of the plans which are already the subject of the order of the Court.

Statement by Governor Faubus of Arkansas

When I assured the President that I expect to accept the decision of the Federal Courts, I entertained the hope that the Department of Justice and the Federal Judiciary will act with understanding and patience in discharging their duties.

Excerpted from "Statement by the President and a Statement by the Governor of Arkansas after their Newport, Rhode Island Meeting." The Arthur Brann Caldwell Papers, Series (5:3), Special Collections, University of Arkansas, Fayetteville.

Governor Orval Faubus Explains His Actions Years Later

I don't think anyone can fully understand the complexities of the situation that existed in Arkansas and many other places in the nation at the time. But I can say that at the beginning of the Little Rock crisis in 1957, I was on excellent terms with all citizens of the state. And my relations with black citizens were especially good for a number of reasons. I had placed leading black citizens on the Democratic State Central Committee, the policy-making body of the Democratic Party in Arkansas, for the first time in the modern history of the state. I had served as governor while all the institutions of higher learning were being integrated. My staff meetings were integrated and this was somewhat unprecedented in Arkansas at that time. We were in the process of equalizing salaries of blacks and whites in state government, which hadn't been done, and in the public schools throughout the state. And I was known as the most understanding man in the history of the state in relation to programs that benefited the poor people.

Many, many of the black people understood when I explained to them that my objective in the Little Rock crisis was to prevent violence and death in the disorders that became imminent. There would have been small, well-organized groups there that morning that school opened, armed to the teeth with repeating rifles and other firearms, determined to halt by extreme means if necessary the entry of the black students into the school. Now, one group—and I have personal knowledge of this and I can even name some of the individuals— unloaded their weapons at a town a short distance east of Little Rock when they learned that the National Guard had been placed on duty. Now, if the guard had not been placed, these determined, armed men would have been there and the well-directed volley from such a well-armed group long skilled in the use of firearms could have left many dead and wounded people. Now, I was not nearly as concerned, which was all in the papers, with the protestations of the Mothers' League, a group formed to oppose integration in Little Rock, or the speeches of the segregationist leaders, as with the intentions of the small, well-armed groups who didn't proclaim their intentions publicly and kept them well concealed.

Now, who was most in danger if such occurred? Well, the blacks themselves would be in most danger. But once it started, everyone would be in danger. (pp. 41–42)

From *VOICES OF FREEDOM* by Henry Hampton and Steve Fayer, copyright © 1990 by Blackside, Inc. Used by permission of Bantam Books, a division of Random House, Inc.

continued

Governor Faubus' Proclamation calling out the Arkansas National Guard

STATE OF ARKANSAS
EXECUTIVE DEPARTMENT

PROCLAMATION

TO ALL TO WHOM THESE PRESENTS SHALL COME — GREETINGS:

WHEREAS,   The Governor of the State of Arkansas is vested with the authority to order to active duty the militia of this State in case of tumult, riot or breach of the peace, or imminent danger thereof; and

WHEREAS,   It has been made known to me, as Governor, from many sources, that there is imminent danger of tumult, riot and breach of the peace and the doing of violence to persons and property in Pulaski County, Arkansas;

NOW, THEREFORE, I, Orval E. Faubus, Governor of the State of Arkansas, do hereby proclaim that a state of emergency presently exists and I do hereby order to active duty Major General Sherman T. Clinger, the Adjutant General of Arkansas, the State Militia units consisting of the Base Detachment at Adams Field and the State Headquarters Detachment of Camp Robinson, and any other units which may be necessary to accomplish the mission of maintaining or restoring law and order and to preserve the peace, health, safety and security of the citizens of Pulaski County, Arkansas.

IN WITNESS WHEREOF, I have hereunto set my hand and caused the Great Seal of the State of Arkansas to be affixed. Done in office in the city of Little Rock this 2nd day of September, 1957.

Simulated original from the Orval Faubus Collection, Series 14, Subseries 3 (496:4), Special Collections Division, University of Arkansas Libraries, Fayetteville.

Real World Investigations for Social Studies
Hoge, Field, Foster, and Nickell

EISENHOWER AND HIS AIDES

Herbert Brownell (President Eisenhower's attorney general and chief adviser during the Little Rock crisis)

President Eisenhower was well aware of the political costs of intervening in the Little Rock situation—or not intervening. He knew for one thing that the leadership in the Congress, both the Senate and the House, would be antagonized if he decided to send troops into Little Rock. That, of course, was important to him, because he had worked fairly closely with the leaders in both houses, which were southern oriented. But he knew that not going into Little Rock would mean that he would be charged, and rightfully charged, with not enforcing the Supreme Court decision in the *Brown* case. Upholding the Constitution was his duty as president, so on balance he never had any hesitation once the crisis developed.

After their meeting in Newport on September fourteenth, President Eisenhower felt let down when Governor Faubus went back to Arkansas and decided against allowing the black children to enter the high school. And the southern governors who had consulted with President Eisenhower to work for a peaceful solution at Little Rock felt let down, and they supported President Eisenhower when he took a firm position.

The FBI was on the spot at Little Rock when the crisis occurred and black children were not allowed to enter the high school there. They gave us hourly reports on what was happening. We felt that it was necessary for local officials to appeal to Washington for assistance before the federal government would send in troops. The mayor of Little Rock did appeal to Washington on the ground that the rioting and the threatened rioting there meant that local law enforcement authorities could not handle the situation. That gave the legal authority which, under the Supreme Court cases, we thought was necessary to have. And that's when the president acted swiftly and surely by sending the troops up the main street of Little Rock and arriving on the scene before anyone realized it. The crisis was solved peaceably without any deaths or any casualties.

He federalized the National Guard to be sure that they were directly under his command. And he had selected the 101st Airborne Division, first, because he had known them and their capabilities when he was commander in chief during World War II and, second, because they were close by and they could be transported quickly and efficiently.

We felt that this was the test case that had to be made in order to dramatize to everyone that when it came to a showdown the federal government was supreme in this area. The situation was as close as you could get to an irreconcilable difference between the North and the South. There'd been nothing like it since the Civil War. (pp. 46–47)

Excerpted from *VOICES OF FREEDOM* by Henry Hampton and Steve Fayer, copyright © 1990 by Blackside, Inc. Used by permission of Bantam Books, a division of Random House, Inc.

continued

Handout 5.7 *continued*

September 27, 1957 Telegram to U.S. Senator Richard B. Russell, Georgia, from President Eisenhower

Few times in my life have I felt as saddened as when the obligations of my office required me to order the use of force within a state to carry out the decisions of a Federal Court. My conviction is that had the police powers of the State of Arkansas been utilized not to frustrate the orders of the Court but to support them, the ensuing violence and open disrespect for the law and the Federal Judiciary would never have occurred. The Arkansas National Guard could have handled the situation with ease had it been instructed to do so. As a matter of fact, had the integration of Central High School been permitted to take place without the intervention of the National Guard, there is little doubt that the process would have gone along quite as smoothly and quietly as it has in other Arkansas communities. When a State, by seeking to frustrate the orders of a Federal Court, encourages mobs of extremists to flout the orders of a Federal Court and refuses to utilize its police powers to protect against mobs persons who are peaceably exercising their right under the Constitution, the oath of office of the President requires that he take action.

Excerpted from "September 27, 1957 Telegram to U.S. Senator Richard B. Russell, Georgia from President Eisenhower." The Arthur Brann Caldwell Papers, Series(5:3), Special Collections, University of Arkansas Libraries, Fayetteville.

EXECUTIVE ORDER 10730, SEPTEMBER 24, 1957

IMMEDIATE RELEASE   September 24, 1957

James C. Hagerty, Press Secretary to the President

- -

THE WHITE HOUSE

U. S. NAVAL BASE
NEWPORT, RHODE ISLAND

EXECUTIVE ORDER

10730

PROVIDING ASSISTANCE FOR THE REMOVAL OF AN OBSTRUCTION

OF JUSTICE WITHIN THE STATE OF ARKANSAS

WHEREAS on September 23, 1957, I issued Proclamation No. 3204 reading in part as follows:

"WHEREAS certain persons in the State of Arkansas, individually and in unlawful assemblages, combinations, and conspiracies, have wilfully obstructed the enforcement of orders of the United States District Court for the Eastern District of Arkansas with respect to matters relating to enrollment and attendance at public schools, particularly at Central High School, located in Little Rock School District, Little Rock, Arkansas; and

"WHEREAS such wilful obstruction of justice hinders the execution of the laws of that state and of the United States, and makes it impracticable to enforce such laws by the ordinary course of judicial proceedings; and

"WHEREAS such obstruction of justice constitutes a denial of the equal protection of the laws secured by the Constitution of the United States and impedes the course of justice under those laws:

"NOW, THEREFORE, I, DWIGHT D. EISENHOWER, President of the United States, under and by virtue of the authority vested in me by the Constitution and statutes of the United States, including Chapter 15 of Title 10 of the United States Code, particularly sections 332, 333 and 334 thereof, do command all persons engaged in such obstruction of justice to cease and desist therefrom, and to disperse forthwith;' and

WHEREAS the command contained in that Proclamation has not been obeyed and wilful obstruction of enforcement of said court orders still exists and threatens to continue:

NOW, THEREFORE, by virtue of the authority vested in me by the Constitution and Statutes of the United States, including Chapter 15 of Title 10, particularly sections 332, 333 and 334 thereof, and section 301 of Title 3 of the United States Code, it is hereby ordered as follows:

-2-

Section 1. I hereby authorize and direct the Secretary of Defense to order into the active military service of the United States as he may deem appropriate to carry out the purposes of this Order, any or all of the units of the National Guard of the United States and of the Air National Guard of the United States within the State of Arkansas to serve in the active military service of the United States for an indefinite period and until relieved by appropriate orders.

Section 2. The Secretary of Defense is authorized and directed to take all appropriate steps to enforce any orders of the United States District Court for the Eastern District of Arkansas for the removal of obstruction of justice in the State of Arkansas with respect to matters relating to enrollment and attendance at public schools in the Little Rock School District, Little Rock, Arkansas. In carrying out the provisions of this section, the Secretary of Defense is authorized to use the units, and members thereof, ordered into the active military service of the United States pursuant to Section 1 of this Order.

Section 3. In furtherance of the enforcement of the aforementioned orders of the United States District Court for the Eastern District of Arkansas, the Secretary of Defense is authorized to use such of the Armed forces of the United States as he may deem necessary.

Section 4. The Secretary of Defense is authorized to delegate to the Secretary of the Army or the Secretary of the Air Force, or both, any of the authority conferred upon him by this Order.

DWIGHT D. EISENHOWER

THE WHITE HOUSE
September 24, 1957

Simulated original from "Executive Order 1073C September 24, 1957." The Arthur Brann Caldwell Papers, Series (5:3), Special Collections, University of Arkansas Libraries, Fayetteville.

Real World Investigations for Social Studies
Hoge, Field, Foster, and Nickell

ARKANSAS NATIONAL GUARD

Camp Joseph T. Robinson, Arkansas
28 September 1957
Annex A (Intelligence) to Opn 0 1

1. Summary of Situation
   a. 2 September through 20 September 1957—National Guardsmen were on duty and have denied entrance to Negro students.
   b. 20 September 1957—Federal District Court issued an injunction against Governor Faubus, General Clinger, and Colonel Johnson from interfering with the integration of Central High School. The National Guard were withdrawn 1840 hours CST. Little Rock city police replaced the National Guard at the school by routine patrol checks.
   c. 50 city police were on duty at Central High School 0700 hours, 23 September, all male crowd of approximately 200 present.

Annex C (Information Program) to Opn 0 1

1. The purpose of this fact sheet is to inform the personnel of the Federalized Arkansas National Guard.

2. The President of the United States has determined that the Arkansas National Guard should be Federalized and partially Mobilized, and that certain Regular Army troops should be used, along with the Arkansas National Guard, to enforce the orders of the US District Court for the Eastern District of Arkansas. The court orders involved are those orders relative to the integration into the Little Rock Central High School of certain Negro students.

3. Our mission is to enforce the orders of the Federal Courts with respect to the attendance at the public schools of Little Rock of all those who are properly enrolled, and to maintain law and order while doing so. It is particularly important that we so conduct ourselves as to carry out the mission promptly and effectively, and at the same time, protect and conserve public property of whatever nature and protect all law abiding citizens in their persons and property. We are required by our orders to assist the civil authorities in enforcing these court orders, not to interfere with the civil authorities in their attempts to enforce those orders, and at all times should conduct ourselves with that thought in mind. Our individual feelings toward these court orders should have no influence on our execution of the mission. Our personal conduct while performing the mission should be exemplary and oppression of those with whom we deal or unlawful damage to or destruction of property is strictly prohibited. The future of the National Guard in Arkansas and possibly that of the Guard Nationwide will be materially effected [sic] by our conduct in accomplishing the mission.

4. Stress daily avoidance in every way of any physical contact involving the civilian populace in general and school children in particular.

5. Regimentation of news media representatives must be avoided. No efforts should be made to control the news media representatives on public property so long as they <u>do</u> <u>not</u> interfere with the carrying out of the military mission.

Excerpted from Annex C (Troop Information Program) to Operations Order No. 1 dated 28 September 1957, contained in Command Report, Operation Arkansas in the archives of the Arkansas National Guard Museum. Reprinted with permission.

Real World Investigations for Social Studies
Hoge, Field, Foster, and Nickell

Handout 5.9

GUIDELINES FOR EVALUATING THE AUTHENTICITY OF DOCUMENTS

- How did you get the document?
- Who gave it to you?
- Has it been altered from its original status?
- Why was it produced?
- Who was/is the author and what are his or her possible biases?
- What was/is the purposes of the document—why was it written?
- Who was/is the intended audience?
- Is the document based on other sources of information? What are they: an eyewitness or secondhand account, a reconstruction or interpretation of an event?
- How likely is it that the author wanted to tell the truth?
- Can you find other documents that discuss the same event or story? Do they agree or disagree with your document?

Based in part on *Qualitative Research and Case Study Applications in Education* (p. 122) by Sharan B. Merriam, 1998, San Francisco: Jossey-Bass Publishers.

LITTLE ROCK CENTRAL CONCEPT WEB

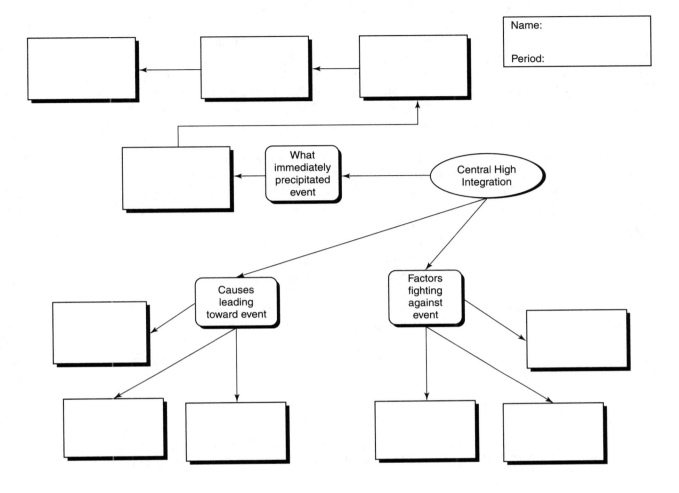

Handout 5.11

PADUCAH, KENTUCKY, INCIDENT: TEEN PLEADS GUILTY BUT MENTALLY ILL IN SCHOOL SHOOTINGS

Paducah, Ky—14-year-old Michael Carneal was charged with murder after shooting into a morning prayer meeting at Heath High School December 1, 1997. The 5'2" school band member stole guns from a neighbor Thanksgiving Day, brought them to school, inserted earplugs, and began firing. Of the eight students Carneal shot, three died and one was paralyzed from the waist down.

Defense attorney Chuck Granner said Carneal believed that his classmates ridiculed him and that the shootings would bring him acceptance. "These feelings of inadequacy were overwhelming to Michael, and he was unable to cope with them. Things that were said about Michael challenged his manhood," the defense team stated. Granner said Carneal understands his feelings at the time of the shooting were wrong. "He deeply regrets the overwhelming pain, the injuries, and the loss of life that his acts have caused," Granner said.

Judge Jeff Hines accepted Carneal's guilty plea with the condition that he will be sentenced to life in prison without the possibility of parole for 25 years. When Carneal turns 18, he will be transferred to an adult prison from the juvenile detention center. He may receive treatment after his mental health is evaluated. Granner characterized Carneal as paranoid, and said that with treatment, "we might have a chance of salvaging a young man."

Adapted by permission of the publisher. "Teen pleads guilty but mentally ill in school shootings," *Associated Press*, 6 October 1998. © by The Associated Press. Reprinted with permission of The Associated Press.

Internet Sources

Find at least two other articles on school shootings on the Internet. The following site contains articles. However, you can do a search using the terms *school violence* and *Columbine shootings* to find additional stories.

dmoz.org/Society/Issues/Violence_and_Abuse/School/Incidents/

An excellent source on this issue, this page of the Open Directory Project provides links to articles on the Columbine, Santana and Thurstone school shootings.

Real World Investigations for Social Studies
Hoge, Field, Foster, and Nickell

ARTICLE ANALYSIS WORKSHEET

1. Problem Identification and Definition: What was the problem or event that was described in this article?

2. Based on the article, what do you think caused the problem?

3. Do you think the article's author left out anything that might have contributed to the problem? If you do, describe.

4. Identify Possible Alternatives and Their Consequences: Identify three events that could have occurred that would have prevented the problem.

a.

b.

c.

Which event would be most effective in preventing violence and hate? Why?

Based in part on Allen (1996).

Handout 5.13

KNOWLEDGE LEADS TO PREVENTION

Dr. Jane Gilgun has conducted extensive interviews with perpetrators of violence on the meaning it had for them. The Columbine school shooting on April 20, 1999, prompted her to post the results of her research at the Minnesota Center on Violence and Abuse so that others could perhaps find ways to prevent further acts of violence. Go to the Web site of the Minnesota Center on Violence and Abuse and read the article titled "Facing Down Violence" written by Dr. Gilgun (http://www.mincava.umn.edu/documents/jgilgun/facing.shtml

Answer the following questions:

1. What are the seven meanings of violence for those who commit these acts?

2. What ways does Dr. Gilgun suggest to prevent acts of violence?

3. What can your group add to these suggestions to help prevent violence?

Real World Investigations for Social Studies
Hoge, Field, Foster, and Nickell

STUDENT RESPONSES TO SCHOOL VIOLENCE

Your task is to find examples of student responses to school violence that will assist your group and the class to develop a plan to stop hate and violence at your school. Begin by visiting the following Web sites and others you may find.

http://www.tolerance.org/teens/index.jsp

A Web site of the Southern Poverty Law Center, this page for students has many excellent materials including stories, newsletters, activities, posters, and much more.

http://bullystoppers.com/index.html

This Web site is a bully and harassment prevention Internet resource that provides free online help to students, parents, and educators. Click any of the links under "Students." These links have, among other things, tips and advice, ways to tell if you are being bullied, 101 comebacks to bullying, and getting help at school.

Do the following:

1. Describe five different methods that have been suggested by the Web sites for dealing with bullying, violence, and other forms of hate.

2. Adapt one of these methods for use at your school and be prepared to describe it to the class.

Real World Investigations for Social Studies
Hoge, Field, Foster, and Nickell

Handout 5.15

HATE PREVENTION PLAN

List your group's topic: _____

1. What factors contribute to allowing (your topic) to cause hate?

2. What can you do personally to prevent this from happening?

3. What can parents do?

4. What can teachers do?

5. What can schools do?

6. What can the government do?

Real World Investigations for Social Studies
Hoge, Field, Foster, and Nickell

6

CHAPTER

Mandatory School Uniforms

A Real-World Exploration of Power, Authority, and Governance

by
John D. Hoge and Stuart J. Foster

OVERVIEW

The lessons in this chapter are developed around the real-world context of a Polk County, Florida, school uniform controversy. In the introduction to the controversy, students learn about the mandatory school uniform policy and the nature of the parents' complaints. The study continues with students encountering the facts related to a class action lawsuit filed on behalf of over 500 Polk County public school parents who sought to have the school board's mandatory uniform policy overturned.

Students are then divided into issues-focused research groups that encounter a variety of facts and prepared statements from the individuals involved in the controversy. The research groups are challenged, through the skillful use of questions, to research their issues further using resources provided in the study packet, their media center, and the World Wide Web. Based on this research, each group is urged to take a stand, pro or con, on the acceptability of the school board's mandatory uniform policy.

The classroom study concludes with a mock school board meeting where the students take on the roles of citizens who speak to each of the issues that they have researched. The school board votes on whether to retain, modify, or repeal its present mandatory school uniform policy. Finally, students are required to make formal recommendations on the formation of a school dress code or uniform policy to a newly created school district.

CONNECTION TO NCSS THEME VI: POWER, AUTHORITY, AND GOVERNANCE

The NCSS recommends that social studies programs include multiple learning experiences about how people create and change structures of power, authority, and governance. This study on mandatory school uniforms helps students develop an understanding of this goal by examining an issue of individual rights in relation to a school board's implementation of a new mandatory school uniform policy.

Students' involvement in this study will help them achieve a variety of valuable social education understandings. Among the most important is the idea that citizens have constitutional rights in many contexts; that the exercise of government authority is often influenced by public opinion; that people often unite in order to gain power for the collective voices; and that government policies should be guided by sound reasoning, empirical evidence regarding need and effect, and the spirit and letter of the law.

METHODS FOCUS: DISTINGUISHING FACT FROM OPINION

The CTL that takes place in this chapter makes use of a range of methods. In this study, however, students must work to distinguish fact from opinion as they conduct their research and analyze people's positions on school uniforms. For example, Lesson One asks students to distinguish the facts of the lawsuit and the school policy. Students then read a collection of newspaper articles and again are challenged to differentiate statements of fact from statements of opinion. In Lesson Two students examine evidence to attempt to answer the question "Are school uniforms really a good idea?"

One of the most common yet most important skills associated with issues-based social studies instruction is the ability to distinguish between statements that have a factual basis and those that represent someone's opinion. Both types of statements are important, but they have different functions. Fact statements are important, but in themselves they remain sterile and lifeless. Opinion statements, on the other hand, are actionable statements that often marshal factual support. For example, government policies regarding the use of marijuana or alcohol contain explicit and implicit opinions that supposedly are justified by the "facts." Distinguishing between fact and opinion is essential if students are to be led to think clearly about social issues.[1]

Facts are discrete bits of information or data that can be verified or corroborated. Fact statements invariably contain references to dates, quantities, or other information that can be tested for accuracy by referring to authoritative sources such as reference books or experts. Facts may also be verified by first-hand observation, scientific replications, and the corroboration techniques used frequently by historians, lawyers, and news reporters. Fact statements often answer the classic news questions: who, what, when, where, and why? (Note, however, that the why question often leads to an individual's interpretation or opinion.) Fact statements can and should be challenged and checked for accuracy. Students should be taught to ask: "How do we know that is true or accurate?" "What sources or methods might be used to verify this fact?" and "How trustworthy are these sources?" Finally, students should be made aware that facts often change over time. For example, crime rates rise and fall, definitions are altered or refined in a way that may change the value of popular economic indices, and even the names and boundaries of nations change over time.

Opinions are statements that express a positive or negative sentiment or value in relation to some object or person. They represent someone's point of view and are often based solely on personal judgment. An opinion may also represent an expert's assessment of something. Considerable factual evidence, solid logic, and complex reasoning often back up such expert opinions. Students should be taught to detect and inspect people's opinion statements. They should be able to describe the part of a statement that identifies it as an opinion. They may be challenged to state the opposite opinion, and they should be told to identify the kinds of evidence that would be needed in order to support an opinion statement. Finally, students should look for

---

[1]See Wilen and Phillips (1995, pp. 135–138) for an example.

inconsistencies in people's opinions and attempt to link people's opinions to statements of their biases.

Here is a brief exercise in distinguishing fact from opinion that uses statements taken from the materials in this chapter. Read each statement and decide if it is an opinion (O) or a fact (F). The answers are provided at the end of the exercise. Note: You may assume that statements that appear to be facts are indeed accurate (i.e., you don't need to mark a statement as O simply because you don't know and can't verify the actual facts).

O   F   1. On May 11, 1999, the Polk County, Florida, school board voted to put into effect a mandatory K–8 school uniform policy.

O   F   2. "I'm assuming somehow we will have to send them [noncompliant students] to the office," [a teacher] said. "I really hate to see little children being deprived of their education, because I'm there to teach and they're there to learn."

O   F   3. Schools with a school uniform policy do not allow students to wear clothing that reflects their religious or cultural beliefs.

O   F   4. School uniforms force large-sized children to wear clothes that are unflattering, difficult to obtain, and harmful to their self-esteem.

O   F   5. Students removed from class for not complying with a school uniform policy are denied access to free pubic education.

O   F   6. Glen Reynolds, the superintendent of the school district, stated that children would be suspended for noncompliance and later threatened to send parents to jail if they disobeyed the policy.

O   F   7. The Polk County School Board policy specified certain colors, fabric types, and styles of clothing.

O   F   8. Exemptions to the new uniform policy were allowed for (a) the uniforms of national youth organizations such as Boy Scouts and Girl Scouts; (b) students who were new to the school district, who would have 30 days to buy their uniforms; and (c) students who objected to the uniform code on the basis of the sincerely held religious beliefs of their families.

O   F   9. "The students feel good about themselves, and they look great," said Principal Eileen Castle.

O   F   10. "I'm really concerned as a teacher how we're going to be monitoring this because we're going to be put in the position of being like a parent," [second-grade teacher Becky] McMann said. "It's going to be very difficult for me telling a second grader, 'You're not wearing the right color or style.'"

Answers: 1–F 2–O 3–F 4–O 5–F 6–F 7–F 8–F 9–O 10–O

Table 6.1 Lesson Overview for "Mandatory School Uniforms"

	GOALS	ACTIVITIES	ASSESSMENTS
LESSON ONE	• Become familiar with the facts and issues of the controversy.	• Read the springboard/grabber story (Handout 6.1). • Identify facts and issues of the school uniform policy and lawsuit. • Work in small groups to read and discuss newspaper articles (Handouts 6.2–6.5). • Complete a written data collection sheet (Handout 6.6). • For homework, students interview their parents to determine their attitudes toward school uniforms.	• Collect and review the students' data collection sheets (Handout 6.6).
LESSON TWO	• Thoroughly research four major issues surrounding the school uniform controversy. • Develop well-grounded positions on the issues.	• Review homework assignments and facts of the case. • Form research groups to read and study the four major questions raised by the policy and lawsuit (Handouts 6.7–6.10). • Research groups organize and take responsibility (Handout 6.11) for the study of the Web sites and articles on their questions (Handout 6.12). • Groups articulate, write, and share their positions on the questions.	• Examine the Task Completion Report (Handout 6.11). • Collect and review each group's position statement.
LESSON THREE	• Present positions on all four research issues at a mock school board meeting. • To conclude the case study learning.	• Elect school board members and set up the room for a mock school board meeting. • Convene the mock school board meeting and hear the positions of the issues groups. • The school board votes to retain, modify, or repeal the district's mandatory school uniform policy. • Students individually produce recommendations for a new school district policy on student dress (Handout 6.13).	• Use the mock school board meeting as a performance assessment. • Examine the final, improved position statements. • Collect and critique each student's policy statement for the new school district (Handout 6.13).

LESSON ONE: Dressed for Success?

Purpose This lesson introduces students to the mandatory school uniform controversy that occurred in Polk County, Florida. Students learn about the policy and the problems that it created. They are challenged to differentiate fact from opinion and to frame the main issues that surrounded this policy controversy.

Duration Two class periods

Materials

Handout 6.1: Dressed for Success?
Handout 6.2: Enforcement Not Uniform
Handout 6.3: Student Branding Outrages Parents
Handout 6.4: Uniform Policy Isn't Made in Shades
Handout 6.5: Teachers Start Work with Many
   Pressures
Handout 6.6: Data Collection Sheet

Procedures

1. Orient your students to the topic of mandatory school uniforms by asking if anyone in the room has ever attended a school that required students to wear uniforms. Give two or three students a chance to share their experiences briefly, or, if no one has any relevant experience, ask two or three students to speculate briefly about what their feelings might be if they were required to wear a uniform to school.

2. Distribute and ask students to read the springboard/grabber article "Dressed for Success?" (Handout 6.1). This article introduces students to a simplified version of the Polk County, Florida, mandatory school uniform policy, the lawsuit that was filed to end the policy, and the perspectives of students and parents who opposed the policy.

3. After students have read Handout 6.1, have them distinguish the facts of the policy and the lawsuit (see "Methods Focus" for help with this task). You may wish to write students' fact statements on the board, chart paper, or a computer for display purposes. Here are some examples of the kinds of fact statements that students might make derived from Handout 6.1:

- On May 11, 1999, the Polk County, Florida, school board voted to put into effect a mandatory K–8 school uniform policy.
- Glen Reynolds, the superintendent of the school district, stated that children would be suspended for noncompliance and later threatened to send parents to jail if they disobeyed the policy.
- The policy specified certain colors, fabric types, and styles of clothing.

(*Have the students formulate other fact statements.*)

4. After clarifying the facts, ask the students to identify the issues and problems that arose from the dress code policy. Point out that some of the issues are hinted at in the questions that were posed in Handout 6.1. Note, too, that issues are statements that can be discussed or debated. As before, you may wish to write students' issue statements on the board, chart paper, or a computer for display purposes. Here are some sample issue and problem statements derived from Handout 6.1:

- Does the school board really have the authority to require students to wear uniforms?

- Will the uniform policy really improve students' behavior and learning?
- Does the policy increase the expense of clothing, and is this fair to low-income families?

(*Have the students formulate other issues and problem statements.*)

5. Once students have identified the facts and issues of the case, give each student one of the four shortened newspaper articles (Handouts 6.2–6.5) to read and discuss. Form the students into groups, but have all four articles read aloud in each group. The students can take turns reading their articles aloud to one another or share a summary of the articles' highlights.

6. When the groups are finished sharing, ask students to return to their seats and write answers to the following questions on their Data Collection Sheets (Handout 6.6).

- *How do parents, students, and school personnel seem to feel about the uniform dress code? What part of your article gave you this impression?* (These questions are designed to help the students identify the *opinions* of the people involved in the case and support their judgments with specific references to the statements in each article that support their ideas.)
- *What problems have come up in this controversy and how important are they?* (This question attempts to get students to identify and summarize the problems caused by the mandatory school uniform policy. Note that some of these will be the same problems identified in the introduction to the policy and lawsuit.)
- *What are the most important issues raised by this mandatory school uniform policy case?* (This question asks the students to prioritize and place a value on the issues they have identified. Students may be asked to rank order this list of issues.)
- *What more would you like to know about this case? What resources might help you find the information you need?* (These questions are designed to lead students into their research groups, which form the focus of Lesson Two.)

7. Conclude this part of the lesson by allowing students to summarize their work briefly on the Data Collection Sheets. Focus on questions 3 and 4 because they lead naturally into the issues research activities of the next lesson.

8. Collect Handout 6.6 for assessment of each student's work.

9. For homework, ask students to interview their parents to determine their views on the topic of

school uniforms. Prepare the students for this task by helping them frame three to five open-ended questions that will guide their interviews. (These questions probably will be related to the questions and problem statements identified above.) You may wish to write these questions on the board and ask the students to copy them so that they can be used in their interviews.

LESSON TWO: Are Mandatory School Uniforms Really a Good Idea?

Purpose This lesson asks students to research four major issues surrounding the school uniform controversy. Students work in groups to establish a knowledge base so that they can intelligently debate the central question: Are mandatory school uniforms really a good idea?

Duration Three class periods

Materials

Handout 6.7: Do School Uniforms Violate Constitutional Rights?

Handout 6.8: Can School Uniform Rules Be Fairly Enforced?

Handout 6.9: Who Should Make School Uniform Policy?

Handout 6.10: Are School Uniforms Effective?

Handout 6.11: Task Completion Report

Handout 6.12: Researching Your Issue (four copies each of the six articles identified and/or computer(s) with Internet access)

Procedures

1. Begin by asking the students to describe briefly what they found out by talking with their parents. Ask if they were surprised by their parents' attitudes toward any of the facts or issues surrounding a mandatory school uniform policy, and have them explain why they were or were not surprised. For clarity, ask the students to review briefly the facts and issues of the case.

2. Divide students into four research groups based on Handouts 6.7 through 6.10. Explain that the task of each group is to research their designated topic and develop a well-grounded position on it. Give each group enough time to read the handout and to consider the points it raises. Encourage the students in each group to divide the responsibilities for researching their topic. For example, one individual may be assigned to investigate and report on a single sub-question or subtopic or students may be assigned responsibility for reading and reporting on one article or Web site. A research team coordinator who oversees the group's work may also be appointed or elected. Students should be asked to complete Handout 6.11 to demonstrate the accomplishment of their work.

3. Provide access to the readings and/or Internet sites identified in Handout 6.12. Monitor each group's work with these resources and answer any questions they may have. Allow sufficient time for thoughtful consideration of these resources.

4. Work with each group to assign unfinished tasks as homework. For example, some students may be assigned to go to the public library to find additional resources and others may volunteer to use their home computers to explore Web sites further.

5. For assessment and closure of the research, require each group to write a one-page position paper that (a) clearly states their opinion(s), (b) offers support with one or more logical arguments, and (c) cites resources that back up their arguments. Adequate in-class time should be devoted to these position statements. Shown below is an abbreviated position statement by students who have been researching the question of whether school uniforms violate students' constitutional rights:

(a) We believe that a school uniform policy does not violate students' First or Fourteenth Amendment rights (b) because these rights are principally exercised through free speech and only minimally shown through the dress that people may wear. A mandatory school uniform policy only limits a minor avenue for self-expression. (c) Supreme court rulings in the cases of *Ferra v. Hendry County School Board* and *Bether School District No. 403 v. Fraser* have supported the idea that schools have a right to restrict what students wear.

6. Ask each group to share their position statement. Encourage supportive and critical comments from other students. If required, urge the groups to improve their position statements, possibly as a homework assignment, before the concluding mock school board meeting to be held in Lesson Three.

LESSON THREE: Hear Our Voices!

Purpose This final lesson gives students an opportunity to present their research findings and options at a mock school board meeting. The meeting may be used as a performance assessment tool to supplement each student's written school uniform policy that is completed in Handout 6.13.

Duration Two class periods

Materials
Handout 6.13: Public Notice
Optional: School board members, administrators, or parents to serve as observers

Procedures

1. Organize a mock school board meeting. The school board should be composed of seven members, with at least one member being selected from each of the four research groups (i.e., all groups should be represented on the school board). If there were students who held minority viewpoints on their topics, they should be given an opportunity to serve on the school board as one or more of the three at-large members. Depending on the knowledge and maturity of your students, you may want to provide them with a brief explanation of the functions typically performed by school boards, paying particular attention to their function as an elected policy-making group that attempts to represent the community's interests and needs. You may also need to stress the relationship between the school board and the school administration, making it clear that, in most cases, superintendents are appointed rather than elected and, as a result, may be fired by the school board. In essence, this explanation should set up the expectation among your students that the school board has the final decision about matters such as dress codes and uniform policies.

2. Begin the meeting by seating the seven school board members at the front of the room. The research groups on the four issues should sit together in the audience and decide which of their members will serve as spokespersons. Announce that you will play the role of moderator and that all students must stand and approach a public microphone (any prop will do) in order to address the board. Limit microphone time to 2 to 3 minutes per person. Speakers may use the one-page position statements prepared at the end of Lesson Two and any other material generated by their research group.

3. Once all of the positions have been heard, the school board members will be free to take questions from the audience and to ask questions among themselves regarding the mandatory school uniform policy. As the moderator, you may need to facilitate this process. At the point where little further information is presented, take a brief administrative recess to allow the school board members to develop one or more motions to retain, modify, or repeal the mandatory school uniform policy. (Research groups can be urged to discuss quietly what they believe should be the outcome of the meeting.) Follow parliamentary procedures to entertain the motions, hear discussion, and conduct the votes that may be necessary.

4. As a final assignment for this lesson, ask each student to write his or her own dress code or uniform recommendations to a new school district that is being formed (Handout 6.13).

Handout 6.1

DRESSED FOR SUCCESS?

On May 11, 1999, the Polk County, Florida, school board put into effect a new districtwide mandatory school uniform policy that dramatically limited what kindergarten through eighth-grade students could wear. The school board's action immediately set off a round of parent complaints and soon led to a lawsuit designed to stop the new policy. The school board's appointed superintendent, Glenn Reynolds, made it clear that students would be suspended for violating the uniform policy and later said he would even consider "sending parents to jail for contributing to the delinquency of a minor" if they refused to dress their children properly according to the new uniform policy.

Black, Blue, Tan, or White

The new districtwide policy stated that the basic uniform for girls would consist of a long- or short-sleeved navy blue or white collared blouse or polo shirt with a dark blue, black, or khaki (tan) skirt, walking shorts, slacks, shorts, and a jumper made of denim, corduroy, or twill fabric. The basic uniform for boys would consist of a long- or short-sleeved navy blue or white collared shirt, such as a polo or oxford dress shirt, and a dark blue, black, or khaki (tan) pair of long pants or walking shorts made of denim, corduroy, or twill fabric. In addition, the new uniform code allowed the principal of each elementary or middle school to designate an official school T-shirt, one additional school color that could be worn on the top, and a school plaid that could be worn on the bottom. Exemptions to the new uniform policy were allowed for (a) the uniforms of national youth organizations such as Boy Scouts and Girl Scouts; (b) students who were new to the school district, who would have 30 days to buy their uniforms; and (c) students who objected to the uniform code on the basis of the sincerely held religious beliefs of their families. The dress code banned all emblems, words, phrases, or insignia except buttons, armbands, or other similar symbols that were worn to exercise the right of free speech guaranteed by the U.S. Constitution.

Questions to Consider

1. How do you think students might feel about having to wear uniforms to school?

2. How do you think parents might feel about having to buy school uniforms?

3. Why would the school board want students to wear uniforms?

The Incidents

The passage of the school district's mandatory uniform code caused many problems once school started. In fact, over 1,000 "loaner outfits" had to be distributed on the first day of school. Here are a few examples of what happened.

Real-World Investigations for Social Studies
Hoge, Field, Foster, and Nickell

A vice principal at Westwood Middle School suspected that a girl was wearing Spandex (a forbidden fabric). In order to test this idea, the vice principal grabbed the girl's pants, opened them, and pulled out the tag. The result was that the girl was sent to in-school suspension for having pants with only a 4 percent spandex content.

Questions to Consider

1. Do you feel that the vice principal's actions were justified and proper? Why or why not?

2. Should any quantity of Spandex content be tolerated? Explain your answer.

A parent said that her second grader had followed the rules at Auburndale Central Elementary School by wearing navy blue pants. However, he got into trouble when he wore a pair that was slightly faded.

Questions to Consider

1. Should faded clothing be tolerated? Why or why not?

2. Is navy blue still navy blue even when it is badly faded? Explain your answer.

A parent sent one of his children to school in a white polo shirt featuring an American flag image and the text "God, please bless America one more time." The child was made to change into a loaner shirt so that he could remain in class. (The loaner shirt had a large *L* that identified him as a uniform code violator.)

Questions to Consider

1. Should patriotic slogans and emblems be allowed? Why or why not?

2. Should loaner clothing be clearly marked? Take a position and explain your answer.

continued

Real-World Investigations for Social Studies
Hoge, Field, Foster, and Nickell

Handout 6.1 *continued*

Many parents chose to send their children to school in uniforms, but with a small sticker or button of protest. Messages ranged from *"Uniforms stink!"* to *"It's not what you wear, it's what you do."* A large number of parents reported that their children were forced to remove the stickers under the threat of severe discipline.

Questions to Consider

1. Why should or shouldn't there be limits on students' right to protest school policies?

2. Who should decide these limits? Explain your answer.

The Lawsuit

A class action lawsuit, filed by an attorney for over 500 families, alleged that the new uniform code (a) placed the school in a position of authority and control over students' dress that is more properly exercised by parents and their children; (b) caused school personnel to take actions that prohibited students from wearing clothing that embodied political, religious, educational, commercial, and other forms of free speech; (c) deflected the schools' attention from their primary educational purpose and mission; (d) prevented students from choosing clothing that expressed their individuality, identity, gender, and ethnic and religious heritage; (e) created extra clothing expense because uniforms had to be purchased in addition to regular clothes; (f) was enforced differently among the schools; and (g) created psychological stress, health, and safety concerns. The lawsuit demanded that the school board overturn its new uniform policy and revert back to its prior dress code, which did not limit students' and families' selections of styles, colors, or materials.

Questions to Consider

1. Who should have authority over what children wear—parents, children, or the school system? Take a position and explain your answer.

2. Why might it be difficult to enforce even a simple uniform code?

3. To what degree are your clothes an expression of your gender, identity, and individuality?

Real-World Investigations for Social Studies
Hoge, Field, Foster, and Nickell

ENFORCEMENT NOT UNIFORM

BARTOW—Enforcing the new mandatory uniform policy has become a nightmare for school administrators. The list of questions is seemingly endless: Is a polo-style shirt acceptable if it has a zipper instead of buttons? Can a student wear popular cargo-style pants or is there a restriction on the number of pockets pants can have? Is a mock turtleneck the same as a collar?

These are just a few of the dozens of questions community relations director Frances McMichael has been asked since school started in Polk County.

"We're having to make decisions about things we never thought about," McMichael said. "We tried really hard to think of all these things." McMichael has been inundated with phone calls from principals confused about when they should punish students for violations of the mandatory uniform policy. "Today we had the issue of mock turtlenecks," McMichael said. "We had a big argument about that. To me, a collar is a collar is a collar."

Some students have worn Capri pants, a fashionable style of mid-calf length pants, to school. These students complied with color and fabric requirements under the uniform policy but left administrators confused about whether the style was acceptable. "We eventually convinced the superintendent that they were just really long shorts," McMichael said.

Despite the confusion, Superintendent Glenn Reynolds and most board members stood behind the new policy. Reynolds praised students and parents for complying with the uniform policy. The District reported about a ninety-nine percent compliance rate Monday, with a final count of twenty-eight students out of about 50,000 elementary and middle school students refusing to wear the uniforms or borrow an approved shirt from their school.

Adapted by permission of the publisher from Karen Cimino, "County dress code not uniform; district officials wade through parents' questions about what conforms to the uniform policy; Polk County School Board," *The Ledger*, 11 August 1999 (Metro). © 2003 by The Ledger. All rights reserved.

STUDENT BRANDING OUTRAGES PARENTS

BARTOW—It's not the "Scarlet Letter," but the "L" drawn on some school-loaned uniforms is very close, according to some angry parents.

On August 25, Lake Wales parent Leah Batson sent her seven-year-old son to Hillcrest school in a teal (bluish-green) shirt, a color not approved in the mandatory uniform policy. However, when she arrived at the end of the school day to pick him up, she was horrified to see him wearing a different shirt with the letter "L" sewn on the sleeve. "He was crying," she said. "I was in shock . . . and really mad. They didn't call me or my husband."

"You tell me what the difference is between an 'L' on a shirt and [a] number on the arm of a Jewish person," said parent Chris Hughes, referring to the Jewish Holocaust victims of Nazi Germany in World War II. Hughes added that branding children who borrow shirts with the letter "L" won't improve their work in class or pride in the school, and may even subject them to teasing or mockery.

School district officials maintain that they do not intend to try to humiliate children because they have to borrow clothes in order to comply with the uniform rules. However, an official said, "The schools have a lot of money invested in these clothes," and they don't want to lose them. During the first week of school in August, uniforms were loaned to 5,497 children.

"Our goal is to have kids in class, but they can't go to class without a uniform on," said Polk County Schools Community Relations Coordinator Francis McMichael. "An easy solution [to the problem for parents] is to make sure the child is in uniform," she added.

Adapted by permission of the publisher from Brian McBride, "Student branding outrages parents," *The News Chief,* 2 September 1999. © 1999 The News Chief.

UNIFORM POLICY ISN'T MADE IN SHADES

LAKELAND—Parent Cyndee Smith applauded when the Polk County School Board ordered elementary and middle school students to wear district-sanctioned uniforms, but now she's starting to change her mind. Her son, Travis, ran afoul of the policy by wearing the wrong shade of green to Highlands Middle School.

Smith said she bought four shirts that were a little more forest green than hunter green and thought they would pass muster. Nevertheless, workers at the school insisted on hunter green. "He went to the office, and somebody told him he couldn't wear that shirt anymore," Smith said.

Smith is frustrated, and she is not alone. Many parents are finding out that following the School Board's controversial directive is not as simple as they had hoped. Teachers and principals are conducting daily inspections of more than 50,000 students for uniform violations, but the School District hasn't disclosed how many shirts and pants school workers have loaned to students because their clothes were deemed improper.

"They make everybody stand up in first period to see if they have the right colors and stuff," said Jeff Keuhner, aged 13, who attends Highlands Middle School. "Then they tell you to go to the office if you aren't wearing the right color or style of clothing. There were about thirty kids in there Thursday."

Adapted by permission of the publisher by Karen Cimino, "Uniform policy isn't made in shades," *The Ledger*, 15 August 1999 (metro). © 2003 The Ledger. All rights reserved.

TEACHERS START WORK WITH MANY PRESSURES

LAKELAND—Teachers have a lot to think about as they prepare to head back to school this year and enforcing the Polk County School District's uniform policy is one major item that has been added to their list.

Polk Education Association President John Taylor said uniforms should be the least concern of parents, students, and teachers as this school year begins. "There are too many other issues in this county for the new uniform code to be the number one concern right now," Taylor said.

Teachers or administrators will have to remove students from class who are out of uniform. The students will be offered a shirt they can borrow for the day and allowed to return to class. If they refuse it, they must stay out of class. Refusal to follow the uniform dress code will lead to in-school and then out-of-school suspensions for students.

Becky McMann, a second-grade teacher at Babson Park Elementary School, said uniforms are the top concern as she heads back to school. "I'm really concerned as a teacher how we're going to be monitoring this because we're going to be put in the position of being like a parent," McMann said. "It's going to be very difficult for me telling a second-grader, 'You're not wearing the right color or style.'" But McMann plans to enforce the policy.

"I'm assuming somehow we will have to send them to the office," she said. "That's school board policy, but I really hate to see little children being deprived of their education, because I'm there to teach and they're there to learn."

Adapted by permission of the publisher from Karen Cimino, "Teachers start work with many pressures," *The Ledger*, 2 August 1999 (News). © 2003 The Ledger. All rights reserved.

DATA COLLECTION SHEET

Q1. How do parents, students, and school personnel seem to feel about the uniform code? What part of your article gave you this impression?

Q2. What problems have come up in this controversy and how important are they?

Q3. What are the most important issues raised by this mandatory uniform policy case?

Q4. What more would you like to know about this case? What resources might help you find the information you need?

Real-World Investigations for Social Studies
Hoge, Field, Foster, and Nickell

Handout 6.7

RESEARCH TOPIC 1

DO SCHOOL UNIFORMS VIOLATE CONSTITUTIONAL RIGHTS?

The First Amendment to the Constitution of the United States guarantees the freedom of speech:

> Congress shall make no law respecting an establishment of religion, or prohibiting the free exercise thereof; or abridging the freedom of speech, or of the press; or the right of the people peaceably to assemble, and to petition the government for a redress of grievances.

Most Americans agree that freedom of speech gives people the right to express themselves in ways other than speech. This includes the right to wear what you want. However, many adults question whether the right to free speech should be given to students and whether this right can reasonably be extended to allow students to wear anything they want.

In addition, Section One of the Fourteenth Amendment guarantees that all citizens of the United States are treated equally under the law:

> No state shall make or enforce any law which shall abridge the privileges or immunities of citizens of the United States; nor shall any state deprive any person of life, liberty, or property, without due process of law; nor deny to any person within its jurisdiction the equal protection of the laws.

People who do not agree with the school uniform policy argue that it violates the Fourteenth Amendment in several ways. Here are some examples of their complaints:

- School uniforms do not allow students to wear clothing that reflects their religious or cultural beliefs.
- School uniforms do not allow special consideration for children with physical handicaps.
- School uniforms force large-sized children to wear clothes that are unflattering, difficult to obtain, and harmful to their self-esteem.
- School uniforms cost additional money. Therefore, the policy discriminates against low-income children by increasing the cost of their "free" (tax-supported) public school education.
- Some children from low-income families are loaned uniforms. However, this clothing often is of poor quality and sometimes is clearly identifiable (e.g., by a large letter *L*). This is humiliating and embarrassing to children. In addition, as the school does not always wash this clothing, it presents a health risk.
- Students removed from class for not complying with the uniform policy are denied access to free public education.

Decisions Made by U.S. Courts

Over the years, judges in state and federal courts have heard hundreds of cases concerning students' First and Fourteenth Amendment rights. Many of these court rulings have sent mixed messages about the proper limits of these rights. Here is a summary of a few cases:

- In 1969, the Supreme Court recognized, in *Tinker v. Des Moines Independent School District*, that students do not lose their constitutional rights while in school. The court ruled that students should not have been suspended from school for wearing black armbands to protest the Vietnam War.

- In 1970, in *Richards v. Thurston,* the First Circuit Court of Appeals ruled that a 17-year-old senior from Marlboro, Maryland, had the right to wear "unusually long hair" in school. The court stated that the student's right to wear his hair as he pleased was a personal liberty that should not be taken away by the school.
- In 1978, in *Ferra v. Hendry County School Board,* the court ruled that school boards have the right to prohibit a student from growing a mustache. The judge argued that "ordinary matters such as these must be left in the hands of the officials who have been duly charged with the operation of our schools."
- In 1986 the Supreme Court, in *Bethel School District No. 403 v. Fraser,* ruled that students did not have the right to wear clothing that was lewd, vulgar, offensive, and against the values of civilized society.

Questions to Consider

1. What do you think about each of these cases? How much authority do you think schools should have over how a person dresses or looks in school?

2. Why do you think judges have differed so much in their decisions?

Constitutional Considerations

School administrators and legal authorities say that schools have to maintain a balance between giving students their First Amendment rights and making sure that they come to school in a manner that does not prevent others from learning. Many people, therefore, suggest that students' dress should be restricted if (a) it is unhealthy or unsafe; (b) it is offensive; (c) it is gang-related; or (d) it disrupts student learning. The difficulty with each of these restrictions is how to decide if, for example, something is offensive.

Consider the following situations. What would you decide if you were the school principal?

- A middle school student wears a T-shirt with the slogan "TEACHERS ARE STUPID."
- An elementary school teacher complains to you that a boy's long hair stops him from working properly.
- Several high school students choose to wear trench coats similar to ones worn by students who killed others at Columbine High School in Colorado in 1999.

continued

Real-World Investigations for Social Studies
Hoge, Field, Foster, and Nickell

Handout 6.7 *continued*

- Cheerleaders at a middle school decide to wear their uniforms to class all day on each game day.
- A middle school student wears the same clothes to school for 2 weeks.
- A high school student wears a large pair of colorful boxer shorts outside of his normal clothing. He is doing this as a protest against the school's dress code.
- A group of fifth-grade students wear sunglasses in school.

Many people who use the Fourteenth Amendment to argue against school uniforms claim that all children are not treated equally under the strict uniform policies. How might a school uniform policy be written to give children in the following categories equal status?

- Children from low-income families
- Children with special physical needs
- Children from different cultural and religious backgrounds

Real-World Investigations for Social Studies
Hoge, Field, Foster, and Nickell

RESEARCH TOPIC 2

CAN SCHOOL UNIFORM RULES BE FAIRLY ENFORCED?

Many school districts that have imposed a uniform policy have had to think about three important questions:

HOW CAN SCHOOLS BE FAIR AND REASONABLE IN APPLYING UNIFORM POLICIES?

A problem faced by school districts is how to be fair and reasonable when applying school uniform policies. In Polk County, Florida, for example, many parents have complained that the schools were not fair and reasonable in their application of the uniform policy. Here are just a few parental complaints:

- Children were sent to the principal for wearing the wrong shade of color (e.g., forest green, not hunter green).
- A child was forced to exchange his shirt for a loaner because it had an American flag on it with the words "God, please bless America one more time."
- Children were forced to change into loaner outfits in front of school personnel.
- Children were isolated from other students for wearing the wrong uniform.

Other parents complained that these incidents humiliated or embarrassed their children in front of others. They also argued that they shifted the focus of the school away from education and placed it inappropriately on compliance with dictated fashion. They stated that teachers were teaching less and that many teachers were afraid to speak out against the uniform policy even though they disliked being cast in the role of "uniform police."

Questions to Consider

1. Is it possible to enforce a school uniform rule fairly? Take a position and explain your answer.

2. How specific should a uniform code be? Should all students be required to follow the uniform code exactly or should they be given some freedom to be different?

3. If children do not wear the correct uniform, what action(s) should school officials take?

Should Students and Parents Have the Right to Opt Out of the Uniform Policy?

The American Civil Liberties Union (ACLU) Director of Public Education, Loren Siegel, argues that an "opt out" choice for parents is essential:

continued

Real-World Investigations for Social Studies
Hoge, Field, Foster, and Nickell

Handout 6.8 *continued*

For a public school uniform to be legal, it has to have an opt out provision. Every child in this country has the right to a public school education, and that right cannot be conditioned upon compliance with a uniform policy. Some parents and children will have religious objections to uniforms. Others won't participate for aesthetic reasons. (Siegel, 1996)

> Similarly, the U.S. Department of Education, in its *Manual on School Uniforms*, notes that "a mandatory uniform policy with no 'opt out' provision could be vulnerable to legal challenge."

Questions to Consider

1. Is it fair that some children are allowed to opt out of a uniform policy? Why or why not?

2. What special circumstances might justify a student's right to opt out?

Should Low-Income Families Be Given Financial Help to Purchase New Uniforms?

In Long Beach, California, the ACLU argued that many parents could not afford the new uniforms (the basic cost for essential items, a white shirt and a pair of pants, was $25). One parent said, "I shop thrift and buy in bulk, and you can't do that with uniforms." Others complained that they simply did not have the money to buy new clothes for three or four children at the start of the new school year.

The U.S. Department of Education's *Manual on School Uniforms* recommends that low-income families be given financial support:

> School districts with uniform policies should make provision for students whose families are unable to afford uniforms. Many have done so. Examples of the types of assistance include: (a) the school district provides uniforms to students who cannot afford to purchase them; (b) community and business leaders provide uniforms or contribute financial support for uniforms; (c) school parents work together to make uniforms available for economically disadvantaged students; and (d) used uniforms from graduates are made available to incoming students.

> (Manual on school uniforms, c. 1996).

Questions to Consider

1. Does a school have the responsibility to provide low-income children with a school uniform? Why? Why not?
2. If children from low-income families are given or loaned school uniforms, how should the school ensure that children are not embarrassed and/or humiliated by the gift or the loan?

RESEARCH TOPIC 3

WHO SHOULD MAKE SCHOOL UNIFORM POLICY?

Who should decide what children wear in school? Read the following opinions about school uniforms and consider the questions that follow.

(a) Should the President Decide?

President Bill Clinton, February 1996

> Quality education is critical to America's future and the future of our children and families. We cannot educate our children, however, in schools where weapons, gang violence, and drugs threaten their safety. We must do everything possible to ensure that schools provide a safe and secure environment where the values of discipline, hard work and study, responsibility, and respect can thrive and be passed on to our children. . . .
>
> Many school districts have made school uniforms an important part of an overall program to improve school safety and discipline. Too often we learn that students resort to violence and theft simply to obtain designer clothes or fancy sneakers. Too often we learn that clothing items worn at school, bearing special colors or insignias, are used to identify gang membership or instill fear among students and teachers alike.
>
> If student uniforms can help deter school violence, promote discipline, and foster a better learning environment, then we should offer our strong support to the schools and parents that try them.
> (Clinton, 1996)

(b) Should State Governors Decide?

Governor William F. Weld (Massachusetts), February 1997

> School uniforms are an idea whose time has come. . . . Little things can add up to a lot. Uniforms may seem like a little thing, but I think they're relevant to self-esteem, possibly even to confidence. (*Boston Globe*, Feb. 12, 1997)

(c) Should Local School Boards Decide?

John Prescott, a local school board member, May 2001

> School uniforms will create a better classroom atmosphere, increase school identity, and reduce gang violence. An orderly school environment is essential to learning. I think all of our schools should adopt official uniform policies.

(d) Should Parents Decide?

Angelica Mendez, parent, January 2001

> A school uniform restricts my child's freedom to wear the colors and styles that are popular. If the school district adopts a mandatory school uniform code teachers will have to look at every child to see that they have the proper uniform on. Teachers will be thinking more about policing the uniform rules than about teaching.

continued

Real-World Investigations for Social Studies
Hoge, Field, Foster, and Nickell

Handout 6.9 *continued*

Darren Holtz, parent, May 2000

I like the idea of school uniforms. It will reduce the hassles of buying school clothes and dressing every morning. Kids won't be so worried about whether they look cool and they won't be harassed for looking different. I think teachers and students will be able to focus more on learning if we have a mandatory school uniform policy.

(e) Should Students Decide?

Penny Wilson, middle school student, March 2000

I hate the idea of having to wear a school uniform. The colors and styles that adults pick are boring and they make everyone look geeky. Wearing a uniform won't make me a better student. It will just make school seem more like prison.

Andrew McFadden, middle school student, April 2002

I really like wearing a uniform because you never have to think twice about what to wear to school. You just put on your uniform and head out for school. It makes school safer, too, because the gang colors are gone and people don't get beat up for what they are wearing.

Questions to Consider

1. Consider each of the five categories separately. What arguments can be made for and against claims that (a) the president, (b) state governors, (c) local school board members, (d) parents, or (e) students should have a say in what clothing can be worn to school?

2. Who do you think should make the final decision on what children should wear in schools? Should elected officials have more authority than parents and children?

Real-World Investigations for Social Studies
Hoge, Field, Foster, and Nickell

RESEARCH TOPIC 4

ARE SCHOOL UNIFORMS EFFECTIVE?

YES! (Uniforms Do Improve Student Behavior)

On July 5, 1994, school uniforms became mandatory in all 70 Long Beach, California, Unified School District elementary and middle schools. The Long Beach school district evaluates the impact of its policy annually. Here is a summary of their results for the first 4 years that the school uniform policy was in use.

Elementary and Middle School Crime Summary (Student Uniforms Required K–8)

SCHOOL CRIME REDUCED	1993–1994 BEFORE UNIFORMS	1994–1995 UNIFORMS REQUIRED	1995–1996 2ND YEAR WITH UNIFORMS	1996–1997 3RD YEAR WITH UNIFORMS	CHANGE
K–8 enrollment	57,497	58,376	59,822	62,039	
Assault/battery*	319	214	53	47	
Assault with a deadly weapon*	6	3	16	11	
Fighting	1,135	554	653	556	–51%
Sex offenses	57	15	5	4	–93%
Robbery/extortion	34	12	13	5	–85%
Chemical substances	71	29	24	20	–72%
Weapons or look-alikes	145	78	28	24	–83%
Dangerous devices	46	23	1	2	–96%
Vandalism†	1,409	1,155	127	93	
Total	3,222	2,083	920	762	–76%

*The statewide category of assault has been revised because of different interpretations of what constitutes assault. Verbal threats without physical contact were sometimes reported as assaults. There is also a new, expanded definition of assault with a deadly weapon as of 1995–1996. Reported now is any item that is actually used in an effort to inflict any bodily harm, i.e., a foot, a fist, a pencil, or a comb.

†Under the new California Safe Schools Assessment School Crime Report, only vandalism over $100 is included. Some prior years' incidents were under $100, so the actual reduction is less than this amount.

Source: http://www.lbusd.k12.ca.us.crime.htm

Many educators and school officials believe that school uniforms are one way of preventing violence in schools. The following article, adapted from *Newsweek* magazine, illustrates how serious the problem is.

In the poor sections of American cities, including New York, Detroit, Newark, N. J., Chicago and Los Angeles, more and more kids are resorting to violence—even killing—for cool clothes. Police began observing the trend two years ago and now say that armed robbery is increasing at an alarming rate. Sometimes it's athletic or leather jackets, other times sneakers. In Detroit, the object of desire is a specific brand of down parka. Last November an 18-year-old was shot to death for his Triple F.A.T. Goose parka and $70 Nike sneakers. In Newark, police said leather or athletic jackets figured in 64 armed robberies between September and December. Two of the victims were shot. In the past six months four Chicago youths were killed for their waist length warm-up jackets that sell for between $90 and $200.

Dressing for success has never been so risky. The combination of crack-quickened tempers, availability of guns and the flashy clothes of the drug culture have taken

continued

Real-World Investigations for Social Studies
Hoge, Field, Foster, and Nickell

fashion awareness to a wicked level. Often the violence is triggered by gang symbols and colors. A brand of sneakers, British Knights, has been adopted by Los Angeles's Crips gang, archrivals of the Bloods. Crips like the shoes because the initials "B. K." can also stand for "Blood Killers." In L.A. last year a little girl unwittingly wore a red sweater, apparently unaware [that] it was also the color favored by the Bloods. Someone, presumably a member of a rival gang, hit her on the head with a rock.

In an effort to stem the tide, several schools have established dress codes. Crenshaw High School in Los Angeles has banned gang garb like bandannas and dangling earrings for boys. In January, the Detroit Board of Education ordered its 259 schools to design and enforce their own mandatory dress codes. Recently, at Boys and Girls High School in Brooklyn, principal Frank Mickens banned excessive jewelry and shearling coats to protect his kids from assault.

NO! (Uniforms Do Not Improve Student Behavior)

Some studies have shown that uniforms may have no direct impact on student behavior:

- Two professors from the University of Notre Dame questioned the Long Beach study. They claimed that *other changes* in Long Beach may have led to improvements in school behavior. In particular, they suggested that a $1 million grant to improve teaching methods in these schools may better explain students' improved behavior. In fact, the Notre Dame study concluded that "our findings indicate that student uniforms have no direct effect on behavioral problems" (Brunsma & Rockgnemore, 1998, n.p.).
- A 1998 Miami-Dade County (Florida) study also reported that mandatory uniforms may not have had a big impact on school children in their district. In middle schools, for example, where uniforms were mandatory, fights nearly doubled from 186 in 1996–1997 to 284 in 1997–1998 (Walters, 1998).

Questions to Consider

1. Why do you think research on the effectiveness of school uniform produces such mixed results?

2. Some people suggest that school uniforms may not fully explain why behavior in the Long Beach school district improved. What other factors might explain the improved student behavior?

3. Some parents and teachers thought that school uniforms were very effective in Long Beach. However, students were not so sure. Why do you think their opinions differed so much?

TASK COMPLETION REPORT

My assigned task was:

In order to accomplish my task, I did the following:

Here is a summary of what I found out:

Name: _____   Date finished: _____

Real-World Investigations for Social Studies
Hoge, Field, Foster, and Nickell

Handout 6.12

RESEARCHING YOUR ISSUE

Below is a list of Web sites and articles that should be used in your research. The Web sites are a rich source for school dress code and uniform information, and you may find these sites easy to use if you have a computer with Internet access. The articles may be obtained and photocopied at your school's media center or community library.

Web sites to Investigate

1. The Polk County School Uniform Web Site

(www.gate.net/~rwms/Uniform.html)

You may want to begin with this site. It looks directly at the issues in Polk County, Florida. Parents who did not want mandatory uniforms in local schools created the Polk County Uniform Policy page. At the Web site you can find links that include information on

- the uniform policy that was enforced by the school district
- the full text of the lawsuit that was filed against the policy
- the position of the ACLU
- a report by Gary Peter Klahr, "The Law on Uniforms", on the constitutionality of uniform policies
- newspaper articles on events in Polk County
- a report on research studies investigating the effectiveness of school uniforms (see "The Raging Debate" link on the home page)

2. The Education Commission of the States

(http://www.ecs.org/)

The Education Commission of the States (ECS) is a government-sponsored Web site that provides a wealth of information on educational issues. Click on the tab for "Education Issues" and then select "Uniforms/Dress Codes" to enter the area where the ECS has organized much of the debate on these topics. Alternatively, you can access additional information on this site by typing in "school uniforms" in the search box. This will lead to dozens of links that offer information on school uniform policy.

3. The U.S. Department of Education

(www.ed.gov/index.html)

This is a massive site administered by the federal government. Click the search tab and enter "school uniforms," and you will see several other links including President Clinton's support for school uniforms. Be sure to look at the "Manual on School Uniforms" and "Student Dress Policies" in the ERIC Digest section of this Web site.

4. The American Civil Liberties Union

(www.aclu.org/)

The ACLU is an organization committed to preserving individual rights. The organization is not in favor of school uniforms and therefore offers a large collection of news releases and summaries of court cases that oppose this policy. To access these resources, click the search box at the bottom of the main page and enter "school uniforms" as your search term.

Articles to Read

Many articles have been written about school uniforms and school dress codes. Here are six selections taken from educational journals or magazines that you may find useful:

Caruso, P. (1996). Individuality vs. conformity: The issue behind school uniforms. *NAASP Bulletin, 80*(581), 83–88.

A very good, brief overview of the arguments for and against uniforms.

Cohn, C. A. (1996). Mandatory school uniforms. *The School Administrator, 53*(2), 22–25.

The superintendent of the Long Beach, California, School District explains the reasons for the alleged success of its uniform policy.

Lane, K. E., Swartz, S. L., Richardson, M. D., & VanBerkum, D. W. (1994). You aren't what you wear. *The American School Board Journal, 181*(3), 64–65.

A brief but useful guide to writing a uniform or dress code policy without violating students' constitutional rights. This is useful for your final assignment.

McCarthy, M. M. (1996). Can educators regulate student appearance in public schools? *Educational Horizons, 75*, 11–14.

A brief look at some of the legal issues related to student appearance and dress in schools.

Paliokas, K. L., Futrell, M. H., & Rist, R. C. (1996). Trying uniforms on for size. *The American School Board Journal, 181*(5), 32–35.

A look at the claims of the effectiveness of the school uniform policy. It also investigates how legal uniforms are and provides a very good list of options that school boards have when designing codes. It is excellent for your final written report.

Stanley, M. S. (1996). School uniforms and safety. *Education and Urban Society, 28*(4), 424–435.

A more detailed article than the one by Caruso (1996) that begins by looking at the apparent success of the school uniform policy in Long Beach, California. The article investigates whether or not school uniforms are effective. A very good list of references is provided at the end of the article.

Handout 6.13

PUBLIC NOTICE BY PUEBLO, ARIZONA, SCHOOL BOARD

The newly formed suburb of Pueblo, Arizona, has elected its first school board and is in the process of establishing a number of policies for the coming school year. As part of their policy formation role, the school board wants citizen input regarding the development of a dress code or uniform policy for all students. Accordingly, the Board seeks written recommendations from citizens regarding whether a dress code or a uniform policy should be adopted and, importantly, the content of such a code or policy should one be adopted. Send your comments to: PUEBLO SCHOOL BOARD, P.O. BOX 1776, PUEBLO, ARIZONA 99675-4579. Clearly state your position on the matter and offer any arguments or support you may have for that position.

Real-World Investigations for Social Studies
Hoge, Field, Foster, and Nickell

CHAPTER

7

Pirates!

From the High Seas to High Tech:
The Great Debate Over Music Piracy

by

Jon Bauer

OVERVIEW

This chapter has been developed around the real-world issue of music piracy. As the Internet proliferated in the 1990s, the ability to send vast amounts of data without regard to distance, borders, or copyright laws touched musicians and the music industry. New technology allowed music CDs to be uploaded by anyone onto the Internet and downloaded by anyone free of charge. Unknown musicians, not wishing to wait to be picked up by a record label, found the Internet to be a cheap and

efficient way to present their music to the public. Sites like MP3.COM provided a cyberstage for tens of thousands of unknown bands, attracting tens of millions of potential fans.

Established musicians and record companies watched in horror. Not only did new technology cut into established artists' royalties by allowing CDs to be uploaded and spread by fans for free, it also threatened to destroy record companies, removing the need for a middleman between future artists and their audiences. Needless to say, ethical and legal issues emerged that may take years to resolve.

This chapter first introduces students to the concept of *piracy* through group research activities on famous historical pirates. Students prepare oral reports on these pirates, covering not only their biographies but also the historical and geographical settings in which they lived. They then discuss the controversy surrounding the lives of many famous pirates and the ethics of their actions.

Following their work on the lives of famous pirates, students are introduced to the contemporary debate on music piracy. Specifically, students explore the historic debate over Napster, the first popular Internet site that allowed millions of fans to swap virtual CDs free of charge. Students learn the various arguments put forth by parties involved in the debate over sites like Napster, from popular artists like Metallica, Dr. Dre, and Chuck D, to the CEOs of record companies, to fans, and to Napster itself. Working in groups, students research the various stakeholders' positions and prepare arguments for a mock senate panel that is convened to explore the issue.

The chapter concludes with an essay in which students take positions to argue whether or not a site like Napster constitutes music piracy. Students are asked to suggest possible solutions to the controversy, including comparisons with the activities of historical pirates discussed in class, and to decide whether they think music fans who download free virtual CDs off sites like Napster are themselves guilty of piracy.

CONNECTION TO NCSS THEME VII: PRODUCTION, DISTRIBUTION, AND CONSUMPTION

This chapter is intended to address the NCSS standard for production, distribution, and consumption by requiring students to think about the way music has been produced, distributed, and consumed in the past and how new technologies are impacting that system.

Tapping students' strong interest in popular music and the Internet, this chapter invites students to think about the ethical, legal, and economic issues surrounding the unbridled free distribution of music. The chapter allows students to research and debate an authentic issue that is likely to touch their lives, and to grapple with the issue just as real-life musicians, fans, music companies, Internet companies, and lawmakers do.

Students' involvement in this study will help them achieve a variety of valuable social education understandings. Among the most important are the key roles that U.S. copyright laws play in protecting intellectual and artistic property; the relationship between an individual's personal ethical behavior and the welfare of our system of free enterprise; and the clash between the desires and values of haves and have-nots.

METHODS FOCUS: CURRENT EVENTS

The contextual teaching and learning that take place in this chapter make use of a range of accepted methods (see "An Introduction to Contextual Teaching and Learning Methods" and other chapters for tips on using a variety of other methods). In this chapter, music piracy and its natural link to technology lends itself to considerations in teaching current events in the age of the Internet.

Current events, also known as *current affairs*, has been a subject of methods textbooks for social studies for many years. John Michaelis's classic textbook *Social Studies for Children in a Democracy* (1963), first published in 1950, devotes an entire chapter to instruction using current events. The *Handbook for Social Studies Teaching* (1967) also contains a chapter on current events and controversial issues. Modern textbooks such as those by Parker (2001) and Ellis (2002) also contain chapters on current events.

The inclusion of current events in the social studies curriculum is widely held as a key means of bringing vitality and reality into the classroom. Teachers are urged to draw parallels between the curriculum and the news in order to help make learning meaningful and because it is believed that citizens of a democracy need to be informed about what is happening in their communities. The practice of requiring students to locate and share topically focused news items has existed for decades in schools around the world. Current events may also enter the classroom when a major event compels teachers to drop their standard curriculum and focus exclusively on developing students' understanding of the news.

Generally speaking, there are several logical and experience-born guidelines that should be used when employing current events instruction. First and foremost, the treatment of current events should be instructional. This means that any use of current events should address real learning goals that are worthy of pursuit and that current events should not exist merely as entertainment or diversion from learning. Following logically from this is the idea that students need guidance in selecting appropriate news items. Limiting students to a particular theme or some well-targeted topics is a good way to gain an appropriate instructional focus for the use of current events.

Next, it is critically important to analyze intellectually the news items that are being discussed. This requires the teacher's attention to and participation in all phases of current events teaching. In particular, teachers must help students fully understand news events by helping them inspect the content and think deeply about its potential significance. This processing may be facilitated by asking a number of standard questions such as:

1. Why is this news item important?

   - How many people does it affect?
   - What does it tell us that we need to know?
   - How does this news relate to trends and developments in our society?

2. How does this news relate to what we have been learning?

   - What concepts or main ideas does it illustrate?
   - What historic, geographic, or economic information do citizens need to know in order to understand this news?
   - What might (name of someone we've been studying) think or say about this news?

3. What can or should we do as citizens about this news?

   - What are the short- and long-term consequences of this news?
   - How should citizens feel about this news, and what actions should they take based on it?

4. What are the positive and negative implications of this news?

   - Which individuals or groups benefit from the content and/or publication of this news?
   - Which groups or individuals suffer from the content and/or publication of this news?
   - Who probably wanted (or did not want) this news reported and why?
   - What does this news tell us about our society, other societies, or the world?

Teachers may wish to discuss these and other analytical questions with students in order to aid them in selecting news items. In turn, students may want to discuss the theme or topics and the questions with their parents for assistance in reading and analyzing the news. If parents become involved, the burden of censorship may be appropriately shared instead of falling entirely on the teacher. However, the issue of censorship is always present when current events are taken up in the classroom. For example, some news fails to get reported because someone, usually a reporter or an editor, decides that it isn't "good enough" to merit publication. At other times, news is withheld or buried on the back pages because editors are concerned about offending powerful people in their communities. Finally, because newspapers carry many sensational crime stories and other reports that may logically be considered inappropriate for middle and high school students, teachers need to know, in advance, the news items that students wish to describe, and they have the right to deny the presentation of any inappropriate items. This denial, of course, is a very serious action, and it should not be taken easily or without explanation to the students, who, it should be noted, are free to discuss the censored news item outside of class.

The Information Age has dramatically influenced the production, content, and distribution of the news and, therefore, the use of current events in the classroom. The proliferation of digital cameras and streaming video, as well as the global reach of the Internet, have greatly expanded people's ability to communicate dramatic events rapidly and widely and to use any spin or point of view they choose. Reputable news organizations have always attempted to follow good journalism practices such as checking sources, verifying facts, gaining the opposition's point of view, revealing any conflicts of interest, limiting the use of "loaded" language, and trying to report enough context so that the news makes sense to their readers. These and other good journalism practices are not necessarily well represented on every Web page that attempts to report the news. Consequently, students must be taught to appreciate good journalism practices and to apply an attitude of critical skepticism in their consumption of news from whatever sources they use. In addition to the above-noted qualities and questions, students must ask:

- Who funds this operation?
- What is its professed mission (and does the content really reflect that mission)?
- Who is on its board of directors or list of editors, and can they be contacted?
- What review processes are used in this publication source?
- How long has this source been in operation, and with whom is it allied?
- What do other sources say about this publication, source, or operation?
- How likely is it that the reported news on this site or source is biased, and what evidence can be gathered to prove such bias?

Just as one would apply specific questions to paper-based current events, students should be taught to apply critical thinking skills to news from Web sites. Students should also be taught to inspect carefully predispositions toward power and privilege that may inappropriately and unnecessarily diminish minority viewpoints or "shoestring" news sources simply because they are not mainstream or well established.

Table 7.1 Lesson Overview for "Pirates!"

	GOALS	ACTIVITIES	ASSESSMENTS
LESSON ONE	• Learn about the concept of piracy through the lives of famous pirates.	• Research and make oral presentations on the lives of famous pirates (Handouts 7.1 and 7.2).	• Evaluate oral presentations.
LESSON TWO	• Learn about music piracy and the controversy surrounding Napster.	• Read about and discuss music piracy and the Napster debate (Handouts 7.3 and 7.4).	• Write answers for the questions on Handouts 7.3 and 7.4.
LESSON THREE	• Research the positions of the various stakeholders in the Napster controversy for presentation before a mock senate panel.	• Divide the class into five teams and distribute Handouts 7.5–7.9. • Research positions. • Prepare for the mock senate panel presentation.	
LESSON FOUR	• Learn about the various positions in the Napster controversy via a mock senate panel discussion.	• The mock senate panel questions each team in turn about the team's position on the Napster controversy. • Teams then respond in turn to arguments made by other teams.	• Write an essay for assessment.

LESSON ONE: Famous Pirates

Purpose This lesson is an introduction to the concept of piracy. It begins with traditional book-based and Internet research on the lives of famous pirates, which lays the groundwork for subsequent lessons dealing with the more difficult concept of music piracy, enabling students to explore the concrete piracy of physical property before moving on to the more abstract piracy of intellectual property.

Duration Two class periods

Materials
Handout 7.1: Famous Pirates
Handout 7.2: Pirate Resources

Procedures
1. Briefly ask the students what they know about pirates: names, when and where they sailed, and why they did what they did. Ask students to define *pirate*.

2. Break up the class into groups or two or three and give students Handouts 7.1 and 7.2. Explain that each group will use books and the Internet to research the life of one famous pirate. Assign a pirate to each group. Go over the questions provided in Handout 7.1 intended to guide research. Point out Web site URLs on Handout 7.2. Emphasize that in addition to using these Web sites, students can enter the names of pirates on google.com, altavista.com, or yahoo.com (or some other search engine) to find information. Explain that each group will be responsible for a 3- to 5-minute oral presentation with at least one visual aid.

3. For homework ask students to complete their research and prepare oral presentations.

4. Have the students give oral presentations. Ask the class to listen for common themes. Point out that high-seas piracy still exists in some areas of the world.

LESSON TWO: Music Piracy and the Debate Over Napster

Purpose This lesson serves initially as a transition from the topic of piracy of the high seas to the piracy of high tech. Students distinguish *physical property* from *intellectual property*. They are then introduced to the concept of a *copyright* and the concept and real-world issue of *music piracy* via the Napster controversy. Discussion enables students to clarify the concepts and issues surrounding the debate over Napster.

Duration One class period

Materials
Handout 7.3: Music Piracy
Handout 7.4: The Debate Over Napster
Classroom computer with Internet connection (optional)

Procedures
1. Give students Handout 7.3. Read the handout together. Clarify the concepts of physical property, intellectual property, copyright, and music piracy.

2. Divide the class into pairs and allow the students to discuss the questions. Follow up with a whole-class check and discussion of each question.

3. Give students Handout 7.4. Check students for background knowledge about Napster. Ask if any student has used Napster, Kazaa, BearShare, LimeWire, or equivalents. Read the handout together. In particular, clarify what Napster and sites like it are, what they do, and why they are both popular and controversial.

4. Divide the class into new pairs and allow students to discuss the questions. Follow up with a whole-class check and discussion of each question.

5. If possible, and if not prohibited by your school's Internet use policy, log on to Napster or a similar site from a computer in your class just to see what you find.

6. Have students write out answers to the questions on Handouts 7.3 and 7.4.

LESSON THREE: Research/Preparation for Senate Panel Discussion

Purpose To research the different positions of stakeholders in the Napster controversy and then utilize this knowledge in a mock senate panel hearing.

Duration Two days (plus additional research time)

Materials
Handout 7.5: Team 1: Musicians Against Napster
Handout 7.6: Team 2: Musicians Supporting Napster
Handout 7.7: Team 3: Napster President Shawn Fanning
Handout 7.8: Team 4: The Recording Industry Association of America (RIAA)
Handout 7.9: Team 5: Senate Panel

Procedures
1. Divide the class into five teams. Provide each team with its corresponding handout from among Handouts 7.5–7.9.

2. Explain to students that music piracy and sites like Napster are very controversial issues with no clear answers. When the U.S. government wishes to explore a controversial issue like that of music piracy, it often convenes a *senate panel*, or a small group of senators assigned to listen to all sides of the controversy and to gather information for possible future action.

3. Have each team read its corresponding handout. Circulate and answer questions each group might have.

4. Point out to the class that the Food for Thought and Questions to Consider sections are intended to get each group to think about its side of the debate and the debate as a whole. Point out that each group has a couple of Web sites to get it started but that the bulk of the research should be done using the keywords provided with a search engine. Make sure that students know how to use a search engine and, if necessary, demonstrate.

5. Allow teams several days to research and prepare. Circulate and advise.

6. For homework ask students to research and prepare.

LESSON FOUR: Senate Panel Presentations

Purpose This lesson provides student teams the opportunity to present their cases to a student senate panel, whose job it is to ask probing questions designed to explore all sides of the Napster debate. The lesson is the culmination of several days of group preparations.

Duration One class period
Materials
Handout 7.10: Essay
Procedures

1. Arrange the room with the senate panel team in the front. Each team will be allowed to present its side of the issue, followed by exploratory questions from the senate panel. Write the two broad questions "Does using Napster and similar Web sites constitute music piracy?" and "Should Napster and similar Web sites be declared illegal and shut down?" on the board. Explain that no one should interrupt a team while it is presenting. Only members of the senate panel will ask questions following presentations.

2. After one round of presentations and questions, each team will be allowed a second round in which to respond to arguments made by other teams.

3. For assessment, ask students to write an essay considering the various points of view on the debate over companies like Napster that came to light in the senate panel presentations. The essay should answer the two broad questions posed in the presentations: Does using Napster or similar Web sites constitute music piracy? Should Napster and similar Web sites be declared illegal and shut down? Remember, it is not important which side you take. What is important is that you defend your side logically and support your opinion with solid evidence.

FAMOUS PIRATES

AAAAARRRGGHHH! Welcome to the world of high-seas plunder. Below is a list of famous pirates. Choose one, and using the Internet and books, prepare an oral presentation with pictures for the class. A list of possible Web sites is included in Handout 7.2, but better Web sites can be found by typing in the name of your pirate at search engines like google.com, altavista.com, or yahoo.com. Ask your teacher for help. Failure to do so will be punished by a walk down the gangplank into shark-infested water!

1. Henry Avery
2. Samuel Bellamy
3. Stede Bonnet
4. Anne Bonny Roberts
5. Cheng I Sao
6. Sir Francis Drake
7. William Kidd
8. Jean Lafitte
9. Henry Morgan
10. Grace O'Malley
11. Mary Read
12. Bartholomew Roberts
13. Calico Jack Rackham
14. Mary Read
15. Edward Teach (Blackbeard)
16. Thomas Tew

Questions to Consider

1. When did your pirate live? Where was your pirate from?

2. What did your pirate do before becoming a pirate?

3. How did your pirate become a pirate? How old was he or she? What motivated his or her actions? Do you sympathize with these reasons. Why?

4. What did your pirate do that made him or her famous?

5. Where and for how long was your pirate operating?

6. How was your pirate regarded in his or her day? Was your pirate feared? Respected? Beloved? Did different people have different opinions? Why?

7. What do you think of your pirate? Do you approve of his or her actions? Why?

Real World Investigations for Social Studies
Hoge, Field, Foster, and Nickell

Handout 7.2

PIRATE RESOURCES

Below are a list of Web sites and books that may be useful for pirate research. Typing in your pirate's name at search engines like google.com may turn up many additional treasures. If you are stumped, just ask your teacher. Happy hunting!

Web sites

http://www.piratesinfo.com/biography/biography.php
Pirate history, types of piracy, and individual pirates.

http://www.ability.org.uk/pirates.html
Extensive, detailed links to sites on individual pirates and related sites.

http://www.sonic.net/~press
Excellent links to sites on pirates, pirate literature, and pirate pictures.

Books

Konstam, A. (1999). *The history of pirates*. New York: Lyons Press.
Marley, D. F. (1994). *Pirates and privateers of the Americas* (2nd ed.). Santa Barbara, CA: ABC-CLIO
Roberts, N. (1994). *Blackbeard and other pirates of the Atlantic coast*. New York: John F. Blair.

MUSIC PIRACY

The heady days of high-seas piracy, of Edward Teach (Blackbeard) and Jean Lafitte, have largely receded into memory. (Some high-seas piracy still remains, especially in the South China Sea and the Strait of Malacca near Malaysia.) Nonetheless, the spirit of piracy remains, having for the most part abandoned the high seas of the 18th century for the high technology of the 21st century. Whereas 18th-century pirates stole *physical property* like ships or gold, however, many 21st-century pirates steal *intellectual property*, or information.

Intellectual property includes a song, or a movie, or a book created from an individual's imagination. Now, just as a person or a company can own a ship or gold, a person who writes a song or a company that makes a movie becomes the *owner* of that song or movie. That person or company can receive a *copyright* from the government. A copyright declares to the world the name of the person or company that owns the song or movie and forbids anyone from copying, distributing, or performing that song or movie without permission from the owner. Just as jumping into a stranger's car and taking it for a ride without permission can be considered stealing, so can copying, distributing, or performing a copyrighted song or a movie without permission.

Music piracy is a good example of new high-tech piracy. Music piracy simply means copying and selling someone else's music. Billions of dollars are made illegally each year by organized criminals, largely in Asia and Russia, who copy music CDs and sell them around the world at prices much lower than those at a CD store. Record companies and musicians lose a lot of money, but stopping illegal CD copying is very difficult. Sometimes it's difficult to say whether or not something actually *is* music piracy. For example, if someone uploads onto the Internet a CD she bought at a shop, and thousands of people download it onto their computers for free, would that be music piracy? Let's look at the case of Napster, a popular, controversial Web site that allows music fans to do just that.

Questions to Consider

1. What's the difference between physical property and intellectual property?

2. What are some examples of physical property? Of intellectual property?

continued

Real World Investigations for Social Studies
Hoge, Field, Foster, and Nickell

3. What is a copyright? Look at some books or CDs and find the copyright notice and marks. What do those copyright notices and marks mean?

4. Why do we have copyrights? Where does someone obtain a copyright?

5. What is a *patent*? Look up the word in a dictionary if you don't know. What's the difference between a copyright and a patent? What are some examples of a patent?

6. Define music piracy. Why is it difficult to define music piracy?

7. If someone downloads a music CD from the Internet, who might get angry? Why?

THE DEBATE OVER NAPSTER

It's hard to believe that an obscure 19-year-old college freshman could pose a serious threat to a powerful global multi-billion-dollar industry. Certainly Shawn Fanning never intended to do so. What started for Shawn as a project to enable friends to exchange CDs easily over the Internet, however, in the blink of an eye made thousands of rich, powerful music moguls blanch in horror. The object of their horror? Napster.

Shawn Fanning's software program, Napster, first hit the Internet in September 1999. It allowed users to search the CD music files stored on the computers of other users. When someone located a song or a CD he or she liked on another person's computer, he or she could download it onto his or her own computer. In a sense, the Napster program created a giant swap meet. If three people got together at someone's house to swap CDs, for example, no one would be bothered. Napster, however, allowed millions of people at once to come together *in cyberspace* to exchange "virtual CDs," and while this was similar in some respects to exchanging CDs at someone's house, the scale of the exchange was altered dramatically. In fact, within a short time it allowed more than 20 million people to swap virtual CDs. That *did* bother some people.

Questions to Consider

1. What do you know about Napster? Are there any similar Internet sites?

2. Why might music fans like a site like Napster?

3. Why might musicians and record companies be upset by a site like Napster?

Within months of Napster's startup, record companies and musicians began to take sides in favor of or in opposition to Napster. Most record companies, of course, opposed Napster and insisted that it be shut down. A group representing large record companies called the Recording Industry Association of America (RIAA) sued Napster for *copyright infringement*, or failure to honor copyright laws. The RIAA insisted that Napster allowed millions of people to obtain free virtual CDs illegally; therefore, Napster itself was illegal. Musicians, on the other hand, were divided. Lars Ulrich, the drummer for the heavy metal band Metallica, claimed that over 300,000 copies of his band's CD had been

continued

Real World Investigations for Social Studies
Hoge, Field, Foster, and Nickell

Handout 7.4 *continued*

illegally downloaded for free through Napster, driving him to sue Napster. Rapper Dr. Dre insisted that Napster prevented artists from making a living. Other musicians disagreed. Chuck D, front man for the rap group Public Enemy, argued that, like it or not, Napster and sites like it would become the radio of the 21st century and completely reshape the music business. Before the Internet and sites like Napster existed, musicians had little choice but to sell their music through record companies. Record companies made a lot of money by selling CDs at a very high price, but now they would have to change. Musicians could sell their works directly to fans without record company middlemen if they wanted, and they could sell the virtual CDs at a much lower price than fans would pay at a music store. Musicians like Fred Durst of Limp Bizkit, Courtney Love, and rock legend Neil Young agreed.

Questions to Consider

1. There are four large record companies in the United States. Why might they be afraid of a Web site like Napster?

2. Musicians seem to be divided in their attitudes toward Web sites like Napster. How do you explain some of these differing ideas?

3. Traditionally, the money paid for a CD at a store goes to record companies, which in turn pay musicians. From a successful musician's viewpoint, what might be good or bad about the traditional system? What might be the viewpoint of a little-known musician?

4. From a fan's viewpoint, what might be good or bad about the traditional distribution system? How can musicians make money without traditional record companies?

Real World Investigations for Social Studies
Hoge, Field, Foster, and Nickell

TEAM 1: MUSICIANS AGAINST NAPSTER

Your team will represent musicians against Napster before a senate panel convened to explore the Napster debate. The senate panel is seeking your opinion on two broad questions: Does using Napster and similar Web sites constitute music piracy? Should Napster and similar Web sites be declared illegal and shut down? Your job will be to gather background information and develop arguments against Napster and similar sites *from a musician's point of view.* Famous musicians like Lars Ulrich and Dr. Dre have come out against sites like Napster. Try to imagine the issue from their point of view. Better yet, imagine that your team is a famous band and consider what the debate would mean to you *personally.*

In order to help you prepare your position, some food for thought, questions to consider, and Web sites are provided below. In addition to going directly to the Web sites provided, you can conduct your own Web searches by entering keywords at search engines like google.com, altavista.com, yahoo.com, or another one you prefer. While defending your position, it is a good idea to imagine the points of view and possible arguments of the other teams, too, so that you can be better prepared to deal with their concerns during the senate panel meeting.

Food for Thought

- Lars Ulrich, drummer for Metallica, presented evidence that 300,000 copies of his band's CDs had been downloaded for free without the band's permission through Napster. Considering that musicians make $1 to $2 on every CD sold at a store, that's a lot of money the band lost.
- U.S. copyright law allows copying for personal use. You can legally share CDs with friends. Copyright law does not, however, allow mass copying, selling, or distribution of someone else's music.
- If Web sites like Napster are shut down, new and similar Web sites could open up tomorrow. If a company opened up outside of the United States, U.S. law could do nothing about it.

Questions to Consider

1. For many fans, a $17 CD is too expensive. Can you blame them for wanting to download virtual CDs through sites like Napster for free? Are record companies, in a sense, stealing from customers?

2. What kind of deal might major bands and others strike with owners of a Web site like Napster?

continued

3. What are the advantages to a band of using a major record company? What are the disadvantages?

4. There are only a few major record companies in the United States. Yet, there are thousands of unknown bands and musicians. If these bands and musicians can use a site like Napster to get their music out to the public, is it fair to shut such sites down?

5. U.S. copyright law allows swapping of CDs for personal use. Why would a site like Napster be considered illegal?

6. Are famous bands and musicians overpaid? A nurse earns about $30,000 a year, but famous bands make millions of dollars. Do famous musicians deserve so much money?

7. Why do some musicians support sites like Napster and others don't?

Web sites

http://www.kentlaw.edu/islt/ulrich.htm
Lars Ulrich explains his position on Napster to the U.S. Senate.

http://www.businessweek.com/ebiz/0005/0525ulrich.htm
Lars Ulrich and Chuck D debate Napster.

Keywords for Search Engines

napster, napster debate, napster and lars ulrich, napster and dr dre, napster and musicians, napster and royalties, napster and law

Real World Investigations for Social Studies
Hoge, Field, Foster, and Nickell

TEAM 2: MUSICIANS SUPPORTING NAPSTER

Your team will represent musicians in support of Napster before a senate panel convened to explore the Napster debate. The senate panel is seeking your opinion on two broad questions: Does using Napster or similar Web sites constitute music piracy? Should Napster and similar Web sites be declared illegal and shut down? Your job will be to gather background information and develop arguments in support of Napster and similar sites *from a musician's point of view.* While famous musicians like Chuck D, Courtney Love, Limp Bizkit, and Neil Young have all come out in support of sites like Napster, keep in mind that there are thousands of little-known or unknown musicians who also support them. Try to imagine the issue from their point of view. Better yet, imagine that your team is a band and consider what the debate would mean to you *personally.*

In order to help you to prepare your position, some food for thought, questions to consider, and keywords to use at search engines like google.com, altavista.com, yahoo.com, or another one you prefer are provided. While defending your position, it is a good idea to imagine the points of view and possible arguments of the other teams, too, so that you can be better prepared to deal with their concerns during the senate panel meeting.

Food for Thought

- Record companies charge fans on average $12 to $17 for new CDs at a store, yet musicians receive only $1 to $2 of that price. The rest of the money goes for packaging, shipment, marketing, and, of course, profits for the record company.
- There are tens of thousands of undiscovered musicians in the United States alone. It is very difficult to get a contract with a major record company, which is necessary for mass radio play. Sites like Napster allow such musicians to get their music out to people without record companies.
- Like it or not, the Internet is here to stay. Even if sites like Napster are shut down, Internet experts say, new companies doing the same thing could open tomorrow. If a company opened up outside the United States, it could not be controlled by U.S. law.

Questions to Consider

1. How can musicians make money if people download CDs from Napster for free?

2. What kind of deal could your band and others strike with a company like Napster?

continued

Real World Investigations for Social Studies
Hoge, Field, Foster, and Nickell

3. What advantage would there be for a band to distribute music through a company like Napster rather than through a traditional record company?

4. Many musicians might lose a lot of money if Web sites like Napster remain. Is that fair?

5. If your music was being traded on the Internet and you received no money, how would you feel? Would you try to stop it?

6. Is it stealing to download someone else's music without permission for free?

7. Why do some musicians support sites like Napster and others don't?

Keywords for Search Engines

music piracy, music swapping, CD burners, MP3 download, Kazaa, BearShare, Morpheus, Grokster, Gnutella, LimeWire, Phex, napster, napster and chuck d, lars ulrich and chuck d, napster and musicians, napster and royalties, napster and law, cd sales and napster, music and money

TEAM 3: NAPSTER PRESIDENT SHAWN FANNING

Your team will represent Napster founder and CEO Shawn Fanning before a senate panel convened to explore the Napster debate. The senate panel is seeking your opinion on two broad questions: Does using Napster or similar Web sites constitute music piracy? Should Napster and similar Web sites be declared illegal and shut down? Your job will be to gather background information and develop arguments in support of sites like Napster *from Napster's/Shawn Fanning's point of view.* Try to imagine that you really are Shawn Fanning, and consider what you would think and feel if you were in his position.

In order to help you to prepare your position, some food for thought, questions to consider, and Web sites are provided below. In addition to going directly to the Web sites provided, you can conduct your own Web searches by entering keywords at search engines like google.com, altavista.com, yahoo.com, or another one you prefer. While defending your position, it is a good idea to imagine the points of view and possible arguments of the other teams, too, so that you can be better prepared to deal with their concerns during the senate panel meeting.

Food for Thought

- Record companies charge fans on average $12 to $17 for new CDs at a store, yet musicians receive only $1 to $2 of that price. The rest of the money goes for packaging, shipment, marketing, and, of course, profits for the record company. Sites like Napster cut out the middleman. Though many fans now download music for free, in the future it may be possible to create a system in which fans pay $3 to $4 to companies like Napster, which in turn give some of the money to musicians. Fans would get inexpensive music, and musicians would get their money. Because sites like Napster would be much cheaper, fans could afford to buy much more music than they can now.

- There are tens of thousands of undiscovered musicians in the United States alone. It is very difficult to get a contract with a major record company, which is necessary for mass radio play. Sites like Napster allow such musicians to get their music out to the public without having to go through large record companies.

- Like it or not, the Internet is here to stay. Even if sites like Napster are shut down, Internet experts say, new companies doing the same thing could open tomorrow. If a company opened up outside the United States, it could not be controlled by U.S. law.

Questions to Consider

1. How can musicians make money if people download CDs from sites like Napster for free?

continued

Handout 7.7 *continued*

2. CDs at music stores are expensive. Are fans justified in downloading free music from Napster or some other site if they can? How would you defend against the charge that fans are, in a sense, using sites like Napster to steal?

3. What advantage would there be for a band to distribute music through a site like Napster rather than through a traditional record company?

4. Companies like Napster claim that they do not sell music, so they are breaking no laws. Sites like Napster are giant cyberspace flea markets. Can you defend this description?

5. Napster and similar companies make money by selling advertising on their Web sites. However, what attracts millions of people to these sites is the work of other people, namely, musicians. Is it right for companies like Napster to profit from other people's work without paying?

6. Why do some musicians support sites like Napster and others don't?

Web sites

http://judiciary.senate.gov/oldsite/1092000_sf.htm
Shawn Fanning explains his position on the Napster debate to the U.S. Senate.

http://www.observer.co.uk/review/story/0,6903,223075,00.html
Article and interview with Shawn Fanning.

Keywords for Search Engines

napster, napster debate, shawn fanning, napster and law, music and law, riaa and napster, napster and senate panel, cd sales and napster, napster and music business

TEAM 4: THE RECORDING INDUSTRY ASSOCIATION OF AMERICA (RIAA)

Your team will represent the RIAA before a senate panel convened to explore the debate over Napster. The senate panel is seeking your opinion on two broad questions: Does using Napster and similar Web sites constitute music piracy? Should Napster and similar Web sites be declared illegal and shut down? Your job will be to gather background information and develop arguments against sites like Napster *from the RIAA's point of view.*

Try to imagine that you work for a large record company, and that companies like Napster may put your company out of business and cost you your job. What would you think and feel?

In order to help you to prepare your position, some food for thought, questions to consider, and Web sites are provided below. In addition to going directly to the Web sites provided, you can conduct your own Web searches by entering keywords at search engines like google.com, altavista.com, yahoo.com, or another one you prefer. While defending your position, it is a good idea to imagine the points of view and possible arguments of the other teams, too, so that you can

be better prepared to deal with their concerns during the senate panel meeting.

Food for Thought

- Record companies charge fans on average $12 to $17 for new CDs at a store, yet musicians only receive $1 to $2 of that price. The rest of the money goes for packaging, shipment, marketing, salaries, and, of course, profits for the record company. Many fans can't afford to pay $17 for CDs, and musicians receive only a small percentage of the CD price.

- There are tens of thousands of undiscovered musicians in the United States alone. It is very difficult to get a contract with a major record company, which is necessary for mass radio play. Companies like Napster allow such musicians to get their music out to the public without having to go through large record companies.

- Like it or not, the Internet is here to stay. Even if sites like Napster are shut down, Internet experts say, new companies doing the same thing could open tomorrow. If a company opened up outside the United States, it could not be controlled by U.S. law.

Questions to Consider

1. Why did musicians need record companies in the past? Are these needs still valid?

2. Many people believe that CDs sold at music stores are expensive. Are fans justified in downloading free music from a site like Napster if they can? How would you defend against the charge that record companies overcharge for CDs?

continued

Real World Investigations for Social Studies
Hoge, Field, Foster, and Nickell

3. When new technologies arise, old technologies die. When automobiles became popular, horse carriage companies went out of business. It's natural to cling to life as long as possible. Is that what record companies are doing by suing companies like Napster?

4. Napster and similar companies claim that they do not sell music, so they are breaking no laws. Napster and similar sites are giant cyberspace flea markets. How would the RIAA argue against this claim? How are sites like Napster breaking the law?

5. Once new technology appears, it can't be uninvented. Can suing a company like Napster solve the RIAA's long-term problems? Would it be smarter to work with the new technology rather than against it?

6. Why do some musicians support sites like Napster and others don't? If record companies are so good for musicians, why do many musicians support sites like Napster?

Web sites

http://www.ascap.com/musicbiz/
Very thorough site explaining the structure of the music business and how artists are compensated.

http://www.riaa.org/Napster.cfm
RIAA site explaining its position against Napster.

Keywords for Search Engines

napster, napster debate, riaa and napster, lars ulrich and chuck d, napster and law, music and law, music and money, cd sales and napster, napster and music business

Real World Investigations for Social Studies
Hoge, Field, Foster, and Nickell

TEAM 5: SENATE PANEL

Your team makes up the senate panel. A senate panel is a small group of senators chosen from within the U.S. Senate to explore complicated, controversial issues of national importance. The job of the senate panel is to listen to all sides of a debate and to ask questions to help everyone get a clearer picture of the issues and concerns. It's not your job to judge who is right or wrong but rather to gather information to help explore two broad questions: Does using Napster or similar Web sites constitute music piracy? Should Napster and similar sites be declared illegal and shut down? In a sense, your job is the most challenging of all: to try to see the debate from everyone's point of view.

In order to help you prepare for the debate, your team will also receive the handouts of the four other teams. It's your job to look over the food for thought items and questions to consider and to go to Web sites for further information. Familiarize yourself with the basics of copyright law, how music was distributed in the past and could be distributed in the future, the price of CDs, how musicians are paid, how record companies make money, and why sites like Napster became so popular with music fans so quickly. As you do so, prepare a list of questions you would like to ask each of the four teams when the senate panel convenes. Remember, there are no clear right or wrong answers. It's your job to help everyone think about a possible fair solution to a sticky, complicated real-world problem that touches and will continue to touch the lives of musicians and music fans everywhere.

Web sites

http://www.ascap.com
Explains the role of ASCAP in the music business.

http://www.music-law.com/home.htm
A lawyer explains the basics of music law.

http://www.edu-cyberpg.com/Music/musiclaw.html
Great source for understanding the basics of music and copyright law.

http://www.kentlaw.edu/islt/ulrich.htm
Lars Ulrich explains his position against Napster to the U.S. Senate.

http://www.businessweek.com/ebiz/0005/0525ulrich.htm
Lars Ulrich and Chuck D debate about Napster.

http://www.riaa.org/Napster.cfm
The RIAA explains its position against Napster.

http://www.riaa.com/Protect-Campaign-1.cfm
RIAA information on music piracy.

Keywords for Search Engines

napster, napster and law, napster and senate panel, napster and congress, napster debate, napster and lars ulrich, napster and chuck d, riaa and napster, cd sales and napster, music and money, music and law.

Real World Investigations for Social Studies
Hoge, Field, Foster, and Nickell

To Be or Not to Be

The Zoo Is the Question

by

Carolyn Lyon

OVERVIEW

The survival of animal and plant species across the world is in jeopardy. This chapter explores the possible role of zoos in reversing the threat to wildlife and tries to determine whether or not zoos have any legitimacy in the modern world. Students first examine and interpret the meaning of a picture showing animals housed in an ark and of a poem concerning animal life in zoos. Then, students conduct an investigation of endangered animal species, which are part of the Species Survival Plan run in American Zoological and Aquarium Association (AZA) accredited zoos. Students then take on the role of detective as they try to determine why a captive population of flamingos is losing the pink coloration in its feathers. After solving this mystery, students consider the role of zoos in today's world. Are zoos morally defensible? If they are, under what conditions can their existence be justified? Students debate this topic and advance a cogent argument on both sides of the issue. Finally, students take on the role of photojournalists as they produce a documentary based on an examination and evaluation of a local zoo.

CONNECTION TO NCSS THEME VIII: SCIENCE, TECHNOLOGY, AND SOCIETY

The NCSS recommends that social studies programs include multiple learning experiences that provide for learning about the important connections among science, technology, and society. This theme appears repeatedly as students study history, government, and economics. However, the NCSS recommends that students be given opportunities to confront issues that challenge established beliefs about society's use of scientific knowledge and technology. By examining historic and present-day zoo practices, students gain important insights into people's understanding of nature and their efforts to both protect and display it. Long gone are the days when virtually any use of science or technology seemed unquestionably good. Once little more than a form of entertainment, zoos have evolved to meet higher standards and use science and technology to benefit both people and animals.

METHODS FOCUS: HIGHER-ORDER THINKING

Curriculum and instruction experts have long advocated fostering various forms of higher-order thinking (HOT) as an important goal of education. HOT instruction has been defined somewhat differently by various authors over the years, but it is often associated with creative, critical, and evaluative thinking directed toward making complex decisions or solving real-world problems (Beyer, 1985; Kerka, 1992). Within the field of social studies, various forms of HOT, along with guidelines for making social studies meaningful (NCSS, 1994) and thoughtful, are held to be essential skills for fulfilling the duties of citizenship in our increasingly complex and diverse democracy (Engle & Ochoa, 1988; Parker, 1996).

Newmann (1990) writes that a classroom disposition toward thoughtfulness is essential for the development of HOT skills. This disposition toward thoughtful reasoning engenders the desire to look below the surface, to search for meaning and connections that are not readily apparent, to explore alternative solutions, and to support claims with evidence.

In order to create a classroom environment where a disposition toward thoughtfulness is nurtured, teachers must understand the components of this milieu. Research indicates that thoughtful classrooms share some distinctive characteristics. Specifically, thoughtfulness is fostered in classrooms where teachers move beyond the use of coverage-oriented lectures, textbook readings, and worksheets that are designed mainly to convey information required for recall-oriented tests. Thoughtfulness is developed when teachers begin to engage students' minds through the use of open-ended questions and the research-oriented activities required to find answers. Thoughtful classrooms are also characterized by the use of various forms of group and cooperative learning tasks that require students to engage in a sustained investigation of important questions, issues, or problems. Teachers closely monitor students' work and engage their classes in deliberative discussions (Hess, 2002) where ideas are clarified, assertions are carefully inspected, and evidence is subjected to rigorous tests for relevance, bias, accuracy, and timeliness. In this type of classroom, the teacher becomes a living example of how a person behaves and responds when he or she has highly developed reasoning skills and uses them not only to arrive at well-informed personal judgments, but also to humanely promote high-quality thinking among everyone as a means of achieving a better society and world. In this way, the teacher serves as a constant reminder, guide, and yardstick of sorts for students as they strive to become thinking, reasoning individuals.

Of course, thoughtful classrooms and instruction aimed at promoting HOT cannot limit students' sources of authoritative information to the readings contained in a single textbook. Students must be encouraged to use a wide variety of primary and secondary source documents that can be found in their media center, in local libraries, or on the Internet. Contacts with experts from industry, advocacy groups, or government may also be necessary and advisable, and these sources of information should be subjected to the same tests for accuracy, bias, and relevance as other sources.

As students begin to develop a more sophisticated understanding of their subject, it is necessary and appropriate for the teacher to help them continue to refine the meanings that they give to key terms and to justify their responses, inferences, and assertions. Only by being so challenged will students come to develop more critical minds and a more sophisticated frame of reference that are keys to thoughtfulness. Requiring students to articulate their thoughts fully by stating them is important. However, it is equally important to use a variety of writing assignments (e.g., case notes, glossaries of terms, position papers, editorials) to further develop students' thinking. As we all have experienced, getting words into writing is an important aid to critical thinking, as well as being a HOT skill that is valuable in its own right.

The kind of HOT instruction being advocated here is clearly challenging and authentic in that it engages students in tasks that are similar to those used by many professionals. HOT instruction can easily be infused into traditional history, government, geography, and economics instruction. For example, in history classes, students can be asked to do more explaining of the past and hypothetical thinking about the context of events. In government classes, students should be challenged to justify why certain policies should be left alone, altered, or eliminated. Geography, economics, government, and history can be elevated to HOT instruction by engaging students in a case-based examination of our society's practices with regard to the storage and/or disposal of hazardous wastes.

According to Potts (1994), teachers who wish to engage students in HOT should frequently challenge students to gather, use, and evaluate information. In doing so, they should explicitly note the relationships among things, develop rules for classifying items similarly, and frequently use and explain analogies. To accomplish this kind of intellectual work, Olsen (1995) recommends a variety of strategies, including concept mapping, KWL (what I *Know*, *Want* to know, and what I *Learned*) charts, encouraging the statement of inferences, and using graphics to organize and express relationships. Wilen and Phillips (1995) stress the use of metacognitive tactics (becoming aware of one's thinking practices, skills, and processes) as an additional tool for increasing students' critical thinking abilities.

It should be noted that values, beliefs, and attitudes play an important role in HOT. Indeed, we cannot advance advocacy arguments, criticisms, or most other forms of HOT in the social sciences and humanities without the interference of personal and cultural biases that find their roots in values, beliefs, and attitudes. Accordingly, teachers should help students explicitly inspect these elements as they play their often hidden roles in our judgments. Wright (1995) reviewed four classic tests of fairness in his article on critical thinking in social studies.

The first and perhaps the most basic test simply asks students to engage in a substitution or role-reversal exercise. In this test, students are asked to reformulate their judgments by switching terms with their polar opposites (e.g., *rich people* in a sentence is altered to read *poor people; athletes* is switched to *nerds;* etc.). If students feel different about the judgment when confronted with the change, they should be led to examine their thinking further. One way of accomplishing this task is to invoke the power of what is often termed a *subsumption test,* which is applied to justify a position on the basis of its logical and perhaps causal

relationship to some other higher value or cause. The final two tests are the *new cases test*, which extends the judgment to a slightly different situation or context, and the *related universal consequences test,* which projects the results of the judgment progressively to more and more situations and contexts to see if its logic and principles hold for everyone everywhere.

Teachers may also relate HOT to the upper levels of Bloom's (1984) taxonomy. Analysis (the ability to break something down into its component parts), synthesis (the combining of parts to create something new), and evaluation (making a judgment about something based on set criteria) are fundamental skills of reasoning and are necessary to the other types of critical thinking discussed above. This chapter employs all three of these HOT skills.

Analysis is demonstrated in the first lesson, which has students look at a cartoon of animals on an ark. Some of the questions asked of students as they scrutinize the drawing are: What does the ark signify? What does the trash in the foreground symbolize? Where is the ark sitting? Is there any significance to its resting place? What message is the artist trying to convey? Justify your answer using specific components of the cartoon. These questions ask students to break the cartoon down into its component parts and examine each one in relation to the other components and in relation to the overall cartoon. In this way, students find meaning in the cartoon that is not expressed concretely in any of the images.

Synthesis is used during Lesson Three, in which students are engaged in a project on endangered species. In order to complete this project, students must gather information from a variety of sources and then determine how to put the pieces together to form a suitable whole. Part of this project is to write a poem about the chosen animal that deals with one or more of the following themes:

- The animal and its struggle to survive in the wild
- The animal's habits
- The animal's life in a zoo
- The animal in relation to human beings

Evaluation is demonstrated in Lesson Six, an investigative documentary of a local zoo. The question students must answer when they have finished their investigation is: Should this zoo continue to exist as it is today or should it be closed? Students gather photographic and other evidence to assess the quality of the local zoo and use the AZA standards as the basis for their evaluation. After comparing their findings to the AZA standards, students make their final determination on whether or not the zoo should be allowed to exist in its present form.

Table 8.1 Lesson Overview for "To Be or Not to Be: The Zoo Is the Question"

	GOALS	ACTIVITIES	ASSESSMENTS
LESSON ONE	• Identify sources of danger that threaten animal survival in the wild. Determine why zoos are often referred to as arks.	• Examine a drawing of an ark (Handout 8.1). • Determine the meaning of the picture as it relates to zoos and wildlife preservation (using the questions in Handout 8.2 as a guide).	• Collect and evaluate students' answers to questions concerning the drawing of the ark.
LESSON TWO	• Consider the consequences of failing to protect animal life outside of zoos.	• Determine the meaning of a poem by norman h russell jr. (Handout 8.3). Compare this poem to the drawing from Lesson One and discuss the similarities and the differences in meaning.	• Evaluate a short essay in which students compare and contrast the meanings of the drawing in Handout 8.1 and the poem in Handout 8.3.
LESSON THREE	• Increase students' knowledge of the role some zoos are taking to preserve endangered animals.	• Select, from Handout 8.4, an animal that has a Species Survival Plan being implemented by American zoos and put together a research project on this animal (using Handout 8.5).	• Evaluate students' research projects and class presentations.
LESSON FOUR	• Solve a mystery involving the care of a fictional zoo's population of flamingos. • Develop an understanding of some of the factors zoos must consider when caring for captive animals.	• Examine a number of factual clues concerning flamingo development and survival in the wild in an attempt to determine why a captive population of flamingos is losing the color in its feathers (Handout 8.6).	• Evaluate justification essays in which students answer the questions of why the zoo's flamingos are losing their pink coloration.
LESSON FIVE	• Weigh arguments for and against the continued existence of zoos. • Develop and defend a position on the existence of zoos.	• Study information that supports either the continued existence of zoos or the eradication of zoos (Handout 8.7), as well as a list of ethical considerations in dealing with captive animals (Handout 8.8). Debate the question "Are zoos morally defensible?"	• Evaluate a paper in which students defend a position on the moral legitimacy of the continued existence of zoos.
LESSON SIX	• Use the tools of photojournalism to examine and evaluate the quality of a local zoo.	• Visit a local zoo. Take photographs of animals and exhibits in the zoo. • Construct a documentary on the zoo based on the photographic and textual evidence students gather.	• Evaluate a documentary about the quality of a local zoo, which students construct using textual evidence presented in Lesson Four, as well as photographs and interview evidence gathered on a field trip (Handout 8.9).

LESSON ONE: Picture Interpretation

Purpose This lesson is designed to have students determine one of the strongest justifications for the existence of zoos and to identify some sources of danger that threaten animal survival in the wild.

Duration One class period

Materials
Handout 8.1: A Modern Ark
Handout 8.2: Questions to Accompany "A Modern Ark."

Procedures Students may do this exercise individually or in groups of two to three. The teacher should make this determination based on the needs of students in his or her classroom.

1. Give each student or group of students a copy of the drawing "A Modern Ark" (Handout 8.1).
2. Students should then try to determine the meaning of this picture. They can be given as little or as much guidance as the teacher deems necessary. A list of questions can be used to guide students in their evaluation of the picture (Handout 8.2). Students' responses to the questions should be written.
3. Guide the class in a discussion of the meaning of the drawing. Written responses may be collected before the discussion or can be left with students to facilitate the discussion.

LESSON TWO: Interpretation of a Poem

Purpose This lesson asks students to analyze a poem. In doing this, students will need to consider the consequences of failing to preserve wildlife and their habitats outside of zoos.

Duration One class period

Materials
Handout 8.3: in the valley of the tiger
Handout 8.1: A Modern Ark (from Lesson One). It will be needed for the homework exercise.

Procedures
1. Read the poem "in the valley of the tiger" by norman h russell jr. (Handout 8.3) to the class.
2. Give a copy of the poem to each student. Have students analyze the poem and write a paragraph explaining what the author was trying to communicate. The teacher might wish to phrase the question this way: "What is the main idea the author is trying to communicate in this poem? Explain thoroughly, using words or phrases from the poem to substantiate your opinion."

3. Divide the class into pairs to discuss their interpretations. Students may add to their paragraphs if they wish to do so.
4. Discuss as a class the meaning of the poem. Collect students' paragraphs before the discussion if desired.
5. For homework have students compare this poem to the drawing they analyzed at the beginning of this unit. Both the picture and the poem make reference to zoos. Have students consider and address the following questions as they write an essay comparing the poem and the drawing:

a. Does the picture express the same feeling as the poem? What is the mood established by each?
b. What message(s) do the picture and poem convey about zoos? In what way(s) is/are the message(s) similar? In what ways do they differ?

Students should use lines from the poem and details of the drawing to substantiate their opinions.

LESSON THREE: Endangered Animal Investigation

Purpose This lesson is designed to increase student knowledge of the plight of endangered animals around the world and of the role some American zoos are playing in protecting and preserving these species. It is hoped that through research, students might be motivated to take action, wherever they can, to protect endangered wildlife and the environment, which supports that life.

Duration Three to 4 days
Materials
Handout 8.4: List of Threatened and Endangered Species That Have Species Survival Plans Run by American Zoos
Handout 8.5: Guidelines for Endangered Animal Research Project
(Handout 8.3, "in the valley of the tiger," from Lesson Two, may be used as an example.)

Procedures Give students a list of endangered species (Handout 8.4). Have each student select an animal he or she is interested in learning more about. Alternatively, students can do this assignment in pairs.

1. Give students the list of project requirements (Handout 8.5). Add any other guidelines necessary to tailor the project to the needs of your classes.

2. Read students the poem "the old man and the orangutan."

the old man
hand over foot up the tallest vine
climbed to the top of the tallest tree
hung by a hand and a foot
scratched himself looked down

the red whiskers grew out of his face
his leathery toes curled
he scratched his hairy back
on the highest limb of the tallest tree
and he looked out and away
where there ought to be mountains

the old man swung down the tree
the old man moved from tree to tree
the jungle reached its fruits
out to him
the old man learned everything there is to know
the old man learned
when they caught him in a net
when they put him in a cage
when they laughed at him
the old man learned
not to fight
not to cry
not to laugh.

Reprinted by permission of the author, norman h. russell, jr.

Students may also use the poem from Lesson Two (Handout 8.3) as an example for the poem they will write as part of their research project. Read both of these poems to students while referring to the project guideline sheet (Handout 8.5). Show students how these poems fulfill the requirements on the handout.

LESSON FOUR: The Case of the Fading Feathers

Purpose Through solving a mystery, students gain an understanding of the difficulties involved in reproducing a natural environment for captive animals. Students analyze a number of seemingly unconnected facts in an attempt to figure out why Lesser Flamingos being kept in the Ersatz Zoo are losing their pink coloration.

Duration One class period

Materials
Handout 8.6: Clues for the Case of the Fading
    Feathers
Manila envelopes
Scissors

Procedures
1. Make copies of Handout 8.6. It is suggested that students do this exercise in pairs, so the number of copies required will be half that of the number of students in the class.

2. The clues in Handout 8.6 should be cut apart so that each pair of students can move them around to show connections. Each pair of students should have all of the clues. Place the clues in a manila envelope. One envelope will be handed to each pair of students at the beginning of the exercise.

3. Explain to students that the Ersatz Zoo (fictional) has in its care a flock of Lesser Flamingos. When the flamingos arrived at the zoo their feathers were pink, but now they have started to fade to white. The zoo has collected information concerning flamingo development and survival in the wild, hoping that these facts contain clues that will lead to a solution to the Case of the Fading Feathers. The students' job is to determine why the feathers are losing their pink coloration and to hypothesize about what the zoo could do to reverse the process.

4. The following questions should be asked of students:
Mystery Questions
- Why are the Lesser Flamingos' feathers losing their pink coloration?
- In the Great Rift Valley in Africa, Greater and Lesser Flamingos occupy much of the same territory, yet the Lesser Flamingos have a darker pink color than the Greater Flamingos. What is the reason for the difference in coloration?

Other Questions
- How can the Ersatz Zoo restore the pink color of the Lesser Flamingos' feathers?
- What does this exercise tell you about zoos and the care of captive animals?

(Answers to these questions can be inferred from the exercise.)

5. Students should be told that they must use the evidence available to justify their solution to the mystery. The strength of their justification should be the emphasis of this exercise.

LESSON FIVE: The Great Zoo Debate

Purpose This lesson is designed to expose students to the arguments for and against the continued existence of zoos. Students will weigh the arguments on both sides of this issue and develop an opinion that they will justify using evidence from the debate.

Duration Two class periods

Materials
Handout 8.7: Debate Information Sheet
Handout 8.8: Ethical Issues in Dealing with
   Captive Animals

Procedures
   1. Pose these questions to students:
      a. Is the continued existence of zoos justified?
      b. If the existence of zoos is justified, under what conditions are they morally defensible?
   2. Divide the class into groups of three or four students.
   3. Have students read the debate information sheets (Handout 8.7). For purposes of this debate, arguments will be made only about zoos accredited by the AZA.
   4. Based on the information sheets (and any outside sources the teacher wishes to add), have students, while in groups, develop arguments that attempt to justify the continued existence of zoos and arguments that support the eradication of zoos. Separate lists should be made of the arguments for and against the existence of AZA-accredited zoos. A recorder should be selected by the group to write the position statements as they are compiled.
   5. Collect the completed lists. Stack together all of the lists supporting the continued existence of zoos and then stack together all of the lists supporting the eradication of zoos.
   6. Divide the class into two groups, one supporting zoos, the other disapproving of them. Give each group the stack of lists containing arguments supporting the position that group will be representing during the debate. Using the lists developed in the smaller groups, students should rank the various arguments according to their relative strengths. The goal is to put together a strong justification of their position.
   7. Once the large groups have completed their work, each group will select two spokespersons to debate the issue of zoos and their place in modern society.
   8. Monitor the debate, making sure that each side has a legitimate opportunity to present its case.
   9. Assign to the other students in the class the task of taking notes on the arguments/evidence presented. Students may also formulate questions to ask the debaters. At the end of the debate, these students will vote on which side made the stronger defense of its position.
   10. Collect papers from students.
   11. Students will now address the second issue: Assuming that the existence of zoos can be justified, under what conditions are they morally defensible? (This issue should be discussed regardless of the outcome of the debate.) Give Handout 8.8 to students. This handout covers ethical concerns when dealing with captive animals. Allow students to discuss the handout, and its implications for zoos, in groups of three or four. Then conduct a whole-class discussion about this issue.
   12. For homework ask students to write a paper in which they state their opinion about the continued existence of zoos. Use evidence from the handouts to justify your position. Consider both AZA-accredited and non-AZA-accredited zoos in your response.

Resources for Lesson Five Handouts

Beck, B. (1995). Reintroduction, zoos, conservation, and animal welfare. In B. Norton, M. Hutchins, E. Stevens, & T. Maple (Eds.), *Ethics on the ark* (pp. 155–163). Washington, DC: Smithsonian Institution Press.

Conway, W. (1995). Zoo conservation and ethical paradoxes. In B. Norton, M. Hutchins, E. Stevens, & T. Maple (Eds.), *Ethics on the ark* (pp. 1–9). Washington, DC: Smithsonian Institution Press.

Geist, V. (1995). Noah's ark II: Rescuing species and ecosystems. In B. Norton, M. Hutchins, E. Stevens, & T. Maple (Eds.), *Ethics on the ark* (pp. 93–101). Washington, DC: Smithsonian Institution Press.

Hancocks, D. (1995). Lions and tigers and bears, oh no! In B. Norton, M. Hutchins, E. Stevens, & T. Maple (Eds.), *Ethics on the ark* (pp. 31–37). Washington, DC: Smithsonian Institution Press.

Hargrove, E. (1995). The role of zoos in the twenty-first century. In B. Norton, M. Hutchins, E. Stevens, & T. Maple (Eds.), *Ethics on the ark* (pp. 13–19). Washington, DC: Smithsonian Institution Press.

Jamieson, D. (1995). Zoos revisited. In B. Norton, M. Hutchins, E. Stevens, & T. Maple (Eds.), *Ethics on the ark* (pp. 52–66). Washington, DC: Smithsonian Institution Press.

Loftin, R. (1995). Captive breeding of endangered species. In B. Norton, M. Hutchins, E. Stevens, & T. Maple (Eds.), *Ethics on the ark* (pp. 164–180). Washington, DC: Smithsonian Institution Press.

Maple, T. (1995). Toward a responsible zoo agenda. In B. Norton, M. Hutchins, E. Stevens, & T. Maple (Eds.), *Ethics on the ark* (pp. 20–30). Washington, DC: Smithsonian Institution Press.

Maple, T., McManamon, R., & Stevens, E. (1995). Defining the good zoo: Animal care, maintenance, and welfare. In B. Norton, M. Hutchins, E. Stevens, & T. Maple (Eds.), *Ethics on the ark* (pp. 219–234). Washington, DC: Smithsonian Institution Press.

McKenna, V., Travers, W., & Wray, J. (Eds.). (1987). *Beyond the bars: The zoo dilemma.* Rochester, VT: Thorsons.

Norton, B. (1995). Caring for nature: A broader look at animal stewardship. In B. Norton, M. Hutchins, E. Stevens, & T. Maple (Eds.), *Ethics on the ark* (pp. 102–121). Washington, DC: Smithsonian Institution Press.

Regan, T. (1995). Are zoos morally defensible? In B. Norton, M. Hutchins, E. Stevens, & T. Maple (Eds.), *Ethics on the ark* (pp. 38–51). Washington, DC: Smithsonian Institution Press.

Wuichet, J., & Norton, B. (1995). Differing conceptions of animal welfare. In B. Norton, M. Hutchins, E. Stevens, & T. Maple (Eds.), *Ethics on the ark* (pp. 235–250). Washington, DC: Smithsonian Institution Press.

LESSON SIX: Photojournalist for a Day

Purpose In this lesson, students use information about the accepted standards of care for captive animals to evaluate the quality of a local zoo. Students will gain experience in using visuals and text materials to make a persuasive presentation of their point of view on an issue. In this case, the issue will be whether or not a local zoo meets the AZA standards for captive animal care.

Duration Field trip plus 2 days for preparation of documentaries and oral presentations

Materials
Handout 8.9: Guidelines for the Photojournalism Project
Disposable cameras
Tri-boards

Procedures
1. Plan a field trip to a local zoo. Consider calling the zoo to see if any of the keepers or other staff members would be willing to answer students' questions.
2. Each student will need a disposable camera. Alternatively, two or three students could share a camera or students could bring cameras from home.
3. Review with students the guidelines for the project (Handout 8.9). Make sure that students understand the purpose of the field trip.
4. Students should wander around the zoo taking pictures of the grounds, the exhibits, and the animals. Remind students that they should photograph objects or animals which demonstrate quality aspects of the zoo as well as aspects of the zoo that appear to fall below AZA standards. Students should also look for evidence of abnormal behaviors by animals at the zoo.
5. When the film is developed, have students, in groups of two or three, put together a documentary on the zoo using photographs and textual evidence (from Lesson Four and from any interviews done with zoo staff) to support their position on the quality of the zoo.
6. Student groups will present their documentaries to the class.
7. Conduct a whole-class discussion of the findings from the exercise. Should this zoo continue to exist as it is? If not, what could be done to change the conditions at the zoo?

A MODERN ARK

Drawing courtesy of Mary Gail Lyon.

QUESTIONS TO ACCOMPANY "A MODERN ARK"

1. What does the ark signify?

2. Why is the word *zoo* written on the side of the ark?

3. Where is the ark sitting? Is there any significance to its resting place?

4. What kinds of animals are on or near the ark?

5. Most of the animals are in pairs. What does this add to the overall meaning of the drawing?

6. Describe the landscape around the ark.

7. What does the trash in the foreground symbolize?

8. What is happening behind and to the left of the ark? What is happening in front of and to the right of the ark? Are these two things related in any way?

9. What message is the artist trying to convey? Justify your answer using specific components of the drawing.

10. Do you think this artist believes that the existence of zoos is justified? Why or why not?

IN THE VALLEY OF THE TIGER

in the valley of the tiger
a stream flows
a tree grows
but it has no leaves

in the ocean of the polar bear
cold currents run
winters come
but there is no ice

on the mountains of the goat
grass grows
calls of crows
but there is no panther

on the earth of the man
grass grows streams flow calls of crows
winters come oceans run
but there is no tiger

Reprinted by permission of the author, norman h. russell, jr.

LIST OF THREATENED AND ENDANGERED SPECIES THAT HAVE SPECIES SURVIVAL PLANS RUN BY AMERICAN ZOOS

Listed below are some of the 139 species of animals that American zoos are breeding as part of a Species Survival Plan (SSP), sanctioned by the AZA. Choose one species from this list to research.

1. Addax
2. African penguin
3. African wild dog
4. Arabian oryx
5. Asian wild horse
6. Bali mynah
7. Black-footed ferret
8. Bonobo
9. Callimico
10. Chacoan peccary
11. Cheetah
12. Chimpanzee
13. Colobus monkey
14. Condor*
15. Cuban crocodiles
16. Elephant*
17. Giant panda
18. Gibbons
19. Golden lion tamarin
20. Gorilla
21. Grevy's zebra
22. Jaguar
23. Lemur*
24. Leopard*
25. Lion
26. Mauritius pink pigeon
27. Mexican grey wolf
28. Micronesian king-fisher
29. Okapi
30. Orangutan
31. Red wolf
32. Red-browed Amazon parrot
33. Rhinoceros*
34. Rock iguana
35. Rodrigues' fruit bat
36. Sloth bear
37. Sun bear
38. Tiger*
39. Tree kangaroos
40. Virgin Islands boa
41. Wyoming toad

Resource

www.aza.org

This is the official Web site of the AZA. This group is responsible for establishing and implementing SSPs in the United States. A complete list of animals that currently have an SSP is given at this site.

---

*More than one species of this animal has Survival Plans run by American zoos. Students choosing one of these animals may choose a particular species or report on more than one if they wish to do so.
  Condor: Andean, California
  Elephant: African, Asian
  Lemur: black, ring-tailed, ruffed
  Leopard: clouded, snow
  Rhinoceros: black, Sumatran, white
  Tiger: Indochinese, Siberian, Sumatran

Real-World Investigations for Social Studies
Hoge, Field, Foster, and Nickell

Handout 8.5

GUIDELINES FOR ENDANGERED ANIMAL RESEARCH PROJECT

Your research project must answer (but should not be limited to) the following questions:

1. What does the animal look like? List physical characteristics.
2. In what parts of the world does the animal live?
3. What is the natural habitat of the animal?
4. On what animal or plant life does your species' survival depend?
5. Why is the animal endangered?
6. How many individual members of the species survive in the wild today?
7. What is now being done to save this animal from extinction? What more needs to be done?
8. Which zoos in the United States are involved in implementing the SSP for this animal? How successful has the plan been up to this point? Do the zoos offer any educational programs which include information about this animal?
9. What are the prospects for reintroducing individual captive-bred animals into the wild?
10. What, if anything, can you do to help preserve this and other animal species?

Your project should include these components:

1. A picture of the animal.
2. A map showing the areas of the world that the species inhabits.
3. A written report answering the questions above and containing any extra information you wish to include.
4. A poem written by you similar to the poem read by your teacher in class. The poem should deal with one or more of the following:

   - The animal and its struggle to survive in the wild
   - The animal's habits
   - The animal's life in a zoo
   - The animal in relation to humanity

CLUES FOR THE CASE OF THE FADING FEATHERS

Brine shrimp is a type of crustacean that lives in hypersaline lakes in which the salt content may be 25 percent, predators and competitors are few, and the production of algae is high.

Flamingos molt (shed and replace) their feathers in intervals ranging from twice a year to once every 2 years. Molted feathers lose their color.

Greater Flamingoes eat brine shrimp (and other crustaceans), brine cysts, and small mollusks.

Some of the lakes in the Rift Valley area are Lake Baringo, Lake Logipe, Lake Magadi, Lake Nakuru, Lake Natron, Lake Turkana, and Lake Victoria.

If human beings eat too many carrots (it must be a very large number), the whites of their eyes turn pink.

Volcanic ash raises the pH level of water. Water with a high pH level will burn the skin of most animals.

Spirulina is a blue-green algae found in alkaline water.

PH Level of Water

1	3	7	10	12
(Acidic)		(Norm)	(Basic/Alkaline)	

Flamingos communicate with a range of visual displays. During courtship, flamingos perform ritualized stretching and preening motions.

Flamingo chicks have gray and white feathers, which begin slowly to turn pink at around 1–2 years of age.

The Lesser Flamingo can be found in the Great Rift Valley along the alkaline (hypersaline) lakes. It has a deep red bill with a black tip.

Female flamingos lay one egg each season. Both parents incubate the egg as well as care for the chick when it is born.

Lesser Flamingos live on a diet consisting almost entirely of microscopic organisms.

The feathers of the Lesser Flamingo are often a deep pink, whereas those of the Greater Flamingo are a much lighter pink.

----

continued

Real-World Investigations for Social Studies
Hoge, Field, Foster, and Nickell

The Greater Flamingo can be found in the Great Rift Valley along alkaline (hypersaline) lakes as well as freshwater lakes. It is bigger (about 18 inches) than the Lesser Flamingo. It has a pink bill with a black tip.

Flamingos can tolerate pH levels as high as 10.5, but they need fresh water (pH 7) to drink and to wash in.

Carotene is a carotenoid (yellow or red) pigment found in carrots as well as other plant material.

Adult brine shrimp feed primarily on phytoplankton (algae) suspended in the water but can also "graze" on blue-green algae or diatoms, microscopic organisms that grow in shallow areas.

Lake Baringo, Lake Magadi, Lake Nakuru, and Lake Natron are surrounded by volcanic rock and ash.

Parent flamingos feed their young a liquid substance called *crop milk* for the first 3–4 months of life. The babies then forage for their own food.

Crop milk is secreted from a flamingo's upper digestive tract. Both male and female birds produce this milk, which is dark red and high in protein and fat.

Flamingos spend much of their time standing in water searching for food.

Spirulina contains high concentrations of vitamin A, vitamin B_{12}, beta-carotene, vitamin D, and vitamin K.

Real-World Investigations for Social Studies
Hoge, Field, Foster, and Nickell

DEBATE INFORMATION SHEET

- Zoos allow human beings to come into contact with animal and plant life to which they would not otherwise have access.
- Looking at wild animals in their own environment gives greater insight into the natural behavior of these creatures than does examination of their habits in captivity.
- Zoos do not explain or demonstrate the interrelationship of various forms of life in an ecosystem.
- The AZA SSP is a captive-breeding program that seeks to sustain a few of the world's most endangered creatures. A total of 139 animals currently have SSPs run by AZA-accredited zoos.
- Zoo collections include many large mammals but comparatively few small life forms.
- The diversity and complexity of animal life are much greater than those shown in zoos.
- AZA member institutions have guidelines for the ethical care of animals. (See Handout 8.8.)
- Usually it is the destruction of natural habitat that endangers animal species.
- In 2003, AZA-accredited zoos and aquariums were managing SSPs for 109 mammals, 23 bird, 13 reptilian and amphibian, 12 fish, and 4 invertebrate species.
- Zoos spend millions of dollars a year on captive breeding programs.
- One purpose of zoos is to save animal species in the hope that one day these species can be reintroduced into the wild.
- The quality and diversity of modern nature videos provide people with previously unimagined access to animal and plant life across the world.
- Individual animals have a right to be free.
- The health and welfare of zoo animals depend on a number of factors, including the quality of the enclosures and the keepers.
- Over 300 million people visit the nation's zoos every year. Tens of millions more participate in zoo education programs.

- In many zoos, enclosures do not allow animals to perform instinctual behaviors such as digging or climbing.
- Each AZA accreditation inspection is conducted by at least two experienced zoo professionals. Institutions must meet high standards in the following areas: animal management, facility cleanliness, veterinary care, conservation efforts, education, and financial stability.
- In the wild, some animals live in close association with others of their species, whereas others have a solitary existence.
- The primary responsibility for the welfare of the animals in a zoo falls on the keepers assigned to them.
- Zoos often exhibit exotic species but do not show local fauna.
- Humans are damaging the earth; humans must embrace the need to repair that damage.
- In the wild, animals spend their waking time searching for food, avoiding enemies, and procreating. These activities are not necessary in zoos; in fact, they are not possible in most animal collections.
- One of the most serious threats to wildlife is human indifference.
- Animals in zoos live within the confines of their enclosures and within the limits of the knowledge, resources, and good will of the staff of these institutions.
- AZA-accredited zoos run many educational programs for children and adults. Many of these programs teach the importance of saving wild habitat.
- Extinction is a natural process that has been occurring since the beginning of time. Survival of the fittest helps to ensure the continuance of life.
- During 2000 and 2001, AZA members were involved in 2,230 conservation projects (1,300 in situ, 610 ex situ, 230 both) that took place in

continued

94 countries. (*In situ* refers to programs carried out in the species' natural habitat; *ex situ* refers to programs carried out in captivity.)

- During 2000 and 2001, AZA members published 1,450 journal articles, books, book chapters, conference proceeding papers, theses/dissertations, and posters.

- Very few species are successfully reintroduced into the wild.

- Most zookeepers receive little or no formal training; turnover rates are high, and the pay is low.

- Many of the animal species that have SSPs will become extinct without human intervention.

- The AZA has a zoo accreditation system. To become and remain a member of AZA, an institution (zoo or aquarium) must submit to on-site inspections once every 5 years.

- No attempt is made in zoos to show the connections between microbes, plant life, minerals, small animals, and large animals. Also missing is any presentation of the effects on an ecosystem of the extinction of one species within that ecosystem.

- Human encroachment and shrinking habitat are forcing wild animals to exist in increasingly small land areas.

- AZA zoos have a strategic collection plan. The goal of this plan is to avoid excessive breeding so that there will be fewer surplus animals. The collection plans evaluate the present and future role of each animal in terms of its breeding and its role in the zoo.

- Animals kept in impoverished conditions tend to develop abnormal behaviors such as pacing (walking back and forth continuously, swaying (rhythmic leaning from side to side), and self-mutilation (hurting themselves by biting, scratching, and picking).

- The goal of the SSP program is to keep enough animals of a given species alive while conservation and restoration efforts are made in the animal's natural environment so that one day this species will have a chance to thrive again in the wild.

Real-World Investigations for Social Studies
Hoge, Field, Foster, and Nickell

ETHICAL ISSUES IN DEALING WITH CAPTIVE ANIMALS
STANDARDS OF CARE AND ABNORMAL BEHAVIOR

Elements of a quality environment

1. Animals are able to follow their basic instincts to climb, dig, swim, fly, nest, and so on.
2. Animals that live communally in the wild have companions to interact and play with.
3. The complexity of the zoo's environment mirrors that of a natural environment. Exhibits contain trees, vegetation, ponds, and so on. The territory is varied.
4. Enclosures are of adequate size to allow relative freedom of movement. Also, the size of the enclosure takes into consideration the flight distance of a given animal (the distance from danger at which an animal will turn and run away). An animal that is not kept farther away from zoo visitors than its natural flight distance can experience intense stress.
5. The enclosure should provide the animals with a place to hide from observation.
6. Keepers should do things to stimulate animals within the captive environment, such as hiding food so that animals must search for it or giving animals toys to play with.

Animals housed in impoverished environments and affected by stress may begin to demonstrate abnormal behavior.

Abnormal Behaviors

1. Pacing (walking back and forth continuously)
2. Walking in a circle or figure eight pattern
3. Head bobbing or a weaving motion of the head
4. Swaying (rhythmic leaning from side to side)
5. Self-mutilation
6. Playing with food or interacting with the public, which can also signal boredom

Handout 8.9

GUIDELINES FOR THE PHOTOJOURNALISM PROJECT

1. Each group must write a paper presenting its evaluation of the local zoo. The paper should respond to the following question: Should this zoo continue to exist as it is today?
2. Students must justify their answers using photographic and textual evidence.
3. Each group must present the visual and textual evidence it has gathered on a tri-board.
4. The tri-board should be neat, with the information displayed in an organized manner.
5. Each group will make a 15-minute presentation of its documentary, including the tri-board.

Note: The teacher should add to or modify the list of guidelines to suit the objectives of the class, time constraints, and the needs of the learners in the classroom.

Internet Resources

www.iucn.org/themes/ssc/index.htm

This is the official Web site of the World Conservation Union. The International Union for Conservation of Nature (IUCN) Red List (available at this site) is a vast inventory of the worldwide conservation status of animals and plants. It evaluates the extinction risk of species and subspecies according to set criteria. It also provides information on distribution, habitats, and threats to the animals and plants listed.

www.zoos-worldwide.com

This Web site contains an extensive (though not comprehensive) list of zoos, aquariums, animal sanctuaries, and wildlife parks around the world. Students can use this site to help locate zoos in their state. The site also provides current information on the birth of animals in U.S. zoos. In addition, it encourages people to write reviews of zoos they have visited and to send them in for display on the Web site. This site could be used as a final step for the photojournalism project in Lesson Five.

Confronting the Cycle of Poverty

by
Joseph R. Feinberg and Carolyn Lyon

OVERVIEW

Although approximately 13 percent of Americans live below the national poverty line (U.S. Census Bureau, 2000), the issue of poverty is frequently neglected in American discourse because the vast majority of the U.S. population lives well above the *international* poverty line. The generally accepted international poverty line is $1 per day, which is difficult for many American children to imagine, much less comprehend. The chapter uses the voices of both adults and children living in poverty to inform and to awaken interest in the problem of poverty. Students are challenged to confront their own biases and discover ways to take action to alleviate the suffering of those caught in the cycle of poverty.

The lessons in this chapter include a simulation exercise, map and graphing activities, analysis of primary source documents from people living in poverty around the world, and activities to help students develop empathy and understanding for the plight of those in poverty. For a summative assessment, students plan budgets to demonstrate their understanding of living on an income near the poverty line.

CONNECTION TO NCSS THEME IX: GLOBAL CONNECTIONS

The NCSS strongly recommends that social studies programs offer a substantial instructional program designed to develop deep understandings of global connections. This study of the cycle of poverty helps students achieve this goal by vicariously experiencing how poverty influences the lives of people everywhere around the world.

Students' involvement in this study will help them arrive at many valuable and fundamental social education understandings. Among them are the causes, consequences, and potential solutions to poverty, the persistent tensions that exist between national interests and global priorities, and poverty's relationship to human rights, the environment, economic competition, and many other global realities. By engaging in this study, students will perhaps take their first steps toward becoming connected in heart and mind to the problem of poverty.

METHODS FOCUS: TEACHING CHILDREN IN POVERTY

The CTL of this chapter focuses on global connections and on poverty as it exists in some of the poorest nations on earth. However, as this introduction makes clear, approximately 13 percent of all Americans (almost 33 million people) live in families with incomes at or below the official U.S. poverty level (defined as $17,000 for a family of four in the year 2000). Indeed, poverty rates approach 30 percent in some areas of the United States, such as Clarke County, Georgia (Shearer, 2002).

Poverty Is Everywhere

Misperceptions about poverty are commonplace. For example, poverty is not just a big-city or urban phenomenon. According to data compiled by the U.S. Census Bureau, 10.8 percent of urban Americans live in poverty compared to 13.4 percent of rural Americans (Miller & Rowley, 2002). Poverty is also more prevalent among minorities, with approximately 3 out of 10 black or Hispanic children under the age of 18 coming from families living at or below the U.S. poverty level (Annual Demographic Survey, 2001). Of course children who come from low socioeconomic status (SES) homes are predominantly educated in public schools, and because roughly 90 percent of all Americans attend public schools, it is highly likely that you will teach children who are experiencing or have experienced poverty.

Poverty and Teaching

Poverty is a social and cultural problem that has profound implications for teaching and learning. A quality education is often the only means of breaking the cycle of poverty, but there are a number of factors related to poverty that may put a child at risk for academic failure. Due to these obstacles, poor chil-

dren generally achieve at lower levels than do children who come from middle- and upper-class homes (Pellino, 2002). To address this achievement gap, teachers must identify and understand the challenges poor children face at home and at school.

Emotional trauma is one obstacle to learning experienced by children from lower SES backgrounds. Many of these children live in dangerous neighborhoods and have little stability in their lives. The emotional climate in which they live is often stressful and marked by a lack of emotional nurturing. This emotional deprivation leads to feelings of fear, depression, and alienation. These feelings can produce students who appear apathetic, surly, suspicious, aggressive, and hostile (Pellino, 2002).

High mobility is another factor related to poverty that can interfere with the learning process. Often children in poverty move from town to town as their parents seek work or attempt to flee from personal or financial problems. Some children live on the streets or in homeless and battered women's shelters. Because of this lack of stability, school attendance often suffers and many times schools do not know how to place students in the proper grade level, subjects, or support services because their parents have no records from previous schools. In addition, students must routinely make new friends and say good-bye to old friends. This takes an emotional toll that can result in children disengaging from the school environment.

Parenting struggles associated with living in poverty also affect the academic development of a child. Much of a child's early behavioral, social, and cognitive development is based on the parent–child relationship. Learning experiences that parents typically provide for children, such as visits to zoos, reading books, watching educational videos, and interaction with well-spoken, highly educated adults, are important for the development of knowledge and skills necessary for academic success. Parents living in poverty usually cannot provide these types of experiences for their children to the extent that middle- and upper-class parents can. In addition, these parents tend to be less involved in the education of their children than are middle- and upper-class parents. Lack of time due to holding down multiple jobs, lack of affordable day care, and negative experiences with their own schooling all contribute to this lack of involvement.

The culture and hidden rules of schooling are another obstacle to learning that poor children must overcome. Hidden rules serve as indicators that people belong to a certain group. Schools tend to operate according to middle-class rules and values; these differ from the hidden rules and values of persons trapped in generational poverty. For instance, many poor children see the driving forces for decision making as relationships, entertainment, and survival. In middle-class values, the driving forces of decision making are work and achievement (Payne, 1996).

When poor children violate the middle-class values and hidden rules of school, teachers become frustrated and can make incorrect judgments about these children. This lack of understanding concerning the culture of generational poverty can cause teachers to label low-income students as "troublemakers" or "uneducable." As a result, these children receive a lower-quality education than that given to middle- and upper-class children.

What Teachers Can Do

What can teachers do to remove obstacles to learning from the paths of poor children? Here are a few basic guidelines:

1. *Establish a classroom environment that is safe and trusting.*

To do this, teachers must work to build relationships with students. Relationships are very important in the culture of poverty; thus, establishing a meaningful relationship with low-income students increases the likelihood that you will have the influence needed to help them learn. In order to do this, it is important that you share information about yourself and take the time to learn about the life experiences, concerns, and interests of students who come from low-income homes.

2. *Construct challenging learning activities focused on students' interests and perspectives.*

Students are more likely to be engaged in learning when the topic is one in which they are interested. Yet, enthralling topics are not enough. Exercises must be intellectually rigorous (see Lessons One, Two, Three, and Five in this chapter). If the learning exercises done with low-income children are not challenging, these students will not develop the skills necessary to succeed in higher education or to function capably in their personal lives. Teachers who give low-income students the necessary support for accomplishing challenging academic tasks provide these students with a sense of self-efficacy that can help them break out of their existing social class and the cycle of poverty.

3. *Use methods such as cooperative learning, group decision making, and journal reflection.*

Methods such as cooperative learning (see Lesson Three in this chapter) and group decision making can help low-income students to build relationships and a sense of community with other children in their classes. Developing a sense of belonging facilitates the learning process. Journal reflections can help children to identify what is important to them, which aids them in setting goals. Also, personal reflections allow students to use their own voices and, through the process, come to understand that their points of view and experiences really matter (or ought to!).

4. *Develop support networks for students and parents.*

Put families in touch with community programs that provide health, social, and recreational services. Support attendance at parent–teacher conferences by providing child care, transportation, entertainment, and refreshments. Invite parents into the classroom, both to observe and to help with learning.

5. *Avoid punishment-oriented remedies to misbehavior.*

Focus your attempts to correct misbehavior on discussing your positive expectations and describing how the offending behavior blocks short-term performance and desired goal attainment. Use the voice of reason rather than the voice of authority and, if possible, approach discipline matters privately and with controlled emotions.

6. *Provide supplemental learning supports.*

Provide extra tutorial assistance, greater than average computer time, and increased access to media center resources and school supplies. Find out if there is a way to support participation in after-school programs and community events.

7. *Don't get stumped by "I don't care!"*

Respond to a student's statement of "I don't care" with expressions of deep concern for your own performance as a professional and the care that you have for every student's well-being and learning. Demonstrate your caring by asking what you can do to improve the situation and help the student be more successful.

8. *Use the curriculum to humanize learning.*

Stress the struggles, values, feelings, and emotions of people encountered in the curriculum or the news and relate these understandings to students' lives. Make it clear that people have risen and fallen from all sorts of circumstances and that although we cannot control the seemingly random operation of luck, we should work to maximize our opportunities and, it is hoped, influence the potential outcomes of our future.

9. *Be persistent and determined.*

Working with children living in poverty can be emotionally draining yet quite rewarding. Teachers must be persistent, determined, and flexible when working with these students. Setbacks are inevitable, but a true sense of accomplishment can be gained with each small step forward toward independence and personal success.

The tasks of engaging poor children in the academic process and of providing for their special needs seem daunting, but these are endeavors that teachers must embrace with vigor. The number and quality of the choices and opportunities these children have in the future may well depend on them.

Table 9.1 Lesson Overview for "Confronting the Cycle of Poverty"

	GOALS	ACTIVITIES	ASSESSMENTS
LESSON ONE	• Learn about the concept of poverty. • Develop a better understanding of poverty by examining charts of world poverty.	• Participate in a game to understand poverty and be introduced to the cycle of poverty (Handout 9.1). • Analyze statistics on world poverty and determine, from an examination of these statistics, some of the causes and effects of poverty (Handouts 9.2 and 9.3).	• Collect and review students' answers to questions (Handout 9.3).
LESSON TWO	• Understand the factors that contribute to poverty. • Learn about poverty from the Internet.	• Analyze quotes from people living in poverty and identify the elements of poverty (Handout 9.4). • Analyze a political cartoon on child labor (Handouts 9.5 and 9.6).	• Collect and examine each group's responses to the questions (Handout 9.4). • Evaluate students' analysis of the political cartoon on child labor (Handout 9.6).
LESSON THREE	• Learn about child labor and how it relates to poverty.	• Read brief narratives about child laborers around the world, answer questions concerning these narratives, and discuss the responses (Handouts 9.7–9.13). • Reanalyze the political cartoon on child labor (Handout 9.5) and then discuss its meaning as a class (Handouts 9.5 and 9.6). • Participate in a child labor simulation activity.	• Collect and review the students' answers for the cooperative learning activity (Handouts 9.12 and 9.13).
LESSON FOUR	• Learn about social action against poverty.	• Investigate social action. • Read the story of Iqbal Masih (Handout 9.14). • Discuss how one middle school made a difference in the fight against poverty (Handout 9.15).	• Collect and evaluate students' responses to the questions (Handout 9.15).
LESSON FIVE	• Learn about poverty in the United States.	• Examine statistics on poverty from the U.S. Census Bureau and construct bar graphs and pie charts to represent the data (Handouts 9.16 and 9.17). • Analyze the graphs and use this information to answer a series of questions about poverty in the United States (Handout 9.18).	• Collect and critique students' graphs and charts. • Collect and evaluate students' answers on the family budget exercise (Handouts 9.19 and 9.20).

LESSON ONE: What Is Poverty? Understanding the Cycle

Purpose This lesson introduces students to the topic of poverty and the many frustrations of living in poverty.

Duration Two class periods

Materials
Handout 9.1: "Poor Me" Game Cards
Handout 9.2: Statistics: World Development Report and UNICEF
Handout 9.3: Examination of World Poverty Statistics
Candy (one large bag of Tootsie Rolls or hard candy). The candy is used as a motivator for a game.

Procedures
1. Prepare to play the game "Poor Me." The purpose of this game is to have students unknowingly experience, in a small way, the frustration of those who struggle every day to escape the cycle of poverty and to make a better life for themselves, only to see their hopes dashed over and over again.
   a. Prepare two sets of game cards (Handout 9.1) as specified in the table and directions below.
   b. Each set should contain a number of cards that is equal to the number of students in the class minus one. Example: 25 students in class = 24 game cards.
   c. The combination of cards in a game set will differ slightly according to the number of students in the class.
   d. Given below is the number of each type of card needed to complete a game set for classes of varying sizes. Also noted is the number of student names that should be called out during each child's turn at the front of the classroom. **P** = Poverty card; **I** = Inheritance card; **ND** = Natural Disaster card; **T/P/C/H/M** = Television/Pig/Cow/Corn/Car/House/ Medical Care cards; **NS** = number of students to be called during a turn at the front of the classroom.

NO. OF STUDENTS	P	I	ND	T/P/C/H/M	NS
16–17	3	1	1	11–12	4
18–20	3	1	1	13–15	5
21	4	1	1	15	4
22–24	3	1	1	17–19	6
25–26	4	1	1	19–20	5
27–30	4	1	1	21–24	6
31–32	5	1	1	24–25	5
33–35	5	1	1	26–28	6

e. The game is set up according to the rules of probability so that the students earn currency points 32–39 percent of the time. The rest of the time they lose currency points. Over the course of the game, students receive enough currency points to maintain their interest in the game, but ultimately they should not receive enough points to keep them out of poverty.

2. How to Play "Poor Me"
   a. Choose one student to come to the front of the room.
   b. Choose two students to assist in the rapid distribution and collection of game cards.
   c. Before the game begins, show the candy that the students can purchase with their currency points. This raises the students' hopes and desires, thus making the game a more frustrating experience for them as they try in vain to stay out of poverty.
   d. Have the two student assistants pass out one game card, face down, to each remaining student.
   e. The student standing in front of the room calls out one name at a time. As soon as a name is called, the student being addressed should show his or her card to the class. As soon as the card is revealed, the student in front rapidly calls another name (within 4 seconds). This process continues until the designated number of cards has been revealed or until a P or ND card appears.
   f. At the end of each round, the two student assistants collect and redistribute the game cards.
   g. Play until every student has had a turn calling names.

3. "Poor Me" rules
   a. The class begins the game with two currency points. Keep track of the points on the board or overhead.
   b. If the student at the front of the room is successful in calling out the required number of names without revealing a P or ND card, the class receives one currency point.
   c. If a P card appears, the class loses one currency point, and the student calling names must sit down immediately. If an ND card appears, the class loses two currency points, and the student calling names must sit down immediately.
   d. If an I card appears, the students are given two currency points and the turn continues.

If the turn is completed without a P or ND card being uncovered, all students receive an additional currency point.

  e. Students are not allowed to look at their cards unless asked to turn them over. If students cheat by looking at their cards or by signaling each other, take one currency point away from the class total.

  f. At the end of the game, the class should be in "poverty," having accumulated no currency points.

4. After the game has been played, discuss with students the frustration of trying to win a prize but slowly moving further and further away from that objective. What range of emotions did students experience? How difficult was it to be given hope in one round of the game, only to have that hope ripped away in the next round? What if your life followed the pattern of this game and the prize was survival? Would it be difficult to maintain hope with such an uncertain future?

5. Divide students into groups of three or four. Give each student a copy of the statistics chart (Handout 9.2) and the question sheet (Handout 9.3). The chart contains information from 12 countries: Some are relatively affluent; others are poverty-stricken. By analyzing the statistics chart and com-paring the numbers in various categories, students will be able to answer the questions in Handout 9.3. In this way, students should be able to determine which of the factors on the chart are related to poverty and to hypothesize about what that relationship might be.

6. Ask each group of students to write an answer to these two questions: What is poverty? What are its causes and effects? Discuss students' answers to these questions, and have the class develop a definition of poverty and a list of some of the causes and effects of poverty.

7. Optional Web activity: The following Web site has 20 questions about world poverty and development (a great interactive quiz): http://www.world bank.org/poverty/quiz/index.htm

Internet References

www.worldbank.org/poverty/wdrpoverty/report/index.htm
Contains the World Bank's full text report on world poverty with a free download

http://www.unicef.org/statis/index.html
UNICEF's excellent statistical data Web page that displays various demographics by country and region

LESSON TWO: Listen to the "Voices of Poverty"

Purpose This lesson asks students to examine the multidimensional aspects of poverty by analyzing quotes from people living in poverty around the world.

Teachers: Please note that some of the quotes are emotionally moving and may upset some students. Encourage students to be respectful during the discussion because some of their classmates may live in similar circumstances. Read all quotes before distributing them to the class, and consider having a discussion about how difficult poverty can be for children and adults even in the United States.

Duration One class period

Materials
Handout 9.4: Voices of Poverty
Handout 9.5: Child Labor Cartoon
Handout 9.6: Questions About the Child Labor
  Cartoon

Procedures

1. Write the following quote on the board or create a transparency of it:

One farmer's family has worked for [another] family for three generations, hard physical labor every day. This man has worked since his birth for the same farmer but has nothing, no savings, not even a bicycle. These people can afford nothing but survival.—South Africa

Facilitate a discussion about the quote. What does one person have to do in order to pay a second person to produce a product (in this case, farm products)? Who makes more money (usually) in such a situation? What happens to the second person's (farm worker's) wages if the price of a product increases? Decreases? Why doesn't the farm worker leave?

2. Write the following quote on the board or create a transparency of it:

A better life for me is to be healthy, peaceful and live in love without hunger. Love is more than anything. Money has no value in the absence of love.—Ethiopia

Facilitate a discussion about this quote. Why is love so important to this person? Why is love "more than anything"? Do you agree? If you were starving, would you agree?

3. Divide the class into six quote. Give each group a set of quotes to read and to analyze (Handout 9.4). This handout contains six different sets of quotes. A different set should be given to each of the six student groups.

4. Have the groups determine whether each quote describes a cause or an effect of poverty and whether the quote expresses the cycle of poverty. Tell the groups that a few quotes express both cause and effect and that most do not convey the cycle of poverty.

5. List on the board the main factors of poverty and discuss additional factors students believe should be added. Have each group decide which elements or factors of poverty are represented in each quote. Instruct students to categorize or group factors that are similar; for example, government services would include sanitation, roads, and water.

6. As much as possible, encourage students to explain or justify their classifications and categories.

7. After groups are given ample time to analyze the quotes (15–30 minutes), a designated member of each group should read each quote to the class and explain the factors of poverty his or her group believes are exhibited in the quotes. Consider having a student list the factors mentioned on the board or overhead.

Some aspects of poverty that students will discover in the quotes will include the following:

   a. Causes
- Lack of educational opportunity/illiteracy
- Lack of material possessions/assets
- Unemployment: no work/jobs
- Population pressure
- Lack of natural resources
- Natural disaster

   b. Effects
- Protection from corruption, crime, violence, discrimination, abuse—inhumane treatment
- Lack of necessities: shelter, housing, clothes, food, water
- Health issues: hunger, thirst, malnutrition, disease
- Lack of basic infrastructure: clean water, sanitation, roads, transportation, and health care
- Powerlessness, vulnerability, lack of psychological well-being
- Political disenfranchisement: belief that the government does not care or will not help

8. Make an overhead transparency of the cartoon (Handout 9.6) and show it to the class. Point out all of the elements in the cartoon, including the soccer ball visible through the open window. Tell students that the soccer ball visible through the window is traveling back and forth outside of the window. (This is an animated cartoon, and the ball is in motion when the cartoon is viewed on a computer.)

9. Distribute Handout 9.6 and have students answer the questions about the cartoon before the next class session.

10. At the beginning of the next lesson (Lesson Three), collect the homework and proceed to the lesson. Tell students that the class will discuss the cartoon after Lesson Three has been completed.

11. After students have completed Lesson Three, return the homework papers (Handout 9.6) to them. On the back of the papers, and leaving their original answers intact, have students revise or add to these answers.

12. When students have completed their revisions, collect the papers; then, hold a class discussion about the meaning of the cartoon and the ways in which the artist uses its various elements to convey meaning. Place the transparency of the cartoon on the overhead projector during the discussion so that students can refer to it.

13. As you grade students' papers, note the additions to and changes in the answers. It should be possible to see whether or not the lesson on child poverty helped students analyze the cartoon.

Resources
Narayan, D., Chambers, R., Shah, M. K., & Petesch, P. (2000). *Voices of the poor: Crying out for change.* New York: Oxford University Press.

Internet Resources
http://www.ilo.org/pubcgi/235photo.pl?keyword =child+labour
A variety of child labor pictures that can be analyzed at this Web site.

http://www.worldgame.org/worldometers/
A set of "worldometers" showing constantly changing meters of world population, energy consumption, food supply, and so on.

www.NETaid.org
NetAid was created to mobilize support through the Internet to end extreme poverty.

www.unicef.org/crcartoons
UNICEF "Cartoons for Children's Rights."

LESSON THREE: Voices of Child Laborers

Purpose This lesson focuses on child labor to show how poverty affects children around the world.
Duration Two class periods

Materials
Handout 9.7: Voices of Child Laborers (Group 1)
   Ruth: A Street Worker in Guatemala

Handout 9.8: Voices of Child Laborers (Group 2)
Suka Maya: A Factory Worker in Nepal

Handout 9.9: Voices of Child Laborers (Group 3)
Belinda: A Migrant Farmworker in the United
States

Handout 9.10: Voices of Child Laborers (Group 4)
Selvakumar: A Silver Factory Worker in India

Handout 9.11: Voices of Child Laborers (Group 5)
Willie: A Newspaper Delivery Boy in the United
States

Handout 9.12: Voices of Child Laborers: Expert
Group Work Questions

Handout 9.13: Learning from Group Experts

Procedures

1. Begin the lesson by asking the following questions: Do any of you work for pay? Why do you work? How much are you paid? Do working conditions vary for children around the world? How is working for your family different from working for a business or a person outside of your family?

2. Introduce the lesson by explaining that it will be about children who work.

3. Jigsaw group learning activity: Divide the class into five groups and give each student a number ranging from 1 to 5 (have students write their numbers down). Each group will become an expert on one narrative (Handouts 9.7–9.11). Instruct the students to read their group's narrative about a child laborer and thoroughly answer the discussion questions (Handout 9.12).

4. After the expert groups have answered the discussion questions, instruct all students with the same number to team up in a specific location.

5. Distribute Handout 9.13. Instruct each expert to read his or her story to the group and guide everyone to answer the questions in the handout.

6. If time permits, discuss students' responses to all the questions and further develop answers on the board or overhead.

7. The following child labor simulation activity is designed to acquaint students with the rigor of the work done by child laborers around the world. The materials needed for this simulation are beads (multicolored); string (must fit through beads); boxes (one for every three students); placemats (one for each student: optional); and bowls (one for each student: optional).

8. Students need to sit on the floor for this exercise, so the desks must be moved to the periphery of the classroom. (Placemats provide a space for students to work, and the bowl prevents beads from rolling across the floor.)

9. Place the boxes (which need to be at least the size of a shoe box) on the floor, evenly spaced apart.

10. Have three students sit around each box. If you are using placemats and bowls, give one of each to every student. Each student should then be given 20 lengths of string. Each piece of string needs to have a knot already tied on one end and must be long enough for 8–10 beads to be strung on it.

11. Each student's task is to make 20 bracelets consisting of 8–10 beads each. The teacher should make up a pattern that all students must follow: for instance, two blue, one green, two yellow, one red, two purple, one white, one black. The student must tie a knot at the open end of the string after finishing the bead pattern.

12. The teacher acts as an overseer, examining the finished bracelets for mistakes in the pattern. Any defective bracelets must be restrung by the student.

13. Before the lesson begins, the teacher should string one bracelet to determine the amount of time it will take the students to complete each bracelet. Multiply that amount of time by 20. This is the amount of class time students should be given to complete the 20 bracelets. It is unlikely that any students will complete the task, but many will keep close enough to the pace to be motivated to continue.

14. Students should be told the following:
   a. The only grades possible on this exercise are A, C, and F.
   b. Students will receive an A if they finish the 20 bracelets in the specified amount of time. Students making an A will also receive a bonus of a candy bar.
   c. Students who do not finish must come back during lunch or after school to complete their task. Students who complete the task during the extra time receive a C.
   d. All students who do not complete the task receive an F.
   e. The teacher does not actually have to make students return during lunch or after school. Students simply must think that this will be required. Also, no grades should be given. The grades and the time constraint are in place only to put pressure on the students.
   f. The number of bracelets students are required to make can be modified by the teacher according to available class time and available materials. It is recommended that students be asked to complete at least 15 bracelets so that they gain an understanding of the immensity and tediousness of the jobs many child laborers must do.

15. For homework instruct students to collect the classified ads section of a newspaper or a booklet on apartments to rent in the area (free in most grocery stores). Students will need this information for Lesson Five.

Sources

Human Rights Watch Children's Rights Project. (1996). *The small hands of slavery: Bonded child labor in India* (p. 67). New York: Human Rights Watch.

Parker, D. L., with Engfer, L., and Conrow, R. (1998). *Stolen dreams* (pp. 28–29). Minneapolis: Lerner.

Pradhan, G. (1993). *Misery behind the looms: Child labourers in the carpet factories in Nepal* (pp. 38–39). Kalimati, Kathmandu, Nepal: CWIN (Child Workers in Nepal Concerned Center).

Strother, D. B. (Ed.). (1991). *Learning to fail: Case studies of students at risk* (pp. 59–69). Bloomington, IN: Phi Delta Kappa, Maynard R. Bemis Center for Evaluation, Development, and Research.

Tierney, N. L. (1997). *Robbed of humanity: Lives of Guatemalan street children* (pp. 32–35). St. Paul: Pangaea.

LESSON FOUR: Challenging the Cycle of Poverty

Purpose This lesson helps students understand how the cycle of poverty can be broken.

Duration One class period

Materials
Handout 9.14: The Story of Iqbal Masih
Handout 9.15: "A Bullet Can't Kill a Dream"

Procedures

1. Obtain a copy of *Stolen Dreams: Portraits of Working Children* by David L. Parker with Lee Engfer and Robert Conrow (Minneapolis: Lerner, 1998). Invite a guest reader to read "The Story of Iqbal Masih" (pp. 9–18). Consider inviting the principal, a drama teacher, or a student with exceptional reading skills. Alternatively, distribute Handout 9.14 and ask volunteers to read it.

2. Divide the class into groups, distribute Handout 9.14 and ash volunteers to read it. to answer the discussion questions. Have students share their group responses with the class. The instructor should facilitate the discussion to ensure that no blaming of the victim occurs and to prevent simplistic and unrealistic solutions to the questions.

3. Instruct students to read "A Bullet Can't Kill a Dream" (Handout 9.15), which is about middle school students inspired to action by the death of Iqbal Masih.

4. Have students answer and discuss the questions that follow the story and provide critically thought out written responses. Again, the instructor should facilitate the discussion to ensure that no blaming of the victim occurs and to prevent simplistic and unrealistic solutions to the questions.

Sources

http://www.digitalrag.com/iqbal/
"A School for Iqbal," is the excellent Web site on the efforts of students at Broad Meadows Middle School and other organizations to fight child labor around the world. Many excellent links to other sites on this topic and inspirational stories related to Iqbal Masih.

Parker, D., with Engler, L., & Conrow, R. (1998). *Stolen dreams: Portraits of working children*. Minneapolis: Lerner.
This book, containing poignant photographs of child laborers and their stories, begins with the story of Iqbal Masih. It includes dramatic statistics about child labor, explanations of the work children perform, the economic reasons that require them to work, and the effects of the work on their lives.

Kuklin, S. (1998). *Iqbal Masih and the crusaders against child labor*. New York: Henry Holt.
A book chronicling Iqbal Masih's life with a chapter on "A School for Iqbal."

LESSON FIVE: Poverty in the United States

Purpose This lesson exposes students to the reality that even in a country as affluent as the United States, there are a large number of poor people.

Duration Two class periods

Materials
Handout 9.16: U.S. Poverty Statistics (1998)

Handout 9.17: Direction Sheet: Graphs of U.S. Poverty Statistics
Handout 9.18: Question Sheet: Analysis of U.S. Poverty Data
Handout 9.19: Budget Sheet
Handout 9.20: Question Sheet for Budget Exercise
Colored pencils
Drawing paper

Procedures

1. Divide the class into groups of two or three students. Ensure that students have colored pencils and drawing paper.

2. Read Handout 9.17 and ensure that each group has access to the Internet or a copy of the Census Bureau statistics (Handout 9.16) (www. census.gov/hhes/poverty/poverty98/table5.html).

3. Draw on the chalkboard examples of pie charts and bar graphs to give students an idea of the types of graphs they can create with the data.

4. After students have completed the graphs, have them discuss the questions in Handout 9.18. The questions require students to analyze the charts they have created in an attempt to gain information about the poor in our society.

5. Discuss students' answers to the questions and the implications of those answers.

6. Give students the budget sheet and the question sheet (Handouts 9.19 and 9.20). Also, ask students to take out the information they have looked up about apartment and food prices in their area.

7. Divide students into groups of three. Have the groups determine the budget for the Jacobs family and then answer the questions concerning the budget.

8. When students are finished with the exercise, hold a class discussion about the difficulty of living just above the poverty line. Also discuss the factors that made it difficult for the Jacobs to improve their financial situation.

9. As a summary activity ask the students to write a one to two page essay that takes a position on the question: Is it possible to eliminate poverty from the world?

References

U.S. Census Bureau. (1998). Percent of people in poverty by definition of income and selected characteristics: 1998. Available online at www.census.gov/hhes/poverty/poverty98/table5.html

"POOR ME" GAME CARDS

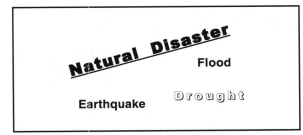

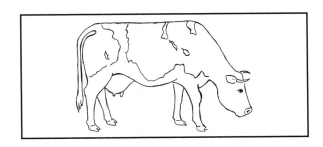

Poverty

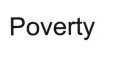

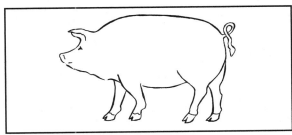

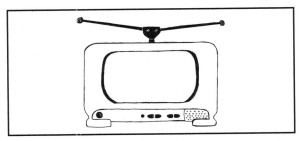

Real-World Investigations for Social Studies
Hoge, Field, Foster, and Nickell

Handout 9.2

STATISTICS: WORLD DEVELOPMENT REPORT AND UNICEF

COUNTRY	TOTAL POPULATION IN MILLIONS	SURFACE AREA (000'S KM²)	TOTAL FERTILITY RATE	INFANT MORTALITY (PER 1,000 LIVE BIRTHS)	PRIMARY SCHOOL ENROLLMENT RATIO (GROSS)	SECONDARY SCHOOL ENROLLMENT (GROSS)	POPULATION DENSITY (PER KM²)
Australia	19	7,741	1.8	5	M 100 F 100	M 100 F 100	2
China	1,250	9,597	1.8	33	M 100 F 100	M 72 F 65	134
Germany	82	357	1.3	5	M 100 F 100	M 99 F 100	235
Guatemala	11	109	4.7	45	M 81 F 75	M 26 F 24	102
India	998	3,288	3	70	M 78 F 64	M 59 F 39	336
Israel	6	21	2.6	6	M 96 F 96	M 84 F 89	296
Japan	127	378	1.4	4	M 100 F 100	M 98 F 97	336
Kenya	29	580	4.2	76	M 89 F 88	M 26 F 22	52
Mexico	97	1,958	2.6	27	M 100 F 100	M 64 F 64	51
Pakistan	135	796	4.8	84	M 99 F 69	M 33 F 17	175
Russian Fed.	147	17,075	1.4	18	M 100 F 100	M 83 F 91	9
United States	273	9,364	2	7	M 100 F 100	M 100 F 100	30

Real-World Investigations for Social Studies
Hoge, Field, Foster, and Nickell

COUNTRY	MATERNAL MORTALITY RATE (PER 100,000 LIVE BIRTHS)	PAVED ROADS (% OF TOTAL)	ADEQUATE SANITATION (% OF POPULATION WITH ACCESS)	INFANTS WITH LOW BIRTH WEIGHT (%)	PERSONAL COMPUTERS (PER 1,000 PERSONS)
Australia	ND	38.7	100	6	411.6
China	55	ND	38	6	8.9
Germany	8	99.1	ND	ND	304.7
Guatemala	190	27.6	85	15	8.3
India	410	45.7	31	33	2.7
Israel	5	100	ND	7	217.2
Japan	8	74.9	ND	7	237.2
Kenya	590	13.9	86	16	2.5
Mexico	55	29.7	73	7	47
Pakistan	ND	57	61	25	3.9
Russian Fed.	50	74.2 #	ND	7	40.6
United States	8	58.8	100	7	458.6

Data compiled from *Statistical Data: Country Tables* (1999–2000). www.unicef.org/statis/country.html and *World Development Report 2000/2001* (2001)
http://www.worldbank.org/poverty/wdrpoverty/report/index.htm

Real-World Investigations for Social Studies
Hoge, Field, Foster, and Nickell

Handout 9.3

EXAMINATION OF WORLD POVERTY STATISTICS

1. The World Bank has divided nations into four categories (based on estimates of 1999 gross national product per capita): high ($9,266+$), upper middle ($2,996–$9,265$), lower middle ($756–$2,995$), and low ($755 or less). The countries examined in Handout 9.2 fit into the above categories as follows: High—Australia, Germany, Israel, Japan, and the United States; upper middle—Mexico; lower middle—China, Guatemala, and the Russian Federation; low—India, Kenya, and Pakistan. Students should keep this classification in mind while examining the world poverty statistics.

2. Study the data in the columns on "Total Population," "Surface Area," and "Population Density."

   • What is the relationship among the data in these three columns?
   • Do the data in any one of these columns appear to correlate with poverty rates in the identified countries?
   • If so, what do you think the connection might be?

3. Inspect the data in the columns on "Total Fertility Rate," "Maternal Mortality Rate," "Infants with Low Birth Weight," and "Infant Mortality."

   • Do any of these factors appear to be related to poverty in the countries listed?
   • If so, are these factors causes or effects of poverty? Why?
   • Can you determine what the specific underlying cause might be for any factors you have identified as being effects of poverty?

4. Look at the data in the columns on "Primary School Enrollment" and "Secondary School Enrollment."

   • Does primary school enrollment relate to poverty rates in the listed countries?
   • Does secondary school enrollment?
   • Can you think of an explanation for the sharp drop in school enrollment from the primary to the secondary level that occurs in some of the listed countries?
   • Is school enrollment a causal factor for poverty, an effect of poverty, or both? Explain.

5. Examine the gender disparity in the "Secondary School Enrollment" column.

   • In which countries is this discrepancy greater than 5 percent?
   • In which of these countries are fewer women than men given a secondary education? Why might this be occurring?
   • How might this gender disparity contribute to poverty?
   • In which of these countries are fewer men than women being educated at the secondary level? Why might this be occurring?

6. Scrutinize the data in the "Adequate Sanitation" column.

   • Does access to adequate sanitation have any relationship to poverty rates?
   • If so, what might this connection be?

Real-World Investigations for Social Studies
Hoge, Field, Foster, and Nickell

7. Study the data in the "Paved Roads" column.

   - Does the percentage of paved roads in these countries correspond to their poverty rates? Explain.

8. Look at the data on "Personal Computers." Countries that have a large number of personal computers (per 1,000 population) have low poverty rates, whereas those with few computers have high poverty rates.

   - Is there a causal link between computer ownership and poverty rates or is this apparent relationship caused by something else?

Based on your examination of these poverty statistics, explain in detail your evaluation of the causes and effects of poverty as revealed in this chart.

Handout 9.4

VOICES OF POVERTY

GROUP 1

1. "Poverty is because of the land; the person who doesn't have any must obligatorily leave to do day labor."—Ecuador
2. "When one is poor, she has no say in public, she feels inferior. She has no food, so there is famine in her house; no clothing, and no progress in her family."—Uganda
3. "The rich is the one who says 'I am going to do it' and does it. The poor, in contrast, do not fulfill their wishes or develop their capacities."—Brazil
4. "I repeat that we need water as badly as we need air."—Kyrgyz Republic
5. "If you don't know anyone, you will be thrown to the corner of a hospital!"—India
6. "It's the cost of living, low salaries, and lack of jobs. And it's also not having medicine, food and clothes."—Brazil

----

GROUP 2

1. "Don't ask me what poverty is because you have met it outside my house. Look at the house and count the number of holes. Look at my utensils and the clothes that I am wearing. Look at everything and write what you see. What you see is poverty."—Kenya
2. "Your hunger is never satiated, your thirst is never quenched; you can never sleep until you are no longer tired."—Senegal
3. "Water is life, and because we have no water, life is miserable."—Kenya
4. "If one does not own land, a house, household property, or domestic animals, then the person is considered to be poor."—Uganda
5. "If you have no relatives among high government officials, people treat you as second-rate. If you have any problems with your business or get in trouble with the police, you will lose your case and won't have your problems resolved. Those who have power and money will always win."—Kyrgyz Republic
6. "Life in the area is so precarious that the youth and every able person has to migrate to the towns or join the army at the war front in order to escape the hazards of hunger escalating over here."—Ethiopia

Real-World Investigations for Social Studies
Hoge, Field, Foster, and Nickell

GROUP 3

1. [I have become like] "a stray dog whimpering in front of the closed doors of relatives in the hope that someone might open the door."—Republic of Georgia
2. "When I leave for school in the mornings I don't have any breakfast. At noon there is no lunch. In the evening I get a little supper, and that is not enough. So when I see another child eating, I watch him, and if he doesn't give me something I think I'm going to die of hunger."—Gabon
3. "Poverty is like living in jail, living under bondage, waiting to be free."—Jamaica
4. "I used to never worry about my illiteracy and the fact that I was not able to send my children to school, as long as we had something to eat. But now . . . I realize that my children are in trouble for life because they cannot get any decent job if they don't know how to read and write."—Swaziland
5. "The unemployed men are frustrated because they no longer can play the part of family providers and protectors. They live on the money made by their wives and feel humiliated because of this."—Kyrgyz Republic
6. "Nobody is able to communicate our problems. Who represents us? Nobody."—Egypt

---

GROUP 4

1. "When my husband died, my in-laws told me to get out. So I came to town and slept on the pavement."—Kenya
2. "Poverty is lack of freedom, enslaved by crushing daily burden, by depression and fear of what the future will bring."—Republic of Georgia
3. "The waste brings some bugs; here we have cockroaches, spiders and even snakes and scorpions."—Brazil
4. "Before, everyone could get health care, but now everyone just prays to God that they don't get sick because everywhere they just ask for money."—Bosnia-Herzegovina
5. "If you don't have money today, your disease will take you to your grave."—Ghana
6. "The municipal congressmen are all thieves. They do not solve anything. There are no schools, no health care. They do not vote issues that interest the people."—Brazil

continued

GROUP 5

1. "The school was okay, but now it is in shambles; there are no teachers for weeks. There is no safety and no hygiene."—Brazil
2. "Often she has to decide who will eat, she or her son."—Ukraine
3. "Poverty is humiliation, the sense of being dependent on them, and of being forced to accept rudeness, insults, and indifference when we seek help."—Latvia
4. "Take the death of this small boy this morning, for example. The boy died of measles. We all know he could have been cured at the hospital. But the parents had no money, and so the boy died a slow and painful death, not of measles but out of poverty."—Ghana
5. "I sold my land and now I have nothing. I can never buy my land back because the prices go up every year."—Tanzania
6. "People place their hopes in God, since the government is no longer involved in such matters."—Armenia

---

GROUP 6

1. "Lack of work worries me. My children were hungry, and I told them 'the rice is cooking,' until they fell asleep from hunger."—Egypt
2. "When food was in abundance, relatives used to share it. These days of hunger, however, not even relatives would help you by giving you some food."—Zambia
3. "The children keep playing in the sewage."—Brazil
4. "If you want to do something and have no power to do it, it is *talauchi* [poverty]."—Nigeria
5. "In my family, if anyone becomes seriously ill, we know that we will lose him because we do not even have enough money for food, so we cannot buy medicine."—Vietnam
6. "For a poor person everything is terrible—illness, humiliation, shame. We are cripples; we are afraid of everything; we depend on everyone. No one needs us. We are like garbage that everyone wants to get rid of."—Moldova

Excerpted from *Listen to the voices* (2001) [online]. Available at http://www.worldbank.org/poverty/voices/listen-findings.htm/.

UNICEF CHILD LABOR CARTOON

From *Cartoons for Children's Rights* (1998) [online]. Available at http://www.unicef.org/broadcast/.
Copyright UNICEF. Reprinted by permission.

Handout 9.6

QUESTIONS ABOUT THE CHILD LABOR CARTOON

1. What is the boy doing?

2. Why did the artist draw so many soccer balls around the boy?

3. Why did the artist draw the shelves so that they appear to come together over the boy's head?

4. Why is there a soccer ball flying through the air outside the window? Why did the artist include this detail in the cartoon?

5. Why do you think the artist put the horizon line near the bottom of this cartoon?

6. How does the darkness in the room add to the meaning of this cartoon?

7. What is the subject of this cartoon?

8. What meaning was the artist trying to convey with this cartoon? What was his or her point? (Give a thorough explanation, using your answers to the above questions as a resource.)

Real-World Investigations for Social Studies
Hoge, Field, Foster, and Nickell

VOICES OF CHILD LABORERS: GROUP 1

Ruth: A Street Worker in Guatemala

My name is Ruth, and my life has been very sad. [Ruth's family lived in a shack made out of corrugated tin and other materials. Her family left El Salvador to avoid war and emigrated to Guatemala.] My father began to fix shoes. He'd go out and take all of us. When my older brother was seven, my father made him his little shoeshine box. And he told him that he was going to shine shoes. Then, after that, my little brother also began, and I came and said to my father that I also wanted to help him because it wasn't right that my brothers also worked and not me. So they decided to dress me as a man. They dressed me like a man and they made a little box for me also.

And sometimes my brother shined or sometimes no or sometimes he would begin to clean car windows and I would begin to ask for money when the cars stopped at the traffic lights. And when we had gathered up a quantity we would arrive at the house already really late, like eleven or twelve at night. And always when we went in my father would hit us. Because we arrive really late and he thought that perhaps we were, like that we had stayed out doing something bad, and no. And we would hand over the money to him, because to him we gave it. [More than 335,000 children are street workers in Guatemala City. They shine shoes, beg for money, and collect garbage along with other types of legal and illegal work.]

Paraphrased and shortened from Tierney, N. L. (1997). *Robbed of humanity: Lives of Guatemalan street children* (pp. 32–35). St. Paul: Pangaea.

Handout 9.8

VOICES OF CHILD LABORERS: GROUP 2

Suka Maya: A Factory Worker in Nepal

One year ago, Suka Maya Magar came to Kathmandu [Katmandu] with a relative to work in a carpet factory to earn money for her poverty-stricken family in Charikot village. The 10-year-old spent her first 3 months in training. She had to work from morning to night learning to weave, but the middleman (boss) fed her only once a day and did not pay her anything. At night she slept on a bare floor scattered with some waste wool.

Even after her training period, Suka Maya was not paid anything. Tired of working long hours on an empty stomach and of the regular nagging and physical abuse of the middleman, she tried twice to run away. Both times she was brought back, and the broker beat her with an iron stick. On the third attempt she succeeded in running away, only to work in another factory. A friend who brought her to the new place had told her that it would be better. So tired was Suka Maya of the previous factory that she thought nothing could be worse. For all of her one year of work in Kathmandu she has not earned even a penny, nor has she had any contact with her family. Although she detests the work here and her health is deteriorating, she is apprehensive about going back home. She thinks her stepmother, who has seven children to feed, would not like to have her back.

Paraphrased and shortened from Pradhan, G. (1993). *Misery behind the looms: Child labourers in the carpet factories in Nepal* (pp. 38–39). Kalimati, Kathmandu, Nepal: CWIN (Child Workers in Nepal Concerned Center).

VOICES OF CHILD LABORERS: GROUP 3

Belinda: A Migrant Farmworker in the United States

My name is Belinda Quintanilla. Three years ago, at the age of 11, I started working in the fields, picking squash and bell peppers at different farms. Each summer, my family migrates from Mission, Texas, to the eastern shore of Maryland. The worst part about migrating is having to adjust everywhere I go, even if I don't like it. Since my first year in school I have had to change schools twice a year. Because I like to read, changing schools has not affected my education too much.

It is terrible working in the fields. I work alongside my parents under the sun, huffing and puffing and aching everywhere. Sometimes there is no clean water available to quench our thirst, and most of the time there is no water for washing our hands and faces before eating or after going to the bathroom.

For me, there is no such thing as a summer vacation. Once school is out, we pack our things and head to Maryland to find work. We have to work every single day when work is available, even if it is ninety degrees or raining. Instead of going home while it rains, we wait under the trees to see if the rain will pass. We have to work because we need the money. It is very dangerous to work in the fields because of all the pesticides that are used to control insects. On the very first day of work this season, I developed a rash all over my legs. The rash made my legs very red and itchy. But even so, I went to work the next day.

Picking squash gets easier day by day, but the pay is low. I have to pick at least 60 buckets to make it worthwhile. A full bucket weighs about 25 pounds. By the way, I don't eat squash because it reminds me of working in the fields.

Although American farm-working children are not bound or beaten, I feel that the loss of young minds is great. No child belongs in the field, and every child deserves an opportunity to enjoy their childhood.

I would like the government to consider regulations and programs that could help children who work in the fields. I am not asking for a handout. I am simply asking for the opportunity to learn and work while helping my parents.

Paraphrased and shortened from Parker, D. L., with Engfer, L., & Conrow, R. (1998). *Stolen dreams* (pp. 28–29). Minneapolis: Lerner.

Handout 9.10

VOICES OF CHILD LABORERS: GROUP 4

Selvakumar: A Silver Factory Worker in India

Selvakumar, a 12-year-old boy, was sent by his parents to the silversmith at the age of 8 because he was "not studying properly." They received a 3,000-rupee [approximately $85] advance for their son; his mother later approached the employer for additional loans, which he gave her. Selvakumar's work schedule varied according to the season. During the months leading up to the holiday of Diwali, the workers are driven at a furious pace, and Selvakumar worked from 7:30 a.m. until midnight or 1:00 a.m. the following morning. After the holidays, the demand for silver drops, and the silver shops return to an 8:00 a.m. to 8:00 p.m. schedule. At the time he left the shop, Selvakumar was earning 350 rupees a month [less than $8].

He described his work as very difficult and very hot. His job was to solder small decorative flowers to the jewelry and solder screws on to earrings. "Very small pieces have to be placed in very small and precise spots. We used small wire for this job, like a bicycle spoke. Sometimes the owner would beat me with this hot wire if he thought I wasn't working properly. He would take the wire and beat me on the arms." After 3 years, Selvakumar ran away from the factory. The first time he ran away, an older brother found him and brought him back. The second time, the owner found him at a shelter for street children, but the shelter's director refused to turn him over to the man. His mother then came and took him back to the factory, but he did not last long. He ran away a third and final time. Selvakumar did not return to his parents' house and assumed they had to pay back the original loan. Selvakumar was interviewed by Human Rights Watch at a shelter for street children.

Paraphrased and shortened from Human Rights Watch Children's Rights Project. (1996). *The small hands of slavery: Bonded child labor in India* (p. 67). New York: Human Rights Watch.

VOICES OF CHILD LABORERS: GROUP 5

Willie: A Newspaper Delivery Boy in the United States

Willie was a 16-year-old tenth grader at the local school. There were about 18,000 people in Willie's small town, approximately 100 miles from the nearest metropolitan city. . . . His clothes were unfashionable and too small; his pants ended above his ankles, his T-shirts were tight, and his jacket sleeves didn't reach his wrists.

Since his mother's death 6 years before the interview and his father's imprisonment 10 years before that, Willie had lived as an only child with his maternal grandparents, his mother's older sister, and her husband. He had two younger half-brothers, but he had not seen them since his mother's death. No one in Willie's family had ever graduated from high school, but they all encouraged Willie's efforts to graduate. Willie's family had limited income, consisting of Social Security benefits and a small amount from Willie's part-time, minimum-wage job. The family paid $62 a month rent for a small white wood-frame six-room house in an old low-income area. The small, neat rooms were arranged so that one had to go through each room to get to the next. One room was a converted one-car garage. There were no interior doors, except to the bathroom. The modest older furniture, mostly from the 1950s and 1960s, was lined up along the walls of each room. The family did not own a car, and Willie did not have a driver's license or driving permit. Willie had a 10-speed bicycle, which he kept in his room.

Willie's aunt had helped him get his part-time job at the local newspaper. According to his grandmother and aunt, Willie considered his job important. His grandmother boasted that Willie's boss said he could do just about anything at work. Willie kept the part-time job for more than 2 years. He did not attend school during the second semester of his sophomore year. Both his aunt and his employer tried to get Willie back in school. They went to school and talked with the administration to ensure that Willie could get back into school. Willie's employer told him he must go back to school and that his job was secure as long as he stayed in school.

Paraphrased and shortened from Strother, D. B. (Ed.). (1991). *Learning to fail: Case studies of students at risk* (pp. 59–69). Bloomington, IN: Phi Delta Kappa, Maynard R. Bemis Center for Evaluation, Development, and Research.

Handout 9.12
VOICES OF CHILD LABORERS: EXPERT GROUP WORK QUESTIONS

Based on what you have learned from the story, answer the following questions:

1. Where does your child laborer work and what does his or her job consist of?

2. What are the working conditions of your child laborer?

3. What is the family life of your child laborer?

4. Why do you think children work?

5. Is it ever good for children to work? Why?

6. What do you think "blaming the victim" means?

Real-World Investigations for Social Studies
Hoge, Field, Foster, and Nickell

LEARNING FROM GROUP EXPERTS

1. From what you have learned about poverty, how does poverty affect these children's lives?

   a. Ruth

   b. Suka Maya

   c. Belinda

   d. Selvakumar

   e. Willie

2. Explain why the children, who are working so hard, cannot get out of poverty.

3. What are the causes or roots of poverty?

4. Without blaming the victims, carefully describe how it might be possible to break the cycle of poverty.

THE STORY OF IQBAL MASIH

Iqbal Masih was a bonded child laborer who lived in Pakistan. His parents were so poor that they couldn't feed their children and so, in exchange for a very small amount of money, they allowed their 4-year-old son to work in a carpet factory. The loan was to be paid through what Iqbal earned, only 3 cents a day, less than $1 a month.

Conditions in the factory were dreadful. The hours were long, often 14 hours a day starting at 6:00 a.m. The work required the children to knot small pieces of thread to the warf threads to make the carpets, which have very intricate designs. It takes more than a million small knots to make one carpet. Lighting was very poor, and in the summer there were no fans and no open windows. The children were not allowed to talk to each other—the owner thought mistakes would be made. Being late, complaining, or making mistakes was met with beatings with a wooden cane, being hung upside down by the ankles tightly bound with rope, and even being chained to the loom.

No education was provided for the children, they were rarely fed enough, and the only break in the day was a 30-minute lunch period. At age 10 Iqbal was only 4 feet tall and weighed less than 60 pounds. The years of bending over the loom had caused his back to curve. His hands were very scarred, calloused, and gnarled from all the years of tying knots.

Because his father left the family, his mother had to borrow more money, and Iqbal soon realized that he could never pay off the loan. He had to find a way out.

When he was 11, Iqbal heard a man speak about laws that prohibited child labor. The man was Ehsan Ulla Khan, who had founded Bonded Labor Liberation Front (BLLF) in 1988 to fight against bonded and child labor in Pakistan.

Iqbal went back to the factory and told the owner that he was breaking the law. Again he was beaten, but Iqbal escaped. Two days later, when the owner came for him, Iqbal stood his ground. Fortunately, Khan helped. He enrolled Iqbal in a school for child laborers like himself. The two began speaking together about the horrors of child labor. By the time he was 12, Iqbal was speaking to very large crowds in Pakistan and India. He was even invited to speak in Europe and America, and in 1994 was awarded a Reebok Human Rights Award. He was also named Person of the Week by *ABC World News* on December 9, 1994.

When people around the world learned how the carpets were made, sales began to drop. The carpet factory owners blamed the organizations that were attempting to prohibit child labor and the "child revolutionary." Iqbal's life was in danger.

In 1995, when he was 12, Iqbal was murdered while riding a bike in the countryside. Though the murderers were never found, many believe he was killed by the "carpet mafia."

BLLF has successfully freed more than 30,000 children from bonded labor and runs its own schools. Despite the good work of this and other organizations there are an estimated 7.5 million children who are bonded laborers. More than 500,000 children like Iqbal work in the carpet industry. Because carpet factory owners, usually rich and influential men in their communities, are often under the protection of the local police, laws against enslaving children are seldom enforced.

Paraphrased and shortened from Parker, D. L., with Engfer, L., & Conrow, R. (1998). *Stolen dreams: Portraits of working children* (pp. 9–18). Minneapolis: Lerner.

Group Discussion Questions

1. What is bonded labor?

2. What is the difference between bonded labor and slavery?

3. Why would parents sell their child into bonded labor?

4. How does child labor contribute to the cycle of poverty?

5. What can be done to prevent child labor? Think about the causes of poverty.

6. If poverty no longer existed, would child labor still exist? Explain your answer.

Real-World Investigations for Social Studies
Hoge, Field, Foster, and Nickell

Handout 9.15

"A BULLET CAN'T KILL A DREAM"

In 1994, seventh-grade students at Broad Meadows Middle School in Quincy, Massachusetts, were fortunate to meet Iqbal Masih just a few months before he was killed. Iqbal told the students that he would like to start a school in his village for children freed from bonded labor. The students at Broad Meadows Middle School decided to make Iqbal's dream come true and began raising money to build his school.

The altruistic students worked before and after school and even worked during vacations to raise money. They sent their message about Iqbal called "A Bullet Can't Kill a Dream" through letters, faxes, fliers, and a Web site (www.digitalrag.com/iqbal/index.html#more). By February 1997, they had raised a phenomenal $143,000 from people in all 50 states and 22 other countries and the "School for Iqbal" was opened. The money raised is also used to buy children out of bondage on the condition that the children are enrolled at the school.

The School for Iqbal was built for 278 of the poorest children, ages 4 through 12, who have never gone to school. The school is located in the city of Kasur, Pakistan, in the Punjab Province where Iqbal was born, sold into bondage, and murdered. The students also established the Iqbal Masih Education Foundation, which will pay all the daily operating expenses for years to come.

The School for Iqbal has a very low dropout rate, and the cycle of poverty is being broken through education and "micro-credit loans." These loans had been made to over 40 Pakistani mothers by August 2001. The mothers create their own small craft business and repay the loan once the business breaks the family out of poverty. Over 90 percent of the School for Iqbal mini-loans have been repaid, which enables more loans to be given to those in poverty.

From Broad Meadows Middle School. *The kids campaign to build a school for Iqbal* [online]. Available at http://www.digitalrag.com/iqbal/

Group Discussion Questions

1. Based on what you have learned about poverty, what can you do to help prevent child labor?

2. What can you do to help end poverty?

3. Why are there few children like Iqbal who take action and fight? (Be careful not to blame the victim.)

4. What tactics can you employ to help bring about change?

Real-World Investigations for Social Studies
Hoge, Field, Foster, and Nickell

U.S. POVERTY STATISTICS (1998)

BY RACE	POPULATION (IN 1,000s)	NUMBER OF PEOPLE IN POVERTY (1,000s)	PERCENT IN POVERTY	PERCENT IN POVERTY			
				NORTHEAST REGION	MIDWEST REGION	SOUTH REGION	WEST REGION
Total (U.S.)	271,059	34,424	12.7	12.3	10.3	13.7	14.0
White	222,837	23,398	10.5	9.5	8.1	10.7	13.8
Black	34,877	9,103	26.1	29.9	27.2	25.3	20.2
Hispanic	31,515	8,068	25.6	29.6	20.3	23.5	26.7

AGE (YEARS)	PERCENT OF TOTAL U.S. POOR
0-6	20.6
7-17	18.1
18-24	16.6
25-44	10.4
45-64	8.0
65-74	9.1
75+	12.2

TYPE OF RESIDENCE	PERCENT OF TOTAL U.S. POOR
In central cities	18.5
Metropolitan area outside of central cities	8.7
Outside metropolitan areas	14.4

FAMILY RELATIONSHIP	PERCENTAGE OF TOTAL U.S. POOR
Married couple	6.2
Married w/children under 18	7.9
Female head of household (FHOH)	33.1
FHOH w/children under 18	40.9

Real-World Investigations for Social Studies
Hoge, Field, Foster, and Nickell

Handout 9.17

DIRECTION SHEET: GRAPHS OF U.S. POVERTY STATISTICS

1. Give students a copy of the U.S. Poverty Statistics chart (Handout 9.16). Also, make sure that each small group has drawing paper and colored pencils.
2. Draw examples of bar graphs and pie charts on the dry erase board so that students will have a form to guide them during the exercise.
3. Students are to construct seven graphs from the census data. Graphs should be structured to represent the following information:

   - Graph 1—The number of people in the United States living below the poverty line:
     a. Total number
     b. Number of blacks
     c. Number of Hispanics
     d. Number of whites
   - Graph 2—People in the United States living below the poverty line as a percentage of the:
     a. Total population
     b. Black population
     c. Hispanic population
     d. White population
   - Graph 3—Percentage of those living in poverty by region:
     a. Northeast
     b. Midwest
     c. South
     d. West
   - Graph 4—Percentage of those living below the poverty line in each region by race:
     a. Northeast: black, Hispanic, white
     b. Midwest: black, Hispanic, white
     c. South: black, Hispanic, white
     d. West: black, Hispanic, white
   - Graph 5—Percentage of those in poverty living in:
     a. Central cities
     b. Metropolitan areas (minus central cities, i.e., suburbs)
     c. Outside of metropolitan areas
   - Graph 6—Percentage of U.S. residents in various age groups who live below the poverty line:
     a. Under age 6
     b. Ages 7–17
     c. Ages 18–24
     d. Ages 25–44
     e. Ages 45–64
     f. Ages 65–74
     g. Ages 75+

- Graph 7—Percentage of those living in various family relationships who are existing below the poverty line:
    a. Married couples
    b. Married couples with children under age 18
    c. FHOH (no husband present)
    d. FHOH (no husband present) with children under age 18
    e. Adults living alone
    f. Adults 65+ years old

Real-World Investigations for Social Studies
Hoge, Field, Foster, and Nickell

221

HANDOUT 9.18

QUESTION SHEET: ANALYSIS OF U.S. POVERTY DATA

1. What type of family, from among those listed in Handout 9.17, seems to have the most difficult time economically? Why might this be the case?

2. What type of family, from among those listed in Handout 9.17, seems best able to avoid living in poverty?

3. Most of the people living in poverty in the United States belong to what race? Does this mean that people belonging to this race are at greater risk of being poor than people of other races? Explain your answer.

4. Americans at greatest risk for being poor are in what age group? How would you explain this?

5. Which age group has the lowest percentage of people living in poverty? What are some possible explanations for this?

6. The percentage of those living in poverty increases sharply in the 75+ age group. Why might this be the case?

7. Does Handout 9.17 reveal anything that surprises you? If so, what?

Real-World Investigations for Social Studies
Hoge, Field, Foster, and Nickell

222

BUDGET SHEET

Tim and Sarah Jacobs head a family of four that is living just above the U.S. poverty line. Their two children, Carly and David, are 4 and 2 years old, respectively. Four months ago, Tim lost his job at an auto parts store and has been staying home with the children, while Sarah works full-time as an office assistant. Sarah's gross income is $19,500 per year. After taxes, Sarah brings home approximately $17,500 per year. Below is a monthly budget for the Jacobs family, which you must help them to complete. Using the classified ads, apartment guides, and the information you gathered about the cost of food, consider the following:

1. What is the total monthly income for the Jacobs family?
2. The Jacobs family cannot afford to spend more than 40 percent of their monthly income on housing. What is the largest amount of money they can afford to pay per month for an apartment? Determine this amount and then locate an apartment with a rent within their budget.
3. How much money does it take to feed a family of four per month? Determine the amount based on your research and write this total in the proper space on the budget sheet.
4. How much money will the family have left to spend on clothing? How much money do you spend on clothing per year? How can a family of four clothe themselves on this budget?

Monthly Income:	_____
Rent:	_____
Food:	_____
Car (one car, including payments, insurance, and maintenance):	$320
Clothing:	_____
Utilities (phone, electricity, water):	$150
Miscellaneous (toiletries, household goods, entertainment):	$80
Debt (from two credit cards):*	$70

---

*The Jacobs have accumulated $2,000 worth of debt on one credit card and $1,500 on another credit card. The annual interest rate for each card is 18 percent. In order to begin paying off the debt, the Jacobs must pay at least $70 a month in addition to any of the budgeted monthly expenses that are purchased with the credit cards.

Handout 9.20

QUESTION SHEET FOR BUDGET EXERCISE

1. Taking into account their current financial situation, should the Jacobs use all of the money in the budget for apartment rent, or should they try to find a cheaper apartment and use the money they save elsewhere? Explain.
2. Sarah Jacobs's father has decided to give his daughter $50 a month to help with expenses. Sarah and Tim decide to either save the money or use it to help pay off their credit card debt. Sarah knows that she can put the money in a savings account at the bank that will pay 3.5 percent interest per year. What should the couple do: Save all of the money, save a portion and use the rest to pay off the debt, or use all of the money to pay off the debt until it is paid in full? Why? Explain your answer.
3. Carly Jacobs wants to take swimming lessons, which will cost the Jacobs $30 a month. Can the Jacobs afford lessons for their daughter? If so, where in the budget will they find the money?
4. Tim Jacobs finds a job working full-time at a warehouse. Making $7 an hour, Tim will bring home a yearly net income of $12,000. How much money will that add to the Jacobs' monthly budget? What would you do with this extra money?
5. Before the money Tim brings home can be added to the budget, a couple of new expenses must be taken into account. Because Tim and Sarah now both work during the day, Carly and David will have to be placed in day care. After checking with a number of day-care facilities in their area, the Jacobs decide to place their children in a center that has a good reputation. The cost of day care for both children is $800 per month. In addition, Tim must ride the bus to and from work. He purchases a bus pass each month costing $20. After paying these new expenses, how much money do the Jacobs have to spend each month? What would you advise them to do with this money?
6. Do you think the amount of money Tim will add to the family is worth all the work he will do? Would you take the job if you were Tim? Discuss reasons that Tim might take the job and reasons that he might decide not to take the job.

Real-World Investigations for Social Studies
Hoge, Field, Foster, and Nickell

10

CHAPTER

Connecting Students to Their Communities Through Service

by

Joseph R. Feinberg

Everyone can be great, because anyone can serve.

–Dr. Martin Luther King, Jr.

OVERVIEW

Older generations have little confidence in today's children and often lament the limited involvement of younger generations in the community. A study by Public Agenda, a nonprofit research and education group, found that American adults are skeptical about whether children, once grown, will make the country a better place. Furthermore, the majority of American adults believe that today's youth fail to learn values such as honesty and respect. Teenagers are also viewed as rude, wild, irresponsible, spoiled, and not friendly or helpful to neighbors. Over two-thirds (65 percent) of those who have regular contact with teenagers describe them disapprovingly (Farkas & Johnson, 1997, p. 9).

The lessons in this chapter connect students to their communities by creating greater understanding, appreciation, and participation in community service. In particular, students learn about other children volunteering throughout history and making a difference in their communities. Only a little guidance is necessary to elicit the civic virtue that all children possess.

At the turn of the 20th century, the social studies curriculum was developed in response to a perceived need for "cultivating an active participatory citizenship" (Wade & Saxe, 1996). The NCSS recently issued a position statement that promotes service-learning as an essential component of social studies education. "Service-learning greatly enhances the potential for social studies teachers to fulfill their mission of educating informed and active citizens who are committed to improving society through a democratic process" (NCSS, 1994, p. 241). Furthermore, *Curriculum Standards for Social Studies* (1994) emphasizes the importance of strengthening the "common good" through citizen action. Service-learning fills a special niche for civics education by addressing societal needs and strengthening the common good through the social studies. This chapter provides a method for coupling classroom learning and community needs with the ultimate goal of meaningful learning and democratic participation.

"'Service learning' is community service with a learning component attached" to classroom activities, assessment, and curriculum (Nickell & Field, 1999). Through service-learning, students explore specific neighborhood and community service options as the class examines projects undertaken by other teenagers in the United States and abroad. The lessons direct students to investigate "mandatory community service" and discuss the controversy surrounding community service requirements. For closure and assessment purposes, the students create a proposal for a community service project and write investigative news reports about mandatory community service.

CONNECTION TO NCSS THEME X: CIVIC IDEALS AND PRACTICES

The primary NCSS curriculum theme addressed by this chapter is Civic Ideals and Practices. Service-learning naturally embraces essential national curriculum standards based on citizenship and citizen action. Students are provided an opportunity to learn beyond the classroom through meaningful analysis of readings and activities concerning community participation and citizen action.

As a result of their participation in this chapter, students will develop a greater understanding of civic action, their role in the community, and the intrinsic rewards of doing something positive and valuable for the community. The ultimate goals of this chapter are to inspire students to overcome apathy and a feeling of isolation and to get them involved in their own community projects.

METHODS FOCUS: SERVICE-LEARNING

Service-learning naturally complements CTL. Students are engaged in real-life problems that are integrated with curricular requirements and involve higher-level thinking through reflection. In addition, students' knowledge is increased, expanding from the classroom to the community around them. Students evaluate and act on societal needs and problems through a variety of informed and researched strategies.

A quality service-learning project, for example, might involve a student or group of students in examining a number of concerns and identifying an appealing real issue. The issue should be selected by the students, not the teacher, to ensure that it is a personally meaningful project for the students. After the issue is identified, teachers or project facilitators should assess how well students understand its social, historical, institutional, and economic aspects. Research reports, discussions, or project proposals (see Lesson Three) establish a preliminary foundation for creating a service-learning project. For example, if the issue is hunger, students could research nutrition and identify, chart, analyze, and discuss the geographical regions of food sources (Fertman, White, & White, 1996, p. 141). In addition, students could examine demographic and economic data to learn about the food needs of the population that they desire to serve. Activities might involve students visiting a grocery store to evaluate the cost and origins of various foods or inviting guest speakers from a local food bank.

After a well-researched understanding of the issue has been established, goals should be created by the students and facilitated by the teacher to direct the purpose of the service project. The purpose of the project will determine the type or category of service-learning that students choose. The three categories of service-learning are direct service, indirect service, and civic action (Fertman et al., 1996, p. 30). Direct service involves personal contact with the individuals being served and ideally occurs over a long period of time. Relationships are more likely to develop through direct contact with those being served, and students feel they are making a significant contribution. Students working with the elderly at a nursing home is an example of direct service. In contrast, indirect service is easier to organize and typically involves channeling resources to an issue, such as raising money or collecting goods to support an organization that helps provide the needs of a community. For example, a project relating to hunger may utilize an indirect approach to provide local food needs by creating a canned-food drive for a local food bank. The third category is civic action, in which students actively work to eliminate or alleviate a societal problem and inform the general public about the issue. Petitioning the local government to fund a homeless shelter and writing letters to the newspaper to promote public awareness of homelessness are examples of civic action.

It is possible to integrate all three types of service into a cohesive service-learning project. Students may first learn about the political and institutional factors through civic action, then progress to indirect service to help provide resources, and culminate in direct service by helping those in need (Fertman et al., 1996, p. 31).

Community partnerships with parents, businesses, and charitable organizations are an important aspect of service-learning. Partnerships support positive and productive interaction with adults, which helps improve awareness and relationships between the two groups. As noted in the Overview, adults have a negative image of children and teenagers, so there is a need for improved relations.

In order to promote meaningful learning, it is essential to encourage students to reflect on their experiences throughout the service-learning process.

Reflection is a fundamental aspect of service-learning. It ensures that students evaluate their experiences and synthesize the information and theories they encounter and create. Without reflection, many of the learning benefits from participating in the service-learning experience are potentially lost.

Reflection can occur throughout the service-learning process. An ideal method of promoting reflection is through student writing or journals that detail learning, misconceptions, and theories. Teachers should periodically respond to written reflections with comments and questions that invite students to develop their understanding further. Other forms of reflection include, but are not limited to, discussions, letters, reports, essays, and project presentations that require clear justification through evaluation and analysis of an issue or problem. For example, a popular and successful reflection technique entails students writing letters to parents, student newspapers, local newspapers, government representatives, government agencies, and businesses to describe the benefits of a service project. The benefits should not only focus on the people who are helped, but should also provide details and an explanation of what students have learned in their own words.

Table 10.1 Lesson Overview for "Connecting Students to their Communities through Service"

	GOALS	ACTIVITIES	ASSESSMENTS
LESSON ONE	• Understand the concept of community service. • Identify the types of community service.	• Groups read community service scenarios and discuss the elements of community service (Handout 10.1). • Students answer questions about the purpose and types of community service (Handout 10.2). • Homework: Students investigate the types of community service options in their community or neighborhood (interview parents and neighbors).	• Collect and review students' answers to scenarios (Handout 10.2).
LESSON TWO	• Explore the historical roots of community service. • Connect past community service to the present.	• The class completes a historical chart on youth community involvement and analyzes a picture of youth protesting (Handouts 10.3–10.5). • Students read and discuss narratives about youth serving in the past and present (Handout 10.4 and 10.6).	• Examine students' charts and answers to questions (Handouts 10.3 and 10.6).
LESSON THREE	• Share reports about community service options researched by each student. • Learn from the Internet about community service resources and organizations.	• The class discusses and classifies findings from the homework investigation. • Students create a community service project proposal (Handout 10.7). • Students research community service information and organizations on the Internet (Handout 10.8).	• Evaluate community service project proposals using the grading rubric in Lesson Three.
LESSON FOUR	• Examine examples of youth performing community service.	• Have the students read, answer questions, and discuss inspiring vignettes about children who perform community service (Handouts 10.9–10.11).	• Collect and review students' answers to the questions (Handout 10.12).
LESSON FIVE	• Research and write about mandatory community service.	• Students read an article to understand and discuss the controversy surrounding mandatry community service (Handout 10.13). • Students create a news article on mandatory community service (Handout 10.14).	• Collect and critique the news articles created by students (Handout 10.14).

LESSON ONE: What Is Community Service?

Purpose This lesson introduces students to the concepts that underlie community service. The class formulates a definition of community service and explains its purpose. Students also learn to identify examples and nonexamples of community service. As a homework project, students investigate the community service options in their neighborhoods or communities.

Duration One class period

Materials
Handout 10.1: Helping Hands
Handout 10.2: Understanding the Concepts

Procedures
1. Have students read the scenarios in Handout 10.1 and write their responses to the questions. Discuss the questions and responses after students have completed them.

2. Have students discuss the basic concepts of community service in groups of three or four using the guide questions in Handout 10.2. Ask the students to share their responses in a class discussion.

3. Homework Assignment: "Community Service Investigators": Give students the first homework assignment that asks them to investigate the community service options available in their neighborhood or community. The investigative report should include a minimum of five suggestions about community service projects, at least two of which are developed through interviews with adults (parents or neighbors). The report should list potential projects that the students are capable of creating, leading, or joining in their neighborhood or community. The findings from this homework are integrated in Lesson Three.

LESSON TWO: Youth Service Past and Present

Purpose This lesson helps students see that young people have always contributed to the development and preservation of democratic ideals through active community involvement and service.

Duration One class period

Materials
Handout 10.3: Historical Chart
Handout 10.4: Roosevelt's World War II Army of Community Service Workers
Handout 10.5: Children on Strike
Handout 10.6: The Children's Peace Statues

Procedures
1. Provide each student with a copy of the Historical Chart (Handout 10.3) and encourage students to fill it out in groups of three or four.

2. Instruct students to read about children who volunteered to help during World War II (Handout 10.4) and answer the questions that follow. Facilitate a discussion based on the questions.

3. Show students the picture of Philadelphia children on strike from a textile factory (Handout 10.5) with signs that read "We want to go to school!" Ask the class what they see in the picture. Next, ask how the children in the picture must have felt about work, school, and their community. The children worked 60 hours a week and wanted a shorter work week, which they won. Did they serve their community by winning a shorter work week?

4. Read the narrative about Sadako Sasaki and the Children's Peace Statues (Handout 10.6) and have students answer the discussion questions.

Teacher's Copy (with Answers) of Handout 10.3	
HISTORICAL EVENT/PERIOD	**HOW DID CHILDREN HELP?**
The American Revolution	Boys were informants and fought in the war against the British; girls made clothes and other supplies for the soldiers.
The Underground Railroad	Boys and girls helped the slaves fleeing from the South. Some scouted the fields for escaped slaves and assisted them to the next safe house.
Industrial Revolution and child labor	Child workers protested working conditions through strikes and walkouts and ultimately improved working conditions.
World War II	Boys and girls engaged in war bond campaigns, scrap and salvage collection drives, victory gardens, conservation and recycling activities.

LESSON THREE: Helping My Community

Purpose In this lesson, students classify and discuss the diversity of service options utilizing their investigative reports from the "Community Service Investigators" homework assignment (Lesson One).

Duration One class period

Materials

Handout 10.7: Service Learning Project Proposal
Handout 10.8: Internet Activity

Procedures

1. Community service classification exercise (Taba, 1966)

   a. Write on the board or overhead the community service options from the homework findings of each student's investigation ("Community Service Investigators," Lesson One).

   b. Ask the students to analyze the list and differentiate the suggestions that have dissimilar characteristics. For example, raising money to install lights in a park is different from raising awareness for a crime prevention project.

   c. Next, group community service options based on similar or common characteristics and then categorize the groups.

2. Write the following slogan (sometimes seen on bumper stickers) on the board or make an overhead:

"Think Globally, Act Locally." Discuss with the class the meaning of this slogan. Facilitate the discussion so that the students understand that without local action, little global improvement will occur.

3. Homework: Handout 10.7: Service Learning Project Proposal. Students create a proposal for their own community service project. Encourage students to research their topic in their community and school library, the Internet, and through discussions with parents, neighbors, or community members. This project proposal provides students with the opportunity and responsibility to strengthen their civic ideals and practices (refer to the NCSS standards). In order for students to better conceptualize their individual projects, students are required to write a detailed description of the project (Handout 10.7), which may be used as a form of assessment or progress grade. A grading rubric is included.

4. Additional Suggested Activity: Research community service options through the Internet (Handout 10.8: Internet Activity). Depending on the availability of computers, students can work in groups or individually. Because Web sites are constantly changing, be sure to visit the Web sites before class to ensure that they have not changed in design or content. This activity is easily modified by changing the directions and questions if necessary.

Grading Rubric for the Community Service Project Proposal

	NOVICE	ACCEPTABLE	EXPERT
Rationale	Justification for the project is unclear and/or of questionable importance.	The purpose of the project is justifiable.	There is a clearly justifiable purpose for the project. There is a need statement and supporting ideas.
Goals	Goals are unreasonable and/or unrelated to the purpose and rationale.	Most goals are attainable and aligned with the rationale. Some may be somewhat unreasonable.	There is a list of attainable goals that are aligned with the rationale.
Steps, procedures, resources	Steps, procedures, and resources are difficult to follow, unclearly described, and/or illogical.	Steps, procedures, and resources are listed but may not be clear or logically sequenced.	Steps, procedures, and resources are organized logically, clearly, and thoroughly.
Timeline	The timeline is incomplete and/or is illogical.	The timeline may not include or provide ample time for all steps; the sequence may not be logical.	The timeline is reasonable and well sequenced.
References	References are absent or minimal.	The list of sources is not extensive or thorough.	There is a list of multiple sources to support the project and goals.

LESSON FOUR: Youth Enjoying Service (Y.E.S.)

Purpose In this lesson, students examine stories of youth performing community service. The stories are likely to make the students realize that anything is possible, even at a young age. The students also discuss how and why some young people succeed in their endeavor to help others.

Duration One class period

Materials

Handouts 10.9: Jon Wagner-Holtz, Founder of Kids Konnected

Handout 10.10: Dwaina Brooks: Feeding the Homeless in Dallas

Handout 10.11: Children's Rain Forest

Handout 10.12: Discussion Questions for Youth Enjoying Service

Procedures

1. Briefly discuss examples of teens making a difference, which introduces Lesson Four.
   a. For example, consider Iqbal Masih and his fight against child bondage in Pakistan, and Broad Meadows Middle School fighting against child bondage and the cycle of poverty from Chapter 9, "Confronting the Cycle of Poverty."
   b. Introduce Jon Wagner-Holtz, who established a hotline for children whose parents have cancer.
   c. Introduce Dwaina Brooks, who organized family and friends to feed the homeless.
   d. Introduce the Children's Rain Forest Network, which was established by Swedish children to preserve the rain forests.

2. Have students read the narratives (Handout 10.9–10.11) of youth enjoying service. First, read the questions (Handout 10.12) so that the students reflect on their answers as they read.

3. Instruct the students to answer the questions after they finish the narratives.

4. Discuss the answers to the questions as a class and write on the board or overhead a summary of the responses.

LESSON FIVE: Mandatory Community Service Reporters

Purpose This lesson introduces the concept of mandatory community service. Many school districts around the country require students to perform a minimum number of community service hours in order to graduate. Mandatory community service is a controversial issue. Students play the role of newspaper reporter and explore both sides of the debate through research, provided readings, and the opinions of classmates and adults concerning mandatory community service.

Duration One class period

Materials

Handout 10.13: Community Service Plan Dividing Students in Dearborn

Handout 10.14: Newspaper Reporter Homework Assignment

Procedures

1. Review the class-established definition of community service from Lesson One.

2. Learn how some schools are mandating community service by reading and discussing an abridged news article (Handout 10.13: "Community Service Plan Dividing Students in Dearborn"). Instruct students to answer the questions that follow the article. Discuss the answers to the questions after students have finished.

3. In class and as a homework assignment (Handout 10.14), have students play the role of newspaper reporter to explore the issues surrounding mandatory community service. Instruct them to interview classmates, teachers, parents, and neighbors about this issue. Have students research the issue and create graphs based on national statistics. Remind students to use correct source citation. Also, encourage students to make their articles more colorful with illustrations, photographs, or cartoons.

4. Additional Suggested Activity: Allow the students to share their "Service Learning Project Proposals" (Handout 10.7) with the class. Presenting each proposal to the class individually or in groups will encourage further refinement of ideas and details. Students should receive positive feedback and constructive criticism to further develop an understanding of their service learning project proposals.
   a. Have the students create professional-quality presentations to convince the class that the proposal is a worthy project.
   b. Have students provide constructive feedback and refine the proposals as a class or in groups.

Handout 10.1

HELPING HANDS

Read the following cases about middle school students and answer the questions at the end.

Toña's Story

My name is Toña and I live in Albany, New York. My grandparents live in North Carolina, so I do not get to see them more than once or twice a year. It occurred to me that there are a lot of grandparents at the local nursing home who also do not get to see their grandchildren. So, I decided to spend some of my spare time visiting the nursing home. A great benefit of going is being able to listen to the many amazing stories that people share about their lives. Also, spending time at the nursing home is fun since I get to participate in various activities, such as board games and cards.

Scott's Story

Some people are really amazed that I spend so much time on my computer. My mother is a computer engineer and she taught me a lot about computers, but I learned some on my own. It is fun showing my friends how to use various computer programs. So, I decided to volunteer after school at a local learning center and tutor beginners on how to use the computer. Tutoring other people is challenging but also fun, and I have discovered that I learn even more about computers by showing someone else!

Abby's Story

My name is Abby, and some people have told me that I am a hard worker. My neighbors pay me to baby-sit on a regular basis because I am reliable and trustworthy. The children I baby-sit are so cute, and I really like watching them. However, I do not work for free unless I have to baby-sit my baby brother. Some of the money I earn is saved for college, but I like to spend most of it on new clothes and shoes.

Max's Story

Ever since I was a little kid, I have enjoyed spending some of my free time at the synagogue. I often volunteer to help set up for services or clean up after a special event like a wedding. Sometimes I assist with maintaining the synagogue's yard by pulling weeds, raking leaves, and planting flowers. I also help the synagogue collect and pack boxes of food for the needy on a regular basis.

Barb's Story

My name is Barb. When I was a young girl I asked my father why there was trash and broken glass around the neighborhood sidewalks. He said, "No one wants to take the responsibility and clean it." Now that I am older, I spend part of each weekend cleaning trash off the sidewalks around my neighborhood. Some of my friends will often help, and we enjoy the satisfaction of seeing that our neighborhood is clean and safe.

Real-World Investigations for Social Studies
Hoge, Field, Foster, and Nickell

Keith's Story

My afterschool job involves working at a local hospital. Helping nurses and doctors is a great experience because I hope to be a doctor when I grow up. The work is demanding, but I am paid relatively high wages. However, giving money to charity is very important to me. So, I give 10 percent of my earnings to my church, 10 percent to a homeless shelter, and another 10 percent to the hospital's burn victim fund.

Questions

1. From what you have just read, describe what each student does in his or her spare time.
   a. Toña
   b. Scott
   c. Abby
   d. Max
   e. Barb
   f. Keith

2. What motivates each student (or what is his or her purpose)?
   a. Toña
   b. Scott
   c. Abby
   d. Max
   e. Barb
   f. Keith

3. From what you have learned, which students are not community service volunteers? Why?

4. Is giving money to charity a form of community service? Why?

continued

Real-World Investigations for Social Studies
Hoge, Field, Foster, and Nickell

Handout 10.1 *continued*

5. What is the purpose of community service?

6. Why would you volunteer for community service?

7. What is the government's responsibility for the community?

8. Why would you work without getting paid?

Real-World Investigations for Social Studies
Hoge, Field, Foster, and Nickell

UNDERSTANDING THE CONCEPTS

1. How would you define community? Where does a community begin and end? Who lives in your community?

2. What does community mean to you?

3. Write the class definition of community in the space below.
   Community:

4. What does service mean to you? Who are you serving?

5. What does it mean to volunteer?

6. What is community service?

7. What can we do to serve our community?

8. What are the barriers to doing community service?

Real-World Investigations for Social Studies
Hoge, Field, Foster, and Nickell

Handout 10.3

HISTORICAL CHART

Based on what you know about the events in the chart below from class, reading books, watching TV, watching old movies, or talking to people, write in the chart how you think children might have helped.

HISTORICAL EVENT/PERIOD	HOW DID CHILDREN HELP?
The American Revolution	
The Underground Railroad	
Industrial Revolution and child labor	
World War II	

ROOSEVELT'S WORLD WAR II ARMY
OF COMMUNITY SERVICE WORKERS

President Franklin D. Roosevelt inspired "every single man, woman, and child" in the country to give up time, money, and goods for the war effort. After the Japanese bombed Pearl Harbor, the United States quickly transitioned into an economy that could fight a war of immense magnitude. Children and schools quickly started projects to raise money, recycle needed materials, grow gardens, harvest crops, and promote health and safety to help their communities during the war effort.

Schools in Massachusetts and Tennessee rallied the entire community to provide scrap and salvage materials needed for the war, such as paper, rubber, metals, and rags. A school in Baltimore, Maryland, collected more than six truckloads of scrap metal, and children in Bloomington, Illinois, recycled enough license plates to build a small tank. The collections were very successful primarily because children had "the opportunity to participate and feel useful" in the war effort.

Victory Gardens and *Victory Squadrons* were organized throughout the country to help plant and harvest crops. Many adults were fighting the war and were needed to make war materials (tanks, guns, planes, etc.). So, kids were needed to plant Victory Gardens to preserve food. Victory Squadrons were released early to pick cotton or harvest crops that adults were unable to collect. The children's "contributions as valuable community service workers paved the way toward keeping home front morale buoyed."

Paraphrased and shortened from Field, S. L. (1996). Roosevelt's World War II army of community service workers: Children and their teachers. *Social Education 60*(5), 280–283.

Discussion Questions

1. Why were children considered "valuable community service workers" during World War II?

2. What are some services children can perform to help their country?

continued

3. Why is it important for children to help?

4. How are kids "valuable community service workers" today?

5. How would you help your community or country?

Real-World Investigations for Social Studies
Hoge, Field, Foster, and Nickell

CHILDREN ON STRIKE

Real-World Investigations for Social Studies
Hoge, Field, Foster, and Nickell

THE CHILDREN'S PEACE STATUES

Children in New Mexico learned about the horrors of the atom bomb that was dropped on Hiroshima, Japan, at the end of World War II. They were moved to action by the true story of one girl, Sadako Sasaki, who was 2 years old during the bombing and 10 years later contracted leukemia. There is no cure for leukemia, which the Japanese called the *atom bomb disease* because many people died from it after the atom bomb was dropped. When Sadako Sasaki was hospitalized for leukemia, she learned about an ancient Japanese legend. According to the legend, someone who folds 1,000 paper cranes will be granted his or her deepest wish. Sadako wished to become well, but she was able to fold only 644 cranes. Before she died, she held up one of her cranes and said, "I will write peace on your wings, and you will fly all over the world." Sadako's classmates and friends folded the remaining 356 cranes and raised money to build a beautiful peace statue of Sadako in Hiroshima. The statue was commemorated in 1958 for all children who were victims of the atomic bombing of Japan.

After hearing about Sadako, third, fourth, and fifth graders in New Mexico were inspired to build a children's statue for peace in the United States. They formed the "Kids Committee to Build a Peace Statue" and were supervised by their teachers. They started a newsletter and held a press conference in Albuquerque, New Mexico. The children also wrote to schools and church youth groups throughout the State of New Mexico to get more kids involved in the project. At a news conference, they decided to build their statue at Los Alamos, where the atom bomb that destroyed Hiroshima was built.

Raising money for the project was very labor-intensive. Kids sold candy and baked goods; they held a walk-a-thon, sold T-shirts, and created alliances with churches and other nonprofit institutions. Most of the money raised came from kids donating or raising a dollar ("Dollar-a-Name Campaign") and signing their names on a peace petition, which collected 90,000 names of children from 50 states and 63 countries (Cranes for Peace Web site, 2001). Kids Committee members worked to spread information on weekends and during the evenings by speaking on the radio and TV, in schools, churches, and bookstores. The more money the children raised, the more work they had to do. Someone had to thank all the people for donations, calculate interest on the money received, and keep track of the kids joining the committee.

The Children's Peace Statue was dedicated in 1995 and is the first national monument in the United States to be created and paid for by children. The statue is currently in Santa Fe, New Mexico, because the Los Alamos City Council has refused to take it.

Cranes for Peace

Peace Day was declared on August 6 by the Japanese on the first anniversary of the bombing of Hiroshima to try to ensure that the horrific, enduring effects of a nuclear war will never be experienced. Children in Japan make origami cranes and drape them over the statue built for Sadako Sasaki every August. As with the peace statue in Japan, children in the United States collect origami cranes to commemorate Peace Day each year on August 6 and hang the cranes on the Children's Peace Statue in New Mexico.

The Peace Statue in Hiroshima is inscribed "This is our cry. This is our prayer. To create peace in the world."

Paraphrased and shortened from Hoose, P. (1993). *It's our world, too! Stories of young people who are making a difference* (pp. 117–125). Boston: Little, Brown; and the Cranes for Peace Web page (http://www.networkearth.org/world/peace.html).

Real-World Investigations for Social Studies
Hoge, Field, Foster, and Nickell

Discussion Questions

1. Why was Sadako Sasaki an inspiring girl?

2. Sadako Sasaki said, "I will write peace on your wings, and you will fly all over the world." What would you write on the paper crane? Why?

3. How did history influence the children who created the Peace Statue in Japan and the United States?

4. Why is peace important today?

5. How can children end the threat of nuclear war?

6. What can you do to promote peace?

continued

Real-World Investigations for Social Studies
Hoge, Field, Foster, and Nickell

7. Optional: Draw or illustrate your own peace statue. Write poetry about peace.

8. Additional Crane Activity for Lesson Two (Duration: 60+ minutes): Although somewhat difficult, your class might want to make origami cranes. For directions, visit the following Web sites:

   http://www.origami-tsuru.com/crane2.htm
   This site provides instructions on how to make an origami crane.
   http://www.pro.or.jp/~fuji/origami/howto/tsuru-eng.html
   A step-by-step illustrated site on how to make an origami crane. Be sure to click on "Start from Crane Base."

   Send the peace cranes to:
   Cranes for Peace
   941-A Rio Vista
   Santa Fe, NM 87501

SERVICE LEARNING PROJECT PROPOSAL

The following questions should be used as a guideline:

1. What is the title of your community service project?

2. Thoroughly describe your community service project.
   a. What is the rationale or justification for the project?

   b. What are the goals of the project?

3. What are the steps, procedures, and resources?

4. How will adults supervise the project?

5. Are there any safety concerns?

continued

Handout 10.7 *continued*

6. How many people will be needed? Are refreshments or snacks for additional voluteers needed?

7. Will the project cost money? If so, how will the money be raised/collected?

8. What tools or materials will be needed?

9. Are any additional items necessary for the completion of the project?

10. What is the timeline for the project? How much time will be required to complete it? Base your estimate on the number of hours per week (e.g., 2 hours to pull weeds and 1 hour to remove trash per week).

Real-World Investigations for Social Studies
Hoge, Field, Foster, and Nickell

INTERNET ACTIVITY

This activity allows you to research a national database of volunteer service opportunities. Follow the directions for each question to learn about the fantastic opportunities and information available for community service.

Follow the directions that guide you through the Web site and answer the questions.

1. Go to http://www.servenet.org/ Enter your zip code in the "Get Involved" section and then click "Go" to learn about community service projects in your area. Describe some of the community service projects in your area.
2. At the top of SERVEnet's Web page, click "About Us" (top left) to learn about Youth Service America (YSA).
   a. What is YSA's commitment, mission, and vision?
   b. What will a strong youth service movement create and foster?
3. At the top of the current SERVEnet Web page, click on "Volunteer Resources." Once the new page opens, click on "Find Youth Service Statistics." Read the information, describe five of the statistical extracts that you find most interesting, and explain why.
4. Next, click on "See Timeline of Service"; the new page displayed will be a timeline on national and youth service in the United States. Read the information on this page and describe at least two historical events that you found interesting.
5. Now go to a new Web site by entering the following address: http://www.serviceleader.org/advice/why.html

   a. Read the page that appears, titled "Why Volunteer."
   b. List the motivations for volunteering that apply to you.

Optional: Research your community service project on the Internet. Be sure to get approval from your teacher for key word searches before you try.
Describe any useful information you found concerning your particular community service project.

Real-World Investigations for Social Studies
Hoge, Field, Foster, and Nickell

Handout 10.9

JON WAGNER-HOLTZ, FOUNDER OF KIDS KONNECTED

When Jon was nine years old, his mother was diagnosed with cancer. Jon describes his difficult circumstances:

> Her illness was extremely tough for me. When she came home from the hospital after surgery, I felt it was my job to be strong for her. After her first chemotherapy treatment, she was very weak and sick to her stomach all the time. I was really angry. My mom was such a good person. How could this be happening to her?

After his mother's recovery, Jon was inspired to establish a support group for kids who had parents with cancer. Jon wrote to the Susan Komen Breast Cancer Foundation to establish a hotline so "that kids could call and talk to other kids who knew what it was like to have a parent with cancer." The Komen Foundation gave him $300 and he called his group Komen Kids.

> I set up a twenty-four-hour hotline in my bedroom and started receiving calls. I probably got around a hundred phone calls, and there were eight or nine kids calling on a regular basis. We felt better knowing we were all experiencing anger, sadness, and fear.

Jon invited eight of the regular hotline callers to discuss his ideas for a support group of kids helping kids. The group decided to hire a psychologist for supervision and held their first meeting with thirty-two kids. The meeting was a success and Jon felt better because he helped another kid.

His group sent flyers [sic] to doctors in his area and they were profiled in the media. As the number of members increased, Jon renamed the group "Kids Konnected," which became its own nonprofit organization. All the programs sponsored by Kids Konnected are free and funded through donations.

Kids Konnected now has eighteen chapters around the country and will help nearly 10,000 kids with a $300,000 budget! Kids Konnected also has a summer camp, which is free to children who have a parent with cancer. They also established Karen's Kids to help children who have lost a parent to cancer. In addition to the hotline, Kids Konnected has a Web site, www.kidskonnected.org, "where kids can go online to get information."

Excerpted from *TEEN WITH THE COURAGE TO GIVE* © 2000 by Jackie Waldman (pp. 1–7) with permission of Conari Press, an imprint of Red Wheel/Weiser.

DWAINA BROOKS: FEEDING THE HOMELESS IN DALLAS

Dwaina Brooks was in the fourth grade when she got the idea of feeding homeless people in Dallas. Her class had been learning about homelessness, and once a week the class called a shelter and talked with people staying there. Dwaina and her classmates asked questions like "Why are you there?" and "What do you need?" She learned, along with her classmates, that most of the homeless people they talked with had ended up in this situation because a bad thing had happened to them, like losing a job, being unable to pay rent, or a family breakup. Dwaina had been sending her lunch money to the shelter, but she knew that didn't help much.

One day as she was talking with a young man, she asked her typical question, "What do you need?" He answered that he needed a job and a place to live. Dwaina told him she couldn't help with these needs and asked him again if there was anything else he needed. The young man told her that he'd like a good meal. Happily, Dwaina knew that was something she could do. She loved cooking and planning meals.

When she got home that night she ran excitedly to her mother, Gail, and asked for her help to make a meal for the people at the homeless shelter. This didn't surprise Dwaina's mother. She had always liked helping others, and she couldn't bear seeing anyone hurt or feeling left out. They got busy, figured out what they could spend (part of it was Dwaina's lunch money), and then bought food and supplies in preparation for making the meal on Friday night. They used coupons and got some donations, and Dwaina's aunts and uncles helped by giving bags of chips, salad dressing, and other items.

On Friday night, Dwaina arrived home from school to find that her mother had laid out an "assembly line" for preparing the sandwiches. Dwaina's two sisters had aprons on and were ready to help. By midnight 105 sandwiches and the chicken were finished, and they loaded up and took the food to the shelter. Dwaina, her mother, and her sisters did this for a year, getting help from their church with deliveries after a while.

Dwaina knew she and her mother were feeding only about half of the men in the shelter and that homelessness was growing, so she asked her fifth-grade teacher if she could speak to the class. Dwaina, who was the class leader, challenged her classmates to help her and her mother. Twenty-three of her classmates agreed to help. Each classmate and his or her family were to bring food, and Dwaina and her mother advised them about where to find bargains and developed a list of items each would bring. That Friday night, 28 people showed up, and by the end of the night 300 sack lunches had been made.

In the 2 years since starting, Dwaina has organized thousands of meals for homeless and other unfortunate people in Dallas. She took something she loved doing and, with the addition of family and friends, turned helping others into an enjoyable activity too.

Paraphrased and shortened from Hoose, P. (1993). *It's our world, too! Stories of young people who are making a difference* (pp. 49–55). Boston: Little, Brown.

Handout 10.11

CHILDREN'S RAIN FOREST

At a small elementary school in rural Sweden, one class listened intently as they were taught about the rain forests. The teacher showed magnificent pictures as she informed her students that half of the world's plants and animals could be found in the rain forests. She read about the importance of the great trees that provide much of the earth's oxygen and prevent the earth from becoming too hot. Students learned that a potential cure for cancer and one-quarter of the medicinal drugs come from rain forest plants. The children were upset when they were told that nearly half of the world's rain forests have been cut down by people who needed wood and by farmers and ranchers for crops and pastures.

The students were horrified that so much could be lost with the massive destruction of the world's rain forests. How could a few children, who lived thousands of miles away, do something to help preserve forests that they might never get to see, forests that might be completely destroyed before they were old enough to see them? One 9-year-old student named Roland wanted to do something and asked whether they could buy the rain forest!

Although the idea of buying a rain forest seemed unrealistic to the teacher, the students were very serious. By coincidence, their teacher was soon introduced to a biologist who worked in a rain forest. When the teacher described her students' idea, the biologist asked if they could buy the one she worked in, a rain forest called Monte Verde (Green Mountain) in Costa Rica. The class was excited about the opportunity and immediately began to brainstorm ideas to raise money. Everything was considered, from dog washing to rabbit-jumping contests. They decided to have a "rain forest evening." At the end of the evening, the students managed to raise $240 and estimated that it was enough to save about 12 football fields' worth of rain forest. They were happy with the results but realized that the plants and animals of the rain forest needed more land to survive.

After another brainstorming of ideas, they wrote letters to prominent people and sold taped songs about the rain forest that the class wrote and recorded. The more creative they were, the more money they raised. They even had a rain forest fair with magicians, pony riding, fortune telling, and a rabbit-jumping contest! The money raised saved nearly 90 acres of the Monte Verde rain forest.

The students decided to form an organization devoted to preserving and protecting the rain forests. They named the organization the "Children's Rain Forest." By early spring of the same year, the students were inspiring the entire country of Sweden to raise money for the rain forests. The Swedish government even gave a grant of $80,000 for the Monte Verde forest.

So far, the Children's Rain Forest has raised over $2 million to preserve over 33,000 acres of rain forest. The International Children's Rainforest Network spans the globe from Sweden to Japan, with children from over twenty countries helping preserve the rain forests.

Paraphrased and shortened from Hoose, P. (1993). *It's our world, too! Stories of young people who are making a difference* (pp. 83–93). Boston: Little, Brown.

Real-World Investigations for Social Studies
Hoge, Field, Foster, and Nickell

DISCUSSION QUESTIONS FOR YOUTH ENJOYING SERVICE

1. Describe how each story shows young people helping.
   a. Jon Wagner-Holz

   b. Dwaina Brooks

   c. Children's Rain Forest

2. Why do these young people give?

3. Why were these young people successful?

4. How old do you have to be to do community service? Why?

continued

Real-World Investigations for Social Studies
Hoge, Field, Foster, and Nickell

5. What have you learned from the stories to create your own community service project?

6. Why is it important to help your community?

Real-World Investigations for Social Studies
Hoge, Field, Foster, and Nickell

COMMUNITY SERVICE PLAN DIVIDING STUDENTS IN DEARBORN

The Dearborn Public School district, which is the largest in metro Detroit, planned to require its high school students to complete 40 hours of community service in order to graduate.

"Most people my age don't help unless they get paid," said Zeinab Hachem, a high school sophomore at Dearborn. Through volunteering her time, Hachem has developed her career goals of being a neurosurgeon. She spends almost 40 hours a week of her summer at Oakwood Hospital in Dearborn volunteering for cat-scan technicians, translating Arabic, and doing other jobs at the hospital. "I think volunteering is a great thing and I'm glad to do it."

Hachem is a supporter of mandatory community service, because volunteering has helped her develop career goals and she is personally fulfilled by helping at the hospital. "The patients are really grateful, and they tell me how nice it is to see young people volunteering."

Jeremy Hughes, the superintendent of Dearborn public schools, said, "All the arguments are valid and I know a lot of people who will be turned off by mandatory community service, but I honestly believe most of the young people will find this to be a tremendous experience."

Steve Parisi, fourteen years old, said, "It's horrible that they would try and make us do volunteer work. We can be good citizens without having to do volunteer stuff."

Parisi felt that forcing students to volunteer would take away from work and social time with friends. We "go to school to learn; this is just more unnecessary work."

Update: As of January 2001, Dearborn public schools "suggest at least 10 hours of voluntary service" but have not established a requirement.

Adapted by permission of the publisher from "Service plan dividing students in Dearborn," Manny Lopez, *The Detroit News*, 8 August 1997 (Metro).© by the Detroit News.

Questions

1. What is mandatory community service?

2. Why does Zeinab Hachem like the idea of mandatory community service?

continued

Real-World Investigations for Social Studies
Hoge, Field, Foster, and Nickell

Handout 10.13 *continued*

3. Why does Steve Parisi dislike the idea of mandatory community service?

4. Why do you think the Dearborn public schools decided not to require community service for graduation?

5. What is your opinion of mandatory community service? Why?

6. What do you recommend to make students good citizens? Be sure to explain how your plan would work.

Real-World Investigations for Social Studies
Hoge, Field, Foster, and Nickell

NEWSPAPER REPORTER HOMEWORK ASSIGNMENT

Become a reporter and create a news article about mandatory community service. Write the article so that it explores both sides of the issue. Interview your classmates, teachers, parents, and neighbors to collect quotes and opinions. Survey students and adults or use data from research and SERVEnet.org to create charts or graphs in the article (be sure to use correct citations for your sources of information). Illustrate your article with photographs, cartoons, or other drawings.

ADDITIONAL TEACHER SOURCES

Hoose, P. (1993). *It's our world, too! Stories of young people who are making a difference.* Boston: Little, Brown.

Mendoza, P. M. (1999). *Extraordinary people in extraordinary times: Heroes, sheroes, and villains.* Englewood, CO: Teacher Ideas Press.

Wade, R. (Ed.). (2000). *Building bridges: Connecting classroom and community through service-learning in social studies.* Washington, DC: National Council for the Social Studies.

ADDITIONAL STUDENT SOURCE

Ajmera, M., Omoludun, O., & Strunk, S. (1999). *Extraordinary girls.* Watertown, MA: Charlesbridge.

References

Introduction

Aronson, E., Blaney, N., Sikes, J., Stephan, C., & Snapp, M. (1978). *The jigsaw classroom.* Beverly Hills, CA: Sage.

Borko, H., & Putnam, R. T. (1998). The role of context in teacher learning and teacher education. In *Contextual teaching and learning: Preparing teachers to enhance student success in and beyond school.* Information series 376 (pp. 35–74). Washington, DC: ERIC Clearinghouse.

Brown, J. S., Collins, A., & Duguid, P. (1989). *Situated cognition and the culture of learning.* Palo Alto, CA: BBN Systems and Technologies Corporation.

Cohen, E. (1994). *Designing groupwork: Strategies for the heterogeneous classroom* (2nd ed.). New York: Teachers College Press.

DeVries, D. L., & Slavin, R. E. (1978). Teams-Games-Tournaments: Review of ten classroom experiments. *Journal of Research and Development in Education, 12,* 28–38.

Driscoll, A. (1995). *Cases in early childhood education: Stories of programs and practices.* Boston: Allyn & Bacon.

Engle, S. H., & Ochoa, S. A. (1988). *Educating citizens for democracy: Decision making in social studies.* New York: Teachers College Press.

Ericsson, K. A., & Smith, J. (Eds.). (1991). *Toward a general theory of expertise.* Cambridge: Cambridge University Press.

Evans, R. W., & Saxe, D. W. (Eds.). (1996). *Handbook on teaching social issues.* Washington, DC: National Council for the Social Studies.

Gardner, H. (1997). Multiple intelligences as a partner in school improvement. *Educational Leadership, 55,* 20–21.

Hunt, M. P., & Metcalf, L. E. (1955). *Teaching high school social studies: Problems in reflective thinking and social understanding.* New York: Harper & Row.

Johnson, D. W., & Johnson, R. T. (1987). *Learning together and alone.* Upper Saddle River, NJ: Prentice Hall.

Johnson, D. W., & Johnson, R. T. (1989). *Cooperation and competition: Theory and research.* Edina, MN: Interaction.

Johnson, D. W., & Johnson, R. T. (1992). Approaches to implementing cooperative learning in the social studies classroom. In R. Stahl & R. Van Sickle (Eds.), *Cooperative learning in the social studies classroom: An invitation to social study.* Bulletin No. 87 (pp. 44–51). Washington, DC: National Council for the Social Studies.

Johnson, D. W., & Johnson, R. T. (1995). *Reducing school violence through conflict resolution.* Reston, VA: Association for Supervision and Curriculum Development.

Johnson, D. W., Johnson, R. T., Holubec, E. J., & Roy, P. (1984). *Circles of learning: Cooperation in the classroom.* Alexandria, VA: Association for Supervision and Curriculum Development.

Johnson, D. W., Johnson, R. T., & Stanne, M. B. (2000). *Cooperative learning methods: A meta-analysis.* Available at http://www.co-operation.com/ The Cooperative Learning Center at the University of Minnesota.

Kagan, D. M. (1993). Contexts for the use of classroom cases. *American Educational Research Journal, 30,* 703–723.

Koballa, T. R., & Tippins, D. J. (2000). *Cases in middle and secondary science education: The promise and dilemmas.* Upper Saddle River, NJ: Prentice Hall/Merrill.

Lave, J., & Wegner, E. (1991). *Situated learning: Legitimate peripheral participation.* Cambridge: Cambridge University Press.

Massialas, B., & Cox, B. (1966). *Inquiry in social studies.* New York: McGraw-Hill.

National Council for the Social Studies. (1994). *Expectations of excellence: Curriculum standards for social studies.* Washington, DC: National Council for the Social Studies.

Newmann, F., & Thompson, J. A. (1987). *Effects of cooperative learning on achievement in secondary schools: A summary of research.* Madison: National Center on Effective Secondary Schools, Wisconsin Center for Educational Research.

Oliver, D. W., & Shaver, J. P. (1966). *Teaching public issues in the high school.* Boston: Houghton Mifflin.

Parker, W. C. (2001). *Social studies in elementary education* (11th ed.). Upper Saddle River, NJ: Prentice Hall/Merrill.

Sharan, S., & Sharan, Y. (1976). *Small group teaching.* Upper Saddle River, NJ: Prentice Hall.

Slavin, R. E. (1978). Student teams and comparison among equals: Effects on academic performance and student attitudes. *Journal of Educational Psychology, 70(4),* 532–538.

Slavin, R. E. (1983). *Cooperative learning.* New York: Longman.

Slavin, R. E. (1986). *Using student team learning* (3rd ed.). Baltimore: Johns Hopkins University, Center for Research on Elementary and Middle Schools.

Slavin, R. E. (1995). *Cooperative learning* (2nd ed.). Needham Heights, MA: Allyn & Bacon.

Slavin, R. E., Madden, N. A., & Leavey, M. (1984). Effects of cooperative learning and individualized instructions on mainstreamed students. *Exceptional Children, 50(5),* 434–443.

Stevens, R. J., Madden, N. A., Slavin, R. E., & Farnish, A. M. (1987). Cooperative integrated reading and composition: Two field experiments. *Reading Research Quarterly, 22,* 433–454.

Vermette, P. J. (1998). *Making cooperative learning work: Student teams in K-12 classrooms.* Upper Saddle River, NJ: Prentice Hall/Merrill.

Vygotsky, L. (1978). *Mind in society: The development of higher psychological processes.* Cambridge, MA: Harvard University Press.

Chapter 1

Dewey, J. (1910). *How we think.* Boston: D. C. Heath.

Engle, S. H., & Ochoa, A. S. (1988). *Education for democratic citizenship: Decision making in the social studies.* New York: Teachers College Press.

Evans, R. W., & Saxe, D. W. (Eds.). (1996). *Handbook on teaching social issues*. Washington, DC: NCSS Publications.

Gerzon, M. (1997). Teaching democracy by doing it! *Educational Leadership, 54*, 6–12.

Griffin, A. (1942). *The subject matter preparation of teachers of history*. Ed.D. diss., Ohio State University.

Hahn, C. L. (1996). Research on issues-centered social studies. In R. W. Evans & D. W. Saxe (Eds.), *Handbook on teaching social issues* (pp. 25–41). Washington, DC: NCSS Publications.

Hernandez, H., & Metzger, D. (1996). Issues-centered education for language-minority students. In R. W. Evans & D. W. Saxe (Eds.), *Handbook on teaching social issues* (pp. 111–120). Washington, DC: NCSS Publications.

Hunt, M., & Metcalf, L. (1955, 1968). *Teaching high school social studies: Problems in reflective thinking and social understanding*. New York: Harper & Brothers.

Ladson-Billings, G. (1996). Multicultural issues in the classroom: Race, class, and gender. In R. W. Evans & D. W. Saxe (Eds.), *Handbook on teaching social issues* (pp. 101–109). Washington, DC: NCSS Publications.

Massialas, B., & Cox, B. (1966). *Inquiry in social studies*. New York: McGraw-Hill.

Newmann, F., & Oliver, D. (1970). *Clarifying public controversy*. Boston: Little, Brown.

Oliver, D., & Shaver, J. (1966). *Teaching public issues in the high school*. Boston: Houghton Mifflin.

Onosko, J. J. (1996). Exploring issues with students despite the barriers. *Social Education, 60*, 22–27.

Passe, J., & Evans, R. W. (1996). Discussion methods in an issues-centered curriculum. In R. W. Evans & D. W. Saxe (Eds.), *Handbook on teaching social issues* (pp. 81–88). Washington, DC: NCSS Publications.

Pugh, S., & Garcia, J. (1996). Issues-centered education in multicultural environments. In R. W. Evans & D. W. Saxe (Eds.), *Handbook on teaching social issues* (pp. 121–129). Washington, DC: NCSS Publications.

Shaver, J. (1996). Afterword. In R. W. Evans & D. W. Saxe (Eds.), *Handbook on teaching social issues* (pp. 380–385). Washington, DC: NCSS Publications.

Chapter 2

Allen, R. F. (2000). Civic education and the decision-making process. *Social Studies, 91*(1), 5–9.

Engle, S. H. (1960). Decision-making: The heart of the social studies. *Social Education 24*(3), 301–304, 306.

Engle, S. H., & Ochoa, A. S. (1988). *Education for democratic citizenship; Decision making in the social studies*. New York: Teachers College Press.

Evans, R. W., & Saxe, D. W. (Eds.). (1996). *Handbook on teaching social issues*. Washington, DC: National Council for the Social Studies.

Massialas, B. G., & Cox, C. B. (1966). *Inquiry in the social studies*. New York: McGraw-Hill.

Newmann, F. M., & Oliver, D. W. (1970). *Clarifying public controversy: An approach to the teaching of social studies*. Boston: Little, Brown.

Senesh, L. (1968). The pattern of the economic curriculum. *Social Education, 32*(1), 47–50, 59.

Chapter 3

Geography Education Standards Project. (1994). *Geography for life*. Washington, DC: National Geographic Research and Exploration.

Lake Sidney Lanier Web site. Retrieved May 3, 2003, from http://lanier.sam.usace.army.mil/Default.htm

U.S. Census (2002). Most of nation's 10 fastest-growing counties in South, Census Bureau reports. Retrieved May 3, 2003, from http://www.census.gov/PressRelease/www2002/cb02-59.html

Chapter 4

Allen, L., Hogan, C. J., & Steinberg, A. (2000). *Knowing and doing: Connecting learning and work*. Providence, RI: LAB, Northeast and Islands Regional Educational Laboratory, 2003.

Baum, W. K. (1995). *Oral history for the local historical society* (3rd ed.). Walnut Creek, GA: Altamira Press.

Borko, H., & Putnam, R. T. (1998). The role of context in teacher learning and teacher education. In *Contextual teaching and learning: Preparing teachers to enhance student success in and beyond school*. Information Series 376 (pp. 35–74). Washington, DC: ERIC Clearinghouse.

Chapin, J. R. (2003). *A practical guide to secondary social studies*. Boston: Allyn & Bacon.

Csikszentmihalyi, M., & Schneider, B. (2000). *Becoming adult: How teenagers prepare for the world of work*. New York: Basic Books.

Field, S. L., & Nickell, P. (2000). The Little Red Hen, Soap Sculpture, and Analyzing Magazines: Activities and lessons used to teach character education in the 1920's and 1930's. *The Educational Forum, 65*(1), 73–79.

Kvale, S. (1996). *InterViews*. Thousand Oaks, CA: Sage.

National Council for the Social Studies. (1994). *Expectations of excellence: Curriculum standards for social studies*. Washington, DC: Author.

Parker, W. (2001). *Social studies in elementary education* (11th ed.). Upper Saddle River, NJ: Prentice Hall.

Rogovin, P. (1998). *Classroom interviews*. Portsmouth, NH: Heinemann.

Steinberg, A. (1997). *Real learning, real work*. New York: Routledge.

Wade, R. R. & Saxe, D. W. (1996). Community service-learning in the social studies: Historical roots, empirical evidence, critical issues. *Theory and Research in Social Education, 24*(4), 331–359.

Yow, V. R. (1994). *Recording oral history: A practical guide for social scientists*. Thousand Oaks, CA: Sage.

Chapter 5

Allen, R. F. (1996). The Engle-Ochoa decision making model for citizenship education. In R. W. Evans & D. W. Saxe (Eds.), *Handbook on teaching social issues* (pp. 51–58). Washington, DC: National Council for the Social Studies.

Foster, S. J., Hoge, J. D., & Rosch, R. H. (1999). Thinking aloud about history: Children's and adolescents' responses to historical photographs. *Theory and Research in Social Education, 27*(2), 179–214.

Fraenkel, J. R., & Wallen, N. E. (2003). *How to design and evaluate research in education*. Boston: McGraw-Hill.

Merriam, S. B. (1998). *Qualitative research and case study applications in education*. San Francisco: Jossey-Bass.

Chapter 6

Boston Globe. (1997, February 12). Weld pushes for uniforms in schools; Files a bill to enable districts to enact mandatory dress codes. Don Ancoin, City Edition, Metro/Region, P. A1.

Brunsma, D. L., & Rockquemore, R. A. (1998). Effects of student uniforms on attendance, behavior problems, substance use, and academic achievement. *Journal of Educational Research 92*(1), 53–62. Also available online at http://www.members.tripod.com/rockqu/uniform.htm. Accessed May 4, 2003.

Clinton, W. J. (1996). Memorandum for the secretary of education. Retrieved May 4, 2003, from http://www.ed.gov/PressReleases/02-1996/whpr26.html

Manual on School Uniforms. (circa 1996). U.S. Department of Education. Retrieved May 4, 2003, from http://www.ed.gov/updates/uniforms.html

Siegel, L. (1996). Point of view: School uniforms. Accessed May 4, 2003, from http://archive.aclu.org/congress/uniform.html.

Walters, S. (1998, September 17). Dade study: School uniforms haven't led to better conduct. *Miami Hearld*, Section A, p. 1.

Wilen, W. W., & Phillips, J. A. (1995). Teaching critical thinking: A metacognitive approach. *Social Education, 59*(3), 135–138.

Chapter 7

Association of Teachers of Social Studies of the City of New York. (1967). *Handbook for social studies teaching* (3rd. ed.). New York: Holt, Rinehart & Winston.

Ellis, A. K. (2002). *Teaching and learning elementary social studies* (7th ed.). Boston: Allyn & Bacon.

Michaelis, J. U. (1963). *Social studies for children in a democracy; recent trends and developments.* (3rd. ed.). Upper Saddle River, NJ: Prentice Hall.

Parker, W. C. (2001). *Social studies in elementary education* (11th ed.). Upper Saddle River, NJ: Prentice Hall/Merrill.

Chapter 8

Beyer, B. K. (1985). Critical thinking: What is it? *Social Education, 49,* 270–276.

Bloom, B. S. (Ed.). (1984). *Taxonomy of educational objectives: The classification of educational goals.* New York: Longman.

Engle, S. H., & Ochoa, A. S. (1988). *Education for democratic citizenship: Decision making in the social studies.* New York: Teachers College Press.

Hess, D. E. (2002). Discussing controversial public issues in secondary social studies classrooms: Learning from skilled teachers. *Theory and Research in Social Education, 30*(1), 10–41.

Kerka, S. (1992). *Higher order thinking skills in vocational education.* ERIC Digest No. 127. Columbus, OH: ERIC Clearinghouse on Adult Career and Vocational Education.

National Council for the Social Studies. (1994). *Expectations of excellence: Curriculum standards for social studies.* Washington, DC: Author.

Newmann, F. M. (1990). Higher order thinking in teaching social studies: A rationale for the assessment of classroom thoughtfulness. *Journal of Curriculum Studies, 22*(1), 41–56.

Olsen, D. G. (1995). "Less" can be "More" in the promotion of thinking. *Social Education, 59,* 130–134.

Parker, W. C. (1996). Curriculum for democracy. In R. Soder (Ed.), *Democracy, education, and the schools* (pp. 182–210). San Francisco: Jossey-Bass.

Potts, B. (1994). Strategies for teaching critical thinking. ED385606. ERIC/AE Digest. Washington, DC: ERIC Clearinghouse on Assessment and Evaluation.

Wilen, W. W., & Phillips, J. A. (1995). Teaching critical thinking: A metacognitive approach. *Social Education, 59,* 135–138.

Wright, I. (1995). Making critical thinking possible: Options for teachers. *Social Education, 59,* 139–143.

Chapter 9

Miller, K., & Rowley, T. (2002, December 4). Rural poverty and rural-urban income gaps: A troubling snapshot of the "prosperous" 1990. Iowa State University, University of Missouri, University of Nebraska: Rural Policy Research Institute.

Payne, R. K. (1996). *A framework for understanding poverty.* Highlands, TX: aha! Process, Inc.

Pellino, K. M. (2002). The effects of poverty on teaching and learning. Retrieved December 3, 2002, from http://www.technology.com/tutorials/teaching/poverty/

Shearer, L. (2002, December 3). Poverty rate too high for Clarke. *Athens Banner-Herald,* Sec. A, p. 1.

U.S. Census Bureau. (2001). Annual demographic survey. Available at http://ferret.bls.census.gov/macro/032002/pov/new01_001.htm

U.S. Census Bureau (2000). Accessed May 4, 2003 at http://www.census.gov/hhes/www/poverty.html

Chapter 10

Farkas, S., & Johnson, J. (1997). *Kids these days: What Americans really think about the next generation.* New York: Public Agenda.

Fertman, C. L., White, G. P., & White, L. J. (1996). *Service learning in the middle school: Building a culture of service.* Columbus, OH: National Middle School Association.

National Council for the Social Studies. (1994). *Curriculum standards for social studies.* Washington, DC: Author.

Nickell, M. P., & Field, S. L. (1999). Real examples of little people doing big things: Lessons in activism and service. *Georgia Council for the Social Studies News and Notes, 29*(1), 1–4.

Taba, H. (1966). *Teaching strategies and cognitive functioning in elementary school children.* San Francisco: San Francisco State College.

Wade, R. H., & Saxe, D. W. (1996). Community service-learning in the social studies: Historical roots, empirical evidence, critical issues. *Theory and Research in Social Education, 24*(4), 331–359.

Index